# LEADING RITES:
## AN EXAMINATION OF RITUALIZATION AND LEADERSHIP IN FACULTY PROFESSIONAL LIFE

# LEADING RITES:
## AN EXAMINATION OF RITUALIZATION AND LEADERSHIP IN FACULTY PROFESSIONAL LIFE

Shah Hasan

Copyright © 2017 by Shah M. Hasan.

| Library of Congress Control Number: | | 2017907669 |
|---|---|---|
| ISBN: | Hardcover | 978-1-5434-2301-3 |
| | Softcover | 978-1-5434-2302-0 |
| | eBook | 978-1-5434-2303-7 |

All rights reserved. No part of this book may be reproduced or transmitted in any form or by any means, electronic or mechanical, including photocopying, recording, or by any information storage and retrieval system, without permission in writing from the copyright owner.

Any people depicted in stock imagery provided by Thinkstock are models, and such images are being used for illustrative purposes only.
Certain stock imagery © Thinkstock.

Print information available on the last page.

Rev. date: 05/17/2017

**To order additional copies of this book, contact:**
Xlibris
1-888-795-4274
www.Xlibris.com
Orders@Xlibris.com
761964

# Contents

Acknowledgments .................................................................xi

CHAPTER 1: INTRODUCTION ...........................................1
  Background of the Study ......................................................1
  What Was the Problem I Was Chasing ................................3
  Why Was This Significant ....................................................4
  Limitations and Delimitations ..............................................4
  Definitions of Some Terms ...................................................5

CHAPTER 2: RITUALIZATION AND LEADERSHIP ............7
  Meaning and Sensemaking ...................................................7
  Ritual and Ritualization .....................................................10
    Ritual in Sacred Time and Sacred Place ........................10
    Ritual as Structure and Performance .............................12
    Ritual as Secular Ceremony ...........................................14
    Ritual in Higher Education ............................................15
  Leadership ..........................................................................18
    Power and Positionality .................................................19
  Classical and Heroic Constructions ...................................20
    Great Man Approaches ..................................................20
    Trait Approaches ............................................................20
    Behavioral Approaches ..................................................20
    Contingency and Situational Approaches .....................22
    Power and Influence Approaches ..................................23
  Emergent and Post-Heroic Constructions .........................24
    Servant Leadership .........................................................25
    Leadership as Social Change ..........................................25
    Leadership and Spirit .....................................................26
  Leadership in the Academic Context .................................28
    Faculty Leadership .........................................................28
    The Socio-Technical System ..........................................29
    The Cultural Systems Perspective ..................................30
    The Cybernetic System Perspective ...............................33
  Leadership and Ritualization .............................................35

## CHAPTER 3: THE STUDY .................................................................. 38
### Naturalistic Inquiry and Qualitative Research ........................... 38
#### Why Qualitative Research? .................................................. 39
#### Phenomenology .................................................................. 42
### Narrative Analysis and Inquiry ................................................ 44
#### Narrative Analysis ................................................................ 45
#### Narrative Inquiry .................................................................. 48
### Participants ................................................................................ 49
#### Selection of Site ..................................................................... 49
#### Selection of Sample .............................................................. 49
### The Researcher Role .................................................................. 50
### Procedures .................................................................................. 52
#### Survey of Interest .................................................................. 52
#### Interviews ............................................................................... 53
### Data Analysis .............................................................................. 54
### Trustworthiness and Authenticity ........................................... 55
#### Trustworthiness ..................................................................... 56
##### Credibility .......................................................................... 56
##### Triangulation .................................................................... 56
##### Transferability .................................................................. 57
##### Dependability .................................................................. 57
##### Confirmability .................................................................. 57
#### Authenticity ............................................................................ 57
##### Fairness .............................................................................. 58
##### Ontological Authenticity ................................................ 58
##### Educative Authenticity .................................................... 58
##### Catalytic Authenticity ...................................................... 59
##### Tactical Authenticity ........................................................ 59
### Ethical Considerations .............................................................. 59
## CHAPTER 4: THE NARRATIVE PROFILE ............................ 62
### Figure, Ground and Sensemaking .......................................... 63
## CHAPTER 5: FRANCESCA ...................................................... 67
#### Early Influences ..................................................................... 69
#### Coming to Wilkinson .......................................................... 70
#### At Wilkinson ......................................................................... 71
#### Election to Dean of the Faculty ......................................... 72
#### From Dean Back to Faculty ................................................ 76
#### Senior Faculty Member ....................................................... 76
#### Looking Back ........................................................................ 77

- CHAPTER 6: PAULA .................................................................82
  - On The Way to Teaching ..............................................83
  - Coming to Wilkinson ...................................................87
  - Early Years at Wilkinson...............................................88
  - Learning from Senior Colleagues...................................91
  - Giving Back ................................................................93
  - Restoring Balance .......................................................96
  - About Student Success.................................................96
  - The Faculty Administrative Role ..................................97
  - Challenging Students and Colleagues.........................100
  - A Stronger Voice........................................................102
  - Rhythms of the Year ..................................................104
  - Academic Ceremony Reflections ................................106
  - Post-Tenure Reflections ..............................................109
  - Leaving a Legacy .......................................................113
- CHAPTER 7: CHARLES..........................................................116
  - Early Influences.........................................................117
  - Coming To Wilkinson................................................120
  - First Years at Wilkinson..............................................122
  - The Academic Good Life ...........................................124
  - Rhythms and Conversations.......................................128
  - The Senior Faculty ....................................................130
  - Comparing Academic and Business Worlds................132
  - The Department Chair ..............................................133
  - Academic Ceremonies ...............................................134
  - Helping Students Succeed .........................................138
- CHAPTER 8: REBECCA..........................................................142
  - Preparing for the Academy ........................................143
  - Building an Academic Network..................................149
  - Network as Nourishment ..........................................154
  - The Fairy Godmother ................................................158
  - Faculty Administrative Work......................................159
  - About Women and Being Scary..................................162
- CHAPTER 9: CROSSINGS AND RITES .................................164
  - Interpreting Narrative................................................164
  - The Sacred and the Non-Sacred .................................166
  - Ritual and Ritualization ............................................168

    The Public and Formal ................................................169
        Academic Ceremonies ..............................................169
        Seasonal Rituals .......................................................171
    The Personal and Informal .........................................173
        Milestones ................................................................173
        Conversations ...........................................................176
        Tenure ......................................................................179
    Secular Ceremony .......................................................181
**CHAPTER 10: PEOPLE AND MEANING** ....................183
    Pivotal Persons ...........................................................183
        Early Influencers ......................................................183
        Opportunity Connectors ..........................................185
        Admirable Role Models ...........................................187
    Ellipses of Significance ...............................................189
        Teaching First ...........................................................189
        Living the Academic Good Life ...............................192
        Leaving a Legacy ......................................................193
        Penetrating Privilege .................................................197
        Being Women ..........................................................198
        Celebrating Student Success .....................................201
**CHAPTER 11: LEADERSHIP** ........................................ 204
    Post-Heroic Explanations ...........................................204
    Formal Administrative Roles ......................................206
    Informal Work ............................................................210
        Assignments .............................................................211
        Commitments ..........................................................213
        Pivotal Persons .........................................................216
    Ritualization and Leadership ......................................218
**CHAPTER 12: IMPLICATIONS** ....................................224
    Reflections of the Study ..............................................225
        The Researcher as Instrument ..................................225
        Joint Construction of Findings ................................227
    Implications for Practice .............................................227
    Implications for Research ...........................................232
    Implications for Me ....................................................233

**References** ........................................................................235

*"If you want to know me, then you must know my story"*
Daniel McAdams, *The Stories We Live By*

# Acknowledgments

This work began many years ago as a dissertation project. The great mystification of doctoral work nurtures the myth that writing a dissertation is like creating one great opus. Instead, as I have come to learn since then, all writing is more like a pilgrimage with a thousand quotidian rituals, entailed together by oftentimes tremulous faith in the project, some duty-bound determination to finish, but most essentially by the thoughtful and generous support of so many others who also attend the journey. There were so many good people who nudged me along this project. I want to acknowledge some of my most significant and generous nudgers.

I want to thank my fellow travelers in my doctoral cohort at Ohio University: Katie Bontrager, Carol Canavan, Libby Daugherty, Jeannette Hale, Jim Kemper, David Litt, Michael Michael, Joanne Risacher, Bonnie Smith, Mokie Steiskal, Mary Vaughn, Molly Weiland, and Michele Welsh. I learned as much from their steady faith in learning and the wisdom of their experiences as I did from our coursework and from our faculty. Over the years these thoughtful companions also became my most steadfast friends and encouragers.

I want to thank the research participants of my study, four very generous and deeply thoughtful members of the faculty of a selective liberal arts college in the Midwest – named for anonymity Wilkinson College. These thoughtful and generous teachers invited me for conversation into the living rooms of their professional and personal lives, an intensely personal narrative space. And inside this hospitable space, they inspired me with their aspirations for good lives of teaching, scholarship, and service to students. I found in their reflections great reserves of devotion to commit to my own life as a teacher and colleague.

I want to note my gratitude to friends and former colleagues, particularly Carole Henry and Bernie Schultz who cheered me on. I remain grateful to former colleagues Steve Ash, Ray Forbes, Martha Shouldis, and Dwayne Todd, for reading early drafts, and for their insights and suggestions. I am also grateful to Stephanie Swope for her many hours of painstaking work on the first-edition transcriptions of my research interview audiotapes.

I want to thank David Descutner, Gary Moden, and Jay Young. As members of my dissertation committee, they served as penetrating and engaged partners, extending themselves generously. I am, of course, most extraordinarily indebted to my dissertation advisor, my teacher, my mentor, and my friend Robert Young. When I met Bob decades ago, I never imagined that he would one day invite me to the doctoral program at Ohio University. And that he would then serve as my dissertation advisor, my "pivotal person" in this important passage in my life. Our intellectual companionship and conversations surrounding ritualization and everything else worth talking about is a treasure of friendship I cherish.

I want to acknowledge a faithful family of relatives, neighbors and friends who aided me in hundreds of little ways, most of them less direct and less visible. Together, they stood watch over this work and me; they helped me stay unfettered, focused and free of distraction to pursue my work. I want to also recognize my brother, Shah Zaman, whose own earlier doctoral work was an admirable model for me of truly inspiring steadfastness and determined faith. I am in awe of how my brother paves his life daily with resolute faith and devotion to the people he loves.

Finally, I want to thank the two angels in my life, my daughter Ellie Hasan and my wife Gigi Boggs. I prize the loyalty of their love, and I honor their never-ending pride and trust in me. I remain grateful for the times they spent, the things they accomplished, and the places they sometime went absent their father and husband as I chased my calling. I thank them for waiting for me. And I love them for believing in me. It is to them, and for them, that I dedicate this work.

Hilliard, Ohio<br>April 2017

# Chapter 1

## Introduction

Several years ago, as part of my doctoral work, I began a study of the self-reflective narratives of four faculty members, Francesca, Paula, Charles, and Rebecca, at Wilkinson College, a selective small liberal arts college in the Midwest. The four research participants as well as their college were assigned fictitious names to protect the anonymity of the participants and the research site. The purpose of this study was to examine the role of ritualization in faculty leadership activities in the particular setting of Wilkinson College. The research participants' narratives were constructed from extended interviews, and I examined their reflections about the personal and professional dimensions of their work as members of the faculty. In this book I examine their stories for patterns of self-described ritualization and what these patterns tell us about how they helped lead their college.

### Background of the Study

While the study of leadership has been an age-old pursuit, attention to the deeper and more spiritual aspects of meaning and purpose in leadership has recently emerged in popular literature. (See for example, Autry, 1994; Bolman and Deal, 1995; Briskin, 1998; Cashman, 1998; DePree, 1989, 1992, 1997; Guillory, 2000; Jaworski,

1996; Koestenbaum, 1991; Lieder, 1997; Moxley, 2000, Nair, 1997; and Owen, 1987, 1999). Many of these authors attempted to connect effective leadership with spiritual and secular meaning making. At the heart of spiritual perspectives on temporal activities is the notion of ritual – a pattern of purposeful action or behavior, often enacted to mark a passage, which effects the creating of spiritual or transcendent meaning external to the pattern of action itself (Driver, 1998).

Ritual as a phenomenon defies clear definition despite being a timeless object of study. However, the variety of approaches to the study of ritual, constructed along understandings of ritual purpose and domain, can be arrayed along a continuum that extends from meaning making in the spiritual and universal, to meaning making in the secular and ordinary. Driver (1998) has described this as the difference between ritual, "the great liturgies and ceremonies of stable institutions…reserved for special occasions" (Driver, 1998, p. 17), and ritualization which "involves both improvisation and the establishment of repeatable form" and "emphasizes the making of new forms through which expressive behavior can flow" (p. 30). This concept of ritualization offers opportunities to explore meaning making in ordinary and every day life passages.

One end of this continuum of approaches to the study of ritual is represented by theorists such as Mircea Eliade (1957, 1958), Victor Turner (1969), and Arnold Van Gennep (1960), who approached the study of ritual as performances that generated transcendent spiritual and universal meanings, primarily in non-Western and "pre-literate" communities. The other end of this continuum is represented by more recent theorists, (such as Driver, 1998; Grimes, 1995, 2000; Moore & Myerhoff, 1977; and Wall and Ferguson, 1998), who approach the study of ritualization in everyday life, primarily in contemporary and secular Western settings. In the context of higher education, Kathleen Manning (1990, 2000) recently described how both ritual and ritualization pervade the college community and professional lives of faculty members at one institution.

A perspective on ritualization prompts the question: How does faculty leadership as a process of influence relate to ritualization as defined above? In the realm of higher education, the study of leadership of faculty members is overshadowed by the ubiquitous study of leadership in academic organizational roles, such as presidents, deans, and chairs (Birnbaum, 1992; Cohen & March, 1986; Fisher, 1984; Fisher, Tack, & Wheeler, 1988; Hecht, Higgerson, Gmelch, & Tucker, 1999; Kerr & Gade, 1986; Vaughan, 1986, 1989; Weingartner, 1996). These studies, however, present strategies for success from the standpoint of positions in academic hierarchies, and do not generally address the leadership work of faculty members extending themselves as professional peers and serving the institution.

Some efforts have been made toward developing theory about how faculty make meaning of their work. For example, Robert Blackburn and Janet Lawrence (1995) have attempted to explain the motivations for satisfying faculty work, drawing largely from survey data, and Earl Seidman (1985) has studied effective teaching in a community college based on qualitative interviews with faculty members. The study of ritualization in the leadership work of faculty members can potentially enrich the larger discussion of meaning and purpose in the inner work of leadership (Koestenbaum, 1991; Mackoff & Wenet, 2001; Moxley, 2000). This is particularly conceptually feasible when higher education faculty leadership is defined as a process of mutual influence and action outside the latticework of role boundaries and authority, and when faculty leadership is examined in the context of a faculty community of colleagues rather than an academic organizational hierarchy.

*What Was the Problem I Was Chasing*

One way to understand the study of the relationship of ritual and faculty leadership is by examining the presence of ritualization in narrative self-descriptions by research participants in leadership work. Within a qualitative research tradition, a "narrative analysis" (Riessman, 1993) and "narrative inquiry" (Clandinin & Connelly, 2001) of interview self-reflections of research participants about ritualization present in their leadership work would generate the following research questions to explore:

1. Are there themes or patterns to how faculty make meaning of their work of leadership?
2. What patterns of ritualization are described by research participants in their reflections of the leadership work of their faculty colleagues?
3. In what ways do the described themes or patterns of leadership experiences correspond with any of the known theoretically derived structures of ritualization?
4. What meanings are attached to the ritualization of the work of faculty leadership?

## Why Was This Significant

When I began the study I thought the examination of ritualization through the interpretive perspectives of faculty members would serve to further expand our understanding of meaning making in faculty leadership. I thought that, within its limitations, this particular study could result in identifying a beginning description of the "structures" of ritualization present in leadership as a process of influence.

An explication of the interaction of ritual and ritualization and leadership in the actions and reflections of faculty members can also extend the understanding of professional peers as leaders in a professional community. For me, this promisesd a fertile patch for cultivating an understanding of the meaning-making perspectives of faculty teaching and leadership in higher education (Palmer, 1998).

## Limitations and Delimitations

Most qualitative inquiry will generate data with very little generalizability beyond the scope of the context of the study, in this instance, a group of faculty members enacting mutually influential leadership in a small selective liberal arts college in the Midwest. This is both a weakness and strength of this study. While a grounded theory approach cannot by definition yield a generalizable theory (Glaser & Strauss, 1967; Strauss & Corbin, 1998), as Patti Lather (1997) has argued, interpretive and constitutive studies can successfully capture phenomena when liberated from positivistic "regulatory" practices of validity. Indeed, I thought the qualitative research approach could liberate this inquiry to generate new ways of exploring leadership that can then be extended in further studies. Naturally, the scope of this study will be bound to the examination of faculty participant interpretations of observed leadership work through the self-reflections of selected participating faculty members/leaders.

## *Definitions of Some Terms*

I use a number of terms in explaining the study that are worthy of better precision. Here below are some of terms and their operating difinitions.

Leadership. Leadership includes identifiable perspectives and observable behaviors that seemingly initiate change and/or seek to influence others' thinking, actions and decisions in service towards a collective and/or mutually beneficial and purposive change.

Ritual. Ritual or rite is an observable pattern of repeated purposeful actions and behavior that appears to generate significant, often public, meaning for the research participants external to the enacted pattern of actions itself.

Ritualization. Ritualization or *secular ceremony* (Moore & Myerhoff, 1971) is also a pattern of purposeful actions and behaviors in everyday life, that research participants described as occurring during passages and transitions of significance that generated often personal meaning for individual participants.

Structures of ritualization. Drawing largely on theoretical classifications of components of ritual and ritualization, structures are predictable and patterned elements and events contained in the flow of ritualization or ritual action.

I use a number of others terms that I define and explicate later in this book, as they are better explained in their contexts.

# Chapter 2

# Ritualization And Leadership

When we explore the relationship between ritualization and leadership, we encoounter the process of meaning making as a means to illuminate the deeper significance that is embedded in the ritualization that is found in faculty leadership work. In this chapter I review various theoretical approaches to ritualization and leadership to construct a framework that supports and contextualizes ritualization in faculty leadership.

## Meaning and Sensemaking

The concept of meaning is such an everyday crude construction that, like beauty and leadership, meaning may be much easier to understand than define; meaning defies rational study. On the one hand, from the interior psychological perspective, discerning meaning has been aggregated with concepts of judgment and decision-making, "the human ability to infer, estimate, and predict…" (Hastie & Dawes, 2001, p. 48). On the other hand, from the exterior sociological perspective, discerning meaning is implicated in the indeterminate *double contingency* processes for how a rational actor determines his/her observable behaviors "contingent on the actions of others, which are in turn contingent upon his actions" (Coleman, 1990, p. 902). As James

Coleman (1990) has interestingly noted, this "greatly complicates the very concept of what constitutes rational or optimal action" (p. 902).

Edmund Bolles' (1991) and Karl Weick's (1995) constructions of sensemaking offer interpretive possibilities for operationalizing meaning making. The narrative descriptions obtained from the transcripts of interviews of research participants would furnish data on their sensemaking of leadership in their academic contexts.

Bolles (1991) located the concept of meaning in human perception. He noted that, in Gestalt psychology, "*figures* are the things we attend to; *ground* is the array of sensations we ignore" (Bolles, 1991, 24). For our purposes, meaning and what is meaningful may be derived, partially, by understanding participant constructions and re-constructions of the perceptual array of figures and ground, and partially by discerning how and why the research participants selected their notions of figures and ground related to faculty leadership.

Another framework for meaning making, from the perspective of communities and organizations, was proposed by Karl Weick (1995), in his concept of *sensemaking*, which he asserted was more a "set of heuristics rather than an… algorithm" (Weick, 1995, p. xii). Weick extended and distinguished his work from Harold Garfinkel's (1967) previous studies, on interpretation and decision-making, and in particular on how jurors retrospectively made sense of the facts. Interpreting facts, Garfinkel (1967) proposed, was largely a phenomenon of retrospectively "assigning outcomes their legitimate history…" (Garfinkel, 1967, p. 115). Weick (1995) proposed that sensemaking could be understood as a process with seven distinguishing properties. The process of sensemaking is:

(1) grounded in identity construction,
(2) retrospective,
(3) enactive of sensible environments,
(4) social,
(5) ongoing,
(6) focused on and by extracted cues, and
(7) driven by plausibility rather than accuracy, (Weick, 1995, p. 17).

According to Weick (1995), sensemaking is *grounded in the sensemaker* because it begins with a singular and mutable self that is shaped and identified in interaction with others (pp. 19-20). Sensemaking is also *retrospective* as an "act of reflection" that corresponds to "a cone of light that spreads backward from a particular present" (p. 26). Specific events and phenomena are remembered and synthesized with meaning in terms of present values, priorities, and projects (p. 27).

Sensemaking is *enactive of sensible environments* in that "people create their environments as those environments create them" (p. 34). Drawing largely on the earlier work of Mary Parker Follett (1924), Weick (1995) asserted that sensemaking emerged from enacted co-determination with the environment. Sensemaking is social and "never solitary because what a person does internally is contingent on others… even monologues and one-way communications assume an audience" (p. 40). Sensemaking is *ongoing* because sensemakers "are always in the middle of things, which become things, only when… people focus on the past from some point beyond it" (p. 43). Here again, is sensemaking metaphorically presented as the retrospecting cone of light.

Sensemaking is *focused on and by extracted cues* because sensemakers interact with their contexts by attending to particular cues. They extract from their contexts "simple, familiar structures that are seeds from which people develop a large sense of what may be occurring" (p. 50). Finally, *plausibility rather than accuracy* drives sensemaking because sensemakers "need to distort and filter, to separate signal from noise given their current projects," and because "sensemaking is about the embellishment and elaboration of an… extracted cue… (which is) linked with a general idea" (p. 56). In short, the process of sensemaking drives toward what appears plausible rather than what is accurate, and on the basis of cues extracted in interaction with the environment. Sensemaking is also an ongoing process of the self in relation to others. These explanations of meaning making (Bolles, 1991) and sense making (Weick, 1995) present useful frameworks for examining how and why the research participants in this study make meaning of leadership through ritualization.

## Ritual and Ritualization

Ritual is like many other phenomena resistant to being contained by language. It has enjoyed multiple definitions, and in most works of scholarship, ritual is operationally defined in accord with the purposes and perspectives of the phenomenon being explained. For the purpose of this review, ritual or ritualization is defined as a pattern of purposeful action or behavior that generates meaning external to the action itself. Gerard Pottenbaum's (1992) definition comes nearest to capturing the phenomena of ritual, which he very poetically suggested, is "the dramatic form through which people in community make tangible in symbol, gesture, word, and song what they have come to believe is the hidden meaning of their experience in relationship with the world, with others, and with their God" (p. 7). Pottenbaum's (1992) definition situates and vivifies ritual in the context of some of the major theories of myth, ritual, and spirituality that are described below.

### Ritual in Sacred Time and Sacred Place

In his classic work on human spirituality, *The Sacred and the Profane*, Mircea Eliade (1957) outlined a theoretical framework for understanding spirituality and myth. Eliade (1957) suggested that the human experience of apprehending and contending with the mysteries of the universe prevents space and time from being experienced as infinitely homogenous; instead space and time are comprehended as punctuated by distinct and bracketed experiences that provide reference and orientation. In fact, "spatial nonhomogeneity finds expression in the experience of an opposition between space that is sacred…and all other space, the formless expanse surrounding it" (Eliade, 1957, p. 20). This is not just a lingual polarity but also an ontological adjacency, because "there is not only a break in the homogeneity of space; there is also revelation of an absolute reality, opposed to the nonreality of the vast surrounding expanse" (p. 21). The spiritual or meaning-making need that is fulfilled by this oppositional propinquity of sacred and non-sacred (profane) space was the human need to find points of reference in an otherwise infinite, chaotic and mysterious universe. The opposition of sacred space and profane space provides punctuation and orientation in an otherwise unmarked and infinite universe.

Sacred space is found in "privileged places, qualitatively different from all others," (Eliade, 1957, p. 24) and can be found in both secular and religious sites. Coming home to a favorite chair, or visiting certain places that have consecrated significant meaning, or going to a temple, or approaching the altar, are some examples of approaching and entering sacred space.

Eliade (1957) also theorized that human experience separates time into sacred and non-sacred (profane) time. Intervals of sacred time are for the most part "liturgical time" and "represent the reactualization of a sacred event that took place in a mythical past" (Eliade, 1957, p. 69). Sacred time is "reversible and recoverable, a sort of eternal mythical present that is periodically reintegrated by means of rites" (p. 70). Entering sacred time often consists of celebrating anniversaries of times and events that engendered significant meaning. Thus, sacred time allows a return to the beginning, a means to stratify temporal continuity with a hierarchy of important moments.

Rituals, according to Lauri Honko (1984) are informed and sanctioned by myths. Myths provide the "ideological content" for meaningful patterns of action (p. 51). Stories that engender meaning are constructed into myths that provide an ontological lens for understanding the world. Rituals, therefore, are symbolic enactments of myth.

The approaching and entering of the sacred in space and time are ways for men and women to turn the chaotic relativity of experience into an orientation of order and hope, grounded in meaning-engendering stories that are constructed into myth. This journey between the thresholds of the sacred and the profane in the context of meaningful myth is sometimes understood in terms of personal or community pilgrimage (Barber, 1991). This pilgrimage captures the elements of transition and transformation fundamental to all ritual (Driver,

1998). Repeating this patterned journey then coheres into a pathway of ritualization, which according to Driver (1998), become "old forms invested with rich symbolic content and carefully guarded by explicit traditions and rules" (Driver, 1998, p. 17).

*Ritual as Structure and Performance*

Another perspective that aids in the pursuit of a working definition of ritual is Arnold Van Genepp's (1960) classification of rites. Van Genepp suggested that among ceremonial patterns, rites of passage might generally be analyzed into "rites of separation, transition rites, and rites of incorporation" (Van Genepp, 1960, p. 11). Van Genepp's ternate passage, which he also called "the territorial passage" (p. 15), is drawn primarily from a socio-cultural perspective of rituals observed in pre-industrial communities. He also proposed to call "the rites of separation from a previous world, preliminal rites, those executed during the transition stage, liminal (or threshold) rites, and ceremonies of incorporation into the new world post-liminal rites" (p. 21).

Preliminal rituals, or rites of separation, such as observed in funeral ceremonies, involve having participants enact symbolic actions to sever old or current connections, with the present or past status, and/or with present or past time.

Following separation, liminal rituals, or rites of transition, such as seen in marriage ceremonies, involve having participants engage in conduct that symbolically and even tangibly transforms their identities. In the liminal phase, participants are suspended outside their normative roles and statuses, and beyond alienation, in an undifferentiated transcendent blending of "lowliness and sacredness, of homogeneity and comradeship… in and out of time… and in and out of secular social structure," which Turner termed "communitas" (Turner, 1969, p. 96). In liminality participants are said to be "outside society, and society has no power over them, especially since they are actually sacred and holy, and therefore untouchable and dangerous, just as gods would be" (Van Gennep, 1960, p. 114). Following transition, post-liminal rituals, or rites of incorporation consummate the three-phase process and involve celebrations of reintegration and return, often with new and mature perspectives and responsibilities. Together in fluid sequence, these three stages of separation, transition, and reintegration constitute the structure of the rites of passage (Van Gennep, 1960).

Van Gennep's (1960) classification of the rites of passage can also be co-located with Eliade's (1957) description of the journey into sacred space or sacred time and back. This would necessitate viewing Van Gennep's (1960) preliminal phase as the stage of purification and preparation before entering the sacred, the liminal phase as the threshold entry into the sacred, and the post-liminal phase as the exiting out of the sacred back into the normal or profane.

Ritual journeys, while they may involve individual or solitary participants, are made in the public context of community, and are often observed by non-participating community members. As such, rituals can also be seen in terms of performance. Indeed, Stanley Tambiah (1980) has suggested that ritual as "a culturally constructed system of symbolic communication… constituted of patterned and ordered sequences of words and acts, often expressed in multiple media…is performative" (Tambiah, 1980, p. 497). According to Tambiah (1980), rituals are performative because they are characterized by features of performance such as "formality (conventionality), stereotypy (rigidity), condensation (fusion), and redundancy (repetition)" (Tambiah, 1980, p. 497). In this sense rituals can be seen as performances (a) because in enacting ritual a participant "saying something is also doing something as a conventional act," (b) because ritual is a "staged performance that uses multiple media by which the participants experience the event intensively," and (c) because "indexical values… [are]… being attached to and inferred by actors during the performances" (p. 497). Ritual performance is public ritual even as it is experienced and interpreted uniquely, personally and individually. After the ritual is the memory of the ritual, remembered uniquely, personally and individually. Only the personal reflection of the ritual participant in their passage narrative (Grimes, 1995, 2000) offers access to how ritual and ritualization has shaped meaning-making.

Eliade's (1957) description furnished purpose for ritual – the pursuit of proximity to the sacred; Van Gennep's (1960) classification provided a structure for ritual – a passage through three phases, Tambiah's (1980) description related ritual to its context – the ambient mythology that surrounds the setting for ritual performance, while Grimes (1995, 2000) perspective affords access to personal meaning-making. The extent to which the work of faculty leadership can be observed and described as performance with purpose, with a structure of entry, engagement, and exit, grounded in an ambient mythology, and implicated in personal meaning-making invites some promising glimpses of a relationship between ritual and leadership.

*Ritual as Secular Ceremony*

Approaching ritual from an anthropological study of everyday life, Sally Moore and Barbara Myerhoff (1977) and Myerhoff (1978) differentiated secular ceremony as a Western phenomenon distinct from more traditional and religious forms of ritual embedded in universal and religious beliefs. Moore and Myerhoff (1977) defined secular ceremony as ritual that communicated everyday beliefs and convictions in a non-religious context. In higher education settings, this definition of secular ceremony would include campus ritualizations such as formal meetings, award ceremonies, alumni reunions, installations, convocations, and commencements. They would also include more personal and individual ritual-like routines that mark or greet transitions of personally meaningful significance. These stand as a category distinct from more formal rituals such as birth and fertility rites, marriage, etc.

Moore and Myerhoff (1977) described secular ceremony as "an act or actions intentionally conducted" (p. 199), with certain properties summarized by Kathleen Manning (2000) as:

(a) repetition in content, form, and occasion;
(b) self-conscious or deliberate action by the participant as part of the distinct behavior or stylized performance;

(c) orderly, stylized action achieved through exaggerated precision, extraordinary actions, or ordinary actions dramatized in unusual ways;
(d) evocative style, presentation, and staging to engage and focus the audience's attention;
(e) a collective dimension expressed in the ritual's message of community and social meaning (p. 46).

The exploration of secular ritualization on campus will differ from more formal campus rites because secular ritualization actions are less formally structured, extemporaneous, and open to interpretation. Secular ritualization engenders meaning for participants that is more local and profound, and less often spiritual and universal.

Ronald Grimes (2000) presented an alternative to exploring ritual through myth and spirituality, suggesting an approach to ritual that examines "passage narratives, accounts told by individuals who narrate their experiences of passage" (Grimes, 2000, p. 9). Recognizing that individual accounts of ritual might appear largely irrelevant to the performance of the rite itself, Grimes (2000) maintained that "the telling and retelling become extensions of the rite itself, stretching it from the original performance in the past until it touches and transforms the present" (p. 10).

Passage narratives are descriptions of ritual experiences that are embedded in what Grimes (2000) called "passage systems, which is to say, assumptions (both shared and contested) about the life course, rites for negotiating this obstacle-laden course, and social arrangements for enacting and perpetuating these rites" (p. 41).

*Ritual in Higher Education*

In the life and work of the faculty at small colleges like Wilkinson, replete with cyclical gestures and ceremonies on campus, the daily passages of leadership influence are surely implicated in the rhythmic life course of institutional experience and the social arrangements of the faculty community (Frost & Taylor, 1996). For members of the faculty, their college community serves as their passage system; their self-reflective narratives on their ritualization and their leadership work serve as their passage narratives. An examination of these passage narratives can therefore offer access to ritualization and leadership.

In her study of ritual and culture at Mount Holyoke College, a women's liberal arts college, Kathleen Manning (1990, 2000), observed that campus rituals provided a "vehicle to communicate and perpetuate the college's purposes, spirit, and ideals" by maintaining a "structure of communal beliefs and ideals" (Manning, 2000, p. 248). She also suggested that for "administrators and faculty," secular ceremony was an "apt form…to communicate the values and ideals of higher education" (pp. 45-46).

In her study Manning (2000) summarized the literature of ritual and identified seven categories of ritual "highlighted due to their prevalence or importance on college campuses" (Manning, 2000, p. 5). Her studies were based on observations at Mount Holyoke College in South Hadley, Massachusetts, and Saint Michael's College in Colchester, Vermont, both liberal arts colleges similar to Wilkinson College in mission and organization. Manning's (2000) study developed non-mutually exclusive categories of ritual that included (1) rituals of reification, (2) rituals of revitalization, (3) rituals of resistance, (4) rituals of incorporation, (5) rituals of investiture, (6) rituals of entering and leaving, and (7) rituals of healing (pp. 5-7).

Campus rituals of reification, such as convocations, functioned to reassure participants that their choices and sacrifices to associate with the College were important and valuable, and "not made in vain" (Manning, 2000, p. 5). Rituals of revitalization, whether formally structured such as presidential inaugurations or informally structured such as meetings, rehearsals, and announcements "revitalize the college's founding values, restate and update underlying assumptions, and enlist new recruits into the belief structure of the institution" (p. 5). Rituals of resistance, such as fraternity and sorority hazing, are seldom institutionally sanctioned but are created by participants to reflect the "true meaning of college living" (p. 5). Rituals of incorporation, such as commencement, provide for a "ceremonial bridge" marking a recognizable change in status and the transition from one relationship with the college to another, such as "crossing from one role (student) to an second role (alumni)" (p. 5). Rituals of investiture, such as the inauguration of a new college president, are public ceremonies that "symbolize the strength of the institution as exemplified by the prominence of the ceremony..." (p. 6). Rituals of entering and leaving, signified by the crossing of thresholds, help participants symbolically classify meaningful locations as inside and outside investing cultural attributions to special locations that can evoke unique responses (Gallagher, 1993). Through these rituals, often embedded in relationships with the architecture of the campus, "students symbolically claimed college ground... the buildings and landscapes... became the material embodiment of college life" (Horowitz, 1984, p. 178). Rituals of healing, such as memorial services, serve to help members of the campus community respond to crisis or tragedy, either on or off campus, and are organized to "help the survivors cope with the pain of loss" (Manning, 2000, p. 7).

Manning (2000) identified four "significant themes" embedded in these categories of campus rituals that included (1) mirroring the College's values, (2) punctuation and mediation of campus life, (3) power, and (4) criticism and parody (Manning, 2000, pp. 8-9). The cyclical and seasonal nature of the work of a residential liberal arts college creates an orderly and predictable procession of rich ritualization.

Eliade's (1957) conception of nonhomogeneity furnishes a universal backdrop for understanding how ritual can be critical to both apprehending and making meaning of our circumstances. Moore and Myerhoff's (1977) five "properties" of secular ceremony (Manning, 2000, p.46) offer a potential framework for developing a line of inquiry to discern structures of ritualization in faculty leadership. It is quite possible that these structures may emerge with a construction that resembles Van Gennep's (1960) three-phase rite of passage. Tambiah's (1980) characterization of ritual as invested with features of performance also offers a potential framework for discerning structures of ritualization in faculty leadership, since, as noted later in this chapter, much of what is described as leadership is often deemed performative.

Manning's (1990, 2000) studies of observed ritual on the campuses of two institutions similar to Wilkinson College, provide both a rationale and basis for structuring this proposed study of ritualization on campus. Unlike Manning's (1990, 2000) studies however, my particular study is domain-limited to the faculty and their leadership activities at Wilkinson. Manning's (1990, 2000) studies involved the description and interpretation of public ceremony and ritual that encompassed the entire campus community, and particularly provided for a seven-category taxonomy of campus ritual. Unlike Manning's (1990, 2000) well-described observations, my study examined ritualization in faculty leadership as interpreted by faculty members, through their own passage narratives (Grimes, 2000). And again unlike Manning's (1990, 2000) studies of ritualized campus occasions, my study examined the less formally structured ritualization (Driver, 1998) and secular ceremony (Moore & Myerhoff, 1977) surrounding faculty leadership as reported by research participants in their passage narratives (Grimes, 2000).

## Leadership

This study of ritualization in faculty leadership requires transcending classical and conventional theoretical constructions of leadership. Narratives that describe leadership as the "heroic" work of extraordinary persons date back as early as the fifth-century BC (Holliday, 2000). Since then most theory and advice on leadership have generally embraced the presumption that leaders occupy positions in a hierarchy. In emerging contrast, more recent constructions present the work of leadership as a process activity, accessible to all partners joined in a community of shared purpose and activity (Moxley, 2000).

*Power and Positionality*

Exploring leadership outside the structures of hierarchies and positions requires constructing broader notions of leadership that include the experiences and perspectives of leaders without formal role authority. In her study of higher education leadership models, Adrianna Kezar (1996) observed that, "constructions of leadership [in higher education] were related to an individual's positionality" (Kezar, 1996, p. 389). In a subsequent treatise on pluralistic notions of leadership, Kezar (2000) noted that for faculty and administrators, "positionality considerations," such as background, campus role, and power conditions, influentially shaped their constructions of leadership (p. 389). She suggested that:

> *Positioned individuals* (assuming that individuals co-construct their location culturally, organizationally, and historically while interacting with others) *possessing multifaceted identities* (assuming that individuals are shaped by formative conditions such as family, culture, community, religion, etc.) *within a particular context* (assuming most contexts are fairly unique and particular) *influenced by conditions of power* (assuming power relationships and dynamics pervade culture, social structures, and history) *construct* (develop understandings based on their situatedness or positionality and particular context and negotiate this understanding with other individuals' understandings) *leadership in unique (individual level) and collective (group level) ways simultaneously* (assuming independent webs of situated individuals connected by their changing positions on various issues) (Kezar, 2000, p.727).

This framework of enumerated positionality considerations offers a useful perspective for distilling faculty leadership from explanations of leadership that include formal roles of authority. Indeed, understanding how faculty members make meaning of ritualization in their leadership work will require excluding positionality considerations in developing the lines of inquiry in this study.

## Classical and Heroic Constructions

The history of the explanation of leadership has proceeded along six major theoretical approaches: (1) Great Man approaches, (2) Trait approaches, (3) Behavioral approaches, (4) Contingency and Situational approaches, and (5) Power and Influence approaches.

<u>Great Man Approaches</u>. Great Man approaches were intertwined in early understandings of polity that located monarchs and royal leaders as mediators between the divine and the human. Leadership was understood and accepted as a hereditary qualification, and therefore accessible only to the presumably heroic chosen few. While the logic of this approach has now been rejected as inappropriate, some vestiges remain today in commonly acceptable expectations of entitlement and obligation for the scions of leaders.

<u>Trait Approaches</u>. Trait theories of leadership were presented on the assumption that leaders possessed individual traits that marked them as naturally capable, and that these traits transcended all contexts. These traits often included physical characteristics (such as height) and personality features (such as self-confidence), specific capabilities (intelligence) and background (career history). The corollary assumption was that non-leaders, often but not always followers, shared common perceptions regarding the traits of successful leadership (Bass, 1981, 1990; Yukl, 1994). More recent constructions extending this approach have included biographical case histories in search of common characteristics and conditions of highly successful and exceptional change agents and leaders (for example Daloz et al, 1996; Gardner, 1995).

<u>Behavioral Approaches</u>. Behavioral theories were attempts to rationally identify and study the notable behaviors that differentiated successful leaders from unsuccessful leaders. They were rooted in the methodological tradition of survey studies, principally at The Ohio State University and the University of Michigan. In the 1950s and 60s, thousands of manager-leaders and subordinate-followers were surveyed across various organizations. Their responses resulted in the patterning of successful leadership behaviors along two independent dimensions

called *consideration* and *initiating structure* (Fleishman, 1973; Halpin & Winer, 1957). Consideration included behaviors that demonstrated support and concern. Initiating structure included task-related behaviors relevant to accomplishing goals and monitoring performance.

In another related study, Douglas McGregor (1960) connected Abraham Maslow's (1954) concept of self-actualization with trust in a managerial perspective called *Theory Y*. A *Theory Y* perspective on leadership that premised followers who wanted to work, and attain goals they were committed to. The opposing perspective was that of *Theory X*, a perspective grounded on the belief that followers disliked work and responsibility, and leadership work required managing control and compliance.

Working independently, Rensis Likert (1961) elaborated on the relationship of leader behavior and group performance, which paralleled McGregor's (1960) "Theory X" and "Theory Y." He identified four basic orientations he called "systems" – *exploitative-authoritative (system 1), benevolent-authoritative (system 2), consultative (system 3)* and *participative (system 4)*. Likert's (1961) *system 1* and *system 4* orientations were similar to McGregor's (1960) *Theory X* and *Theory Y* perspectives. Likert (1961) constructed his *systems* by combining two categories of behaviors: *Job-centered* and *Employee-centered* dimensions. The Job-centered categories of behaviors included *goal emphasis* behaviors that attended to accomplishing group goals, and *work facilitation* behaviors concerned with clarifying roles and managing resources. Employee-centered categories of behavior included *leader support* behaviors that demonstrated concern for subordinates, and *interaction facilitation* behaviors to manage conflict and relationships in the group.

Robert Blake and Jane Mouton (1964) summarized these studies in their profiling of effective leadership along two vectors – (1) *concern for people* and (2) *concern for production*. While this bipolar conceptualization has endured remarkably in subsequent thinking on leadership, behavioral approaches in general were ultimately rejected because their assumptions of universally successful leadership behaviors did not sufficiently cross over different situations.

Contingency and Situational Approaches. Contingency and Situational theories of leadership attempted to extend behavioral approaches in terms of situation and context. An early notable example is Fred Fiedler's (1967) *contingency model*, which was based on the premise that leaders have consistent profiles of behaviors that are associated with successful leadership in certain situations. Hence leadership effectiveness was best attained through thoughtful and managed selection of effective leader-situation matches. Another model inside the contingency approach is *path-goal theory* (Evans, 1970; House & Dressler, 1974), which posits the recommendation that successful leaders furnish or ensure available rewards for goal attainment and then focus on behaviors that support followers along their path to accomplishing their goals.

The *situational leadership* model (Hersey & Blanchard, 1969, 1982) is rooted in the Ohio State and Michigan behavioral approach studies (Fleishman, 1973; Likert, 1961), and ranges effective leadership along two axes, *task behaviors* and *relationship behaviors*. Four combinations of high and low degrees of task and relationship behaviors are ideally matched with categorical situations of increasing follower *task maturity*, also known as *follower readiness*. Therefore, a combination of high task and low relationship behaviors (Telling) is ideally matched with followers with low task maturity/follower readiness. A combination of low task and low relationship behaviors (Delegating) is ideally matched with followers with high task maturity/follower readiness. In the situational leadership model, the key to successful leadership work is to adapt the appropriate combination of behaviors to its respective situation of follower task maturity and readiness. Leadership in this model is most effective when the appropriate combination is utilized.

More recently Lawrence Miller (1989) has proposed a model, which suggests that successful leadership behavior profiles correspond with the life cycle phase of the organization of followers. Earlier in the rapid growth phase of the life cycle of the organization, leadership is effective when it is inspiring and innovative requiring leadership profiles of the *prophet* and *barbarian*. Later in the life cycle, as growth declines, and as specialization, systems, and security increase in the organization, effective leadership is required in terms of the profiles of the *builder and explorer* and the *administrator*. According to Miller (1989), as the organization's creative energy gives way to the orthodoxy of past strategy and structure, the congruent leadership profiles of the *bureaucrat* and the *aristocrat* prevail, thus leading to the gradual demise of the organization. In the higher education context, the contingency and situational approaches and the life cycle approach have extended into models about viewing effective leadership as situationally responsive to multiple organizational realities (Bensimon, 1991) or to distinct academic cultures (Bergquist, 1992).

Power and Influence Approaches. Power is defined as the "capacity" for effecting change, whereas influence is the "degree of actual change" (Hughes, Ginnett, & Curphy, 1996, p. 119). Power and influence theories considered the sources and quantities of power, and explored how successful leaders use strategies of influence (Cialdini, 1993, 1995), how they generate and use power (Kotter, 1985), and how leaders use symbols and other representations of authority (Pfeffer, 1992), sometimes even to accomplish inappropriate or immoral outcomes (Milgram, 1974). An early taxonomy of social power identified five sources of power available for leaders to influence followers: (1) *expert* power based on knowledge, (2) *referent* power based on role modeling and relationships, (3) *legitimate* power based on organizational role, (4) *reward* power based on control over desired resources, and (5) *coercive* power based on ability to administer negative sanctions (French & Raven, 1959).

James MacGregor Burns (1978) drew a distinction between *power-wielders* and *leaders*. Power-wielders influenced followers to accomplish goals that are important mostly to the power-wielder. Leaders mobilized followers and marshaled resources to accomplish goals that would benefit followers, themselves, as well as others. Burns (1978) also described leadership as recognizable in two forms: *transactional* leadership and *transformational* leadership. Transactional leadership transpires in a mutually beneficial relationship of exchange between the leader and follower. Burns (1978) characterized this kind of leadership as transitory and effective, but in pursuit of *modal values* of mutual exchange. Transactional leadership typically maintains status quo and does not elicit change. Transformational leadership, in contrast, attempts to change the status quo by developing a vision for the future that appeals to the values and sense of purpose of followers. Transformational leaders teach followers to become leaders, pursuing humanistic and moral *end values* related to making a difference in the world.

Some elements of power and influence approaches, such as expert and referent power (French & Raven, 1959), social influence (Cialdini, 1995), and transformational leadership (Burns, 1978), begin to transcend perspectives on leadership based solely on leaders as roles in a hierarchy. When leadership is examined outside this paradigm of leaders as roles, where all community partners are leaders and partners jointly and severally engaged in a shared purpose, this concept presents more promising possibilities for examining leadership related to faculty work, ritualization, and meaning making.

## *Emergent and Post-Heroic Constructions*

James Rost (1991) differentiated emergent and post-heroic constructions of leadership from classical and heroic constructions by describing the latter as embedded in the industrial paradigm with theories that were "structural-functionalist, management-oriented, personalistic in focusing only on the leader, goal-achievement dominated, self-interested and individualistic in outlook, male-oriented, utilitarian and materialistic in ethical perspective, and rationalistic, technocratic, linear, quantitative, and scientific in language and methodology" (Rost, 1991, p. 27). Post-industrial explanations of leadership, grounded in the emergent and post-heroic constructions explicated below, represent a different direction.

Unlike the classical and heroic tradition described above, through which one can trace a linear evolution, post-heroic constructions are a family of explanations without a cohering motif. Post-heroic explanations

(Rost, 1991) focus on leadership as an activity or process, rather than leadership as an appointed role. All members of the community are presumed potentially both leaders and followers working towards a shared purpose. Post-heroic explanations also presume different preferences for organizations. Gareth Morgan (1989) has proposed a continuum of organization profiles that ranges from the mechanistic and bureaucratic profile organized for stability to the organic network profile organized for flexibility and change. Flexibility and change, while increasingly preferred as the appropriate organizational responses in more recent circumstances, necessitates post-heroic perspectives on leadership. The object of leadership in post-heroic explanations is to influence making change, most particularly social change. Three particular explanations relevant to this proposed research study are described below.

Servant Leadership. An early post-heroic explanation was Robert Greenleaf's (1977) notion of servant leadership, which was more homily than explanation of how leadership can be successful only in the form of a posture of service to others. Effective servant leadership is therefore distinguished by the servant-leader's motives: to help make a difference by focusing on the needs of others. By assisting others to grow their capabilities to learn more, to create change, and to work with others, the servant-leader is able to help effect transformations in the community (organization). Among other prescriptions, the servant-leader is exhorted to "become more the manager of a process that gets the job done and less the administrator of day-to-day operations" (Greenleaf, 1977, p. 151). Servant leadership is a potentially useful explanation to help examine faculty leadership, particularly since this explanation focuses on the work of individuals in a community of professional equals (Spears, 1995, 1998; Astin & Astin, 1999).

Leadership as Social Change. Emanating from a feminist study in the qualitative tradition, Helen Astin and Carole Leland (1991) interviewed 77 women they identified as leaders, and proposed a model of leadership based on social change. Their work was subsequently explained in the form of a social change framework of leadership (Higher

Education Research Institute, 1996) that could be applied to both positional and non-positional leadership. In a subsequent elaboration of their transformative leadership framework, Alexander Astin and Helen Astin (2000) defined leadership as a "purposive process… inherently value-based…[that is]…ultimately concerned with fostering change" (Astin & Astin, 2000, p. 8). The leader, therefore, is viewed as a "change agent" (p. 8), and leadership values are grounded in the contextual aspirations toward which the change is being pursued. Robert Young (1997) has outlined a thorough taxonomy of significant values prized in the milieu of higher education, and therefore very probably embedded in the aspirations for social change leadership among the faculty.

Effective leadership, in the social change framework, is defined as a *group process* that requires that "(a) the group function according to certain principles and values, and that (b) individual members of the group exemplify certain qualities and values…" (Astin & Astin, 2000, p. 11). The group principles necessary to advancing the leadership process include (1) engendering *collaboration*, (2) agreeing on *shared purpose*, (3) engaging in *disagreement with respect*, (4) clarifying the *division of labor*, and (5) maintaining a mutually beneficial collaborative *learning environment* (pp. 11-12). For individuals, the qualities also necessary to the process include (1) facilitating *self-knowledge*, (2) maintaining *authenticity and integrity*, (3) supplying and sustaining *commitment*, (4) listening and cultivating *empathy and understanding of others*, and (5) promoting and utilizing *competence* (pp. 12-13).

In the social change framework for leadership, each of the ten group and individual qualities are deemed to be in dynamic and reinforcing interaction with each other. The emphases on leadership as a process and grounded in values extend this social change framework outside of conventional constructions of leadership as heroic activity.

<u>Leadership and Spirit</u>. Another post-heroic approach proposed by Russ Moxley (2000), and grounded in action research at the Center for Creative Leadership, explores the role of spirit and meaning making in communities and organizations. Noting that "spirit is as natural as anything else in the natural world… [and] an essential part of each of us"

(Moxley, 2000, p. 25), Moxley distinguished the "spirited" organization from the "dispirited" organization in the table on the next page.

Dispirited organizations, according to Moxley (2000), evolve as the consequence of coercive power and hierarchical arrangements. Spirited organizations, in contrast, are nurtured by a *partnership model* that requires (1)

| Spirited | Dispirited |
| --- | --- |
| Use all four energies (mental, physical, emotional, spiritual) at work | Use physical and mental at work |
| Work is a vocation | Work is a job |
| Sense of connectedness to others; community or family used as metaphor | Sense of separation and disconnectedness; more competition than cooperation and community |
| Congruence between personal and organizational mission and values; work has meaning and purpose | Lack of congruence between personal and organizational mission and values; lack of meaning and purpose |
| Energized and animated workers | Workers drained of energy |
| Workers involved in the activity of leadership | Leadership exercised in a top-down way |

(Moxley, 2000, p. 39).

balance of power, (2) shared purpose, (3) shared responsibility, (4) respect for the person, and (5) partnering in the nitty-gritty (pp. 75-77). *Balance of power* is maintained by eschewing "positional and coercive power" and when "all individuals claim their personal power and use it help co-create win-win situations and reach a shared goal" (p. 75). *Shared purpose* is encouraged by honoring disagreement and conflict, "but underneath there is a shared commitment to a larger mission" (p. 75). *Shared responsibility* is maintained by mutual expectation, where "all the participants share responsibility and accountability for the work of the partnership," regardless of their authority (p. 75). *Respect for the person* is codified by prizing the "belief in the inherent worth and value of every person" and assuming that "everyone has gifts and skills and energies to offer to the process of cocreation" (p. 76). *Partnering in the nitty-gritty* is embedded in the architecture and processes of the organization so that all situations are responded to by "individuals working as partners, rather than as boss and subordinate" (p. 77). Together these requirements create the conditions for people in organizations to experience "more vitality and energy… [where]… spirit is experienced, elegantly weaving individuals and their relationships" (p. 77).

Heroic and classical constructions of leadership have dominated explanations of leadership and management, but these constructions are inextricably linked to understandings of organizations as hierarchies and a leader-follower polarity that assumes leadership as an exclusive and elite activity. Constructions of leadership for the purpose of this research study will need to extend beyond heroic explanations in order to help access and interpret the mutually influencing leadership of a professional community of faculty members.

## Leadership in the Academic Context

*Faculty Leadership*

Judith Little (2000) has described a school education analog of college and university faculty leadership, called "teacher leadership," where "teachers are expected to exert the kind of influence on one another that would enhance success and satisfaction with students" (Little, 2000, p. 393). In a historical analysis of the evolution of the profession of teaching in both schools and post-secondary institutions, Gerald Grant and Christine Murray (1999) delineated how "schoolteaching and professing" have institutionalized differently over time, and yet they shared the "essential acts of teaching" (p. 32). Schoolteachers and college and university faculty share the essential acts of "knowing the student, engaging and motivating, modeling, judging and evaluating, and reflecting and renewing" (Grant & Murray, 1999, pp. 32-56). The authors examine a number of promising examples in the "slow revolution" of professional teachers providing peer-based leadership of their work with students and learning.

Astin and Astin (2000) have woven the individual and group qualities of their model of transformative leadership (described earlier) into the three roles of faculty members – teacher, scholar, and provider of service to the institution, describing an elaborate model for the "faculty leader" (Astin & Astin, 2000, pp. 34-41). The exploration of faculty leadership is even further refined when we examine its fluid and fertile context – the systems and cultural perspectives on describing leadership in the academy.

When universities and colleges are roundly criticized for their lack of effectiveness, Max Weber's (1947) efficient machine bureaucracy is often the comparison ideal in mind. However, the academic organization's unique "messiness" of multiple missions is more suitably understood through alternative frames such as "cultures" and "cybernetic systems." The result of this alternative analysis is a revised appreciation of the more complex relationships between organizational effectiveness and organizational structure in college and university organizations.

*The Socio-Technical System*

The idea of viewing organizations as systems was advanced by Fred Emery and his collaborator Eric Trist, who both worked at the London Tavistock Institute in the 1950s and 1960s. Emery and Trist (1960) introduced the phrase "socio-technical system" to describe an organization that comprised of people interacting with each other (a social system) and choosing tools and techniques (a technical system) to obtain organizational outcomes. Emery borrowed the concept of the organization as an "open system" from Ludwig von Bertalanffy (1950, 1968), who proposed that many of the systems found in the biological and physical sciences expressed a design where all things influenced all other things. Since all the elements of a system functioned simultaneously as both cause and effect in their mutual influence, von Bertalanffy (1950, 1968) argued that identifying cause and effect chains would be impossible. Emery and Trist (1960) suggested that this was equally applicable in the reality of human systems in organizations.

Relationships between organizational effectiveness and organizational structures are predicated on the foundational concept of the organization as a socio-technical system. In the logic of this model, high performance is obtained when the "design of the technical system and the design of the social system of work were congruent" (Nadler & Gerstein, 1992, p.115). Thus the Weberian bureaucracy is a highly efficient socio-technical system. However, such logic fails to include the nuanced variations of the academic organization.

Emery and Trist (1960) described the organization as an open system that imports and converts a set of inputs -- mostly intellectual, physical, and financial capital -- into a set of exported outputs -- products and services. This continuous exchange provides feedback and renews the system. The college and university organization can be described as an open system with its structure shaped as a loosely-coupled confederation of autonomous specialized units – from academic departments of entomology to operational departments of parking services, each with their own inputs, processes, and outputs. The focus of college and university leadership on goals and values, and the evaluation of organizational effectiveness, still leaves faculty and operational managers with internal control over their processing of outputs.

*The Cultural Systems Perspective*

The attempt to understand the academic organization and to make sense of the apparently mysterious and irrational actions of human systems essentially evolved to viewing the organization as a culture, "the abstract values, beliefs, and perceptions that lie behind people's behavior" (Haviland, 1993, p. 29). Edgar Schein (1985) elaborated culture as a pattern of basic assumptions – invented, discovered, or developed by a given group as it learns to cope with its problems of external adaptation and internal integration – that has worked well enough to be considered valid and, therefore, to be taught to new members as the correct way to perceive, think, and feel in relation to those problems (p. 9).

This way of viewing the organization assumes that general and regular behaviors of the organization/system can be better understood by exploring elements of the organization's culture. When related to Emery and Trist's (1960) description of the socio-technical system, Schein's proffered function of culture appears to assist in defining how the system ought to process input into output, shape the contours of the social system, and thereby influence the technical system. The implications for organizational leadership become increasingly sophisticated: that "managing" the culture of the organization can be an effective way to manage the organization's ability to change, and to adapt and innovate.

William Bergquist (1992) has suggested that the academy could be characterized in four distinct cultures. These four cultures – the collegial, the managerial, the developmental and the negotiating culture are invisible, but deeply influence the interactions of the various members of the academic institution.

The assumptions of the *collegial culture* emphasize the independence of faculty professionals and strong "tolerance for and even encouragement of autonomous activity" (Bergquist, 1992, p. 43). Academic freedom resides as a strong value embedded in long tradition. Leadership is facilitated by people who assume "first among equals" roles, and who convene established quasi-political and protracted deliberations in pursuit of consensual decisions (p. 45).

In contrast to the serendipitous change and chaos of the collegial culture, Bergquist (1992) suggested that the second distinct culture -- the *managerial culture* -- embraces both the clarity of educational outcomes and evaluation of performance (p. 58). The managerial culture dominates community colleges, two-year colleges, and smaller public institutions, although Bergquist has argued that more and more institutions are likely to see the features of this distinct culture ascending in the future. Trends in academic organizations such as amplified size and complexity, more detailed statewide planning and evaluation of performance, the increased presence of part-time faculty members, and reduced financial support are leading to replacing the collegial culture with the managerial culture (pp. 66-68).

The interaction of the collegial and managerial cultures often results in two hybrid variations – the developmental culture and the negotiating culture. The *developmental culture* is a "healing" culture. Combining elements of both the collegial and the managerial, and grounded in principles from behavioral sciences, the developmental culture seeks to apply "rationality to personal and organizational life" and is often the dominant culture of populist institutions with non-traditional students and faculty (p. 102). Another outcome of the interaction of collegial and managerial cultures is the *negotiating culture*, which upholds the two major values of equity and egalitarianism (p.152). Wedded to the premise of ultimate compatibility between personal and organizational well being, institutions with a dominant negotiating culture are characterized by active collective bargaining and other processes for maintaining a balance of power (p.160).

Bergquist (1992) concluded that all institutions contain elements of all four cultures, therefore, leadership strategies for managing the culture of the organization require nurturing and integrating useful elements of each culture to assist with the institution's future adaptation and survival (pp. 170-171). The unique traditions and culture of the academic organization can therefore also be compared to Emery and Trist's (1960) socio-technical system although, as Schein (1985) has suggested, much of this cultural system remains invisible. Leadership, therefore, is concerned with leveraging the structural elements of the cultural system. In the structure of academic organizations, however, these structural elements appear connected to each other in an "intelligent" cybernetic system.

*The Cybernetic System Perspective*

Drawing on the earlier work of Katz and Kahn (1978) on social systems, Robert Birnbaum (1988) outlined three definitional characteristics of systems: interacting components, boundaries that delineate the system from the environment, and inputs and outputs of the system (Birnbaum, 1988, pp. 31-33). Permeable boundaries and complex sets of inputs and outputs (p. 34) characterize the academic organization as a system. Another feature is loosely coupled interactions between units or subsystems of the system. This means that while they are responsive to each other, departments of the academic organization retain their own intentions and wills. Birnbaum describes this loose coupling in responsiveness as far less "deterministic" and much more "probabilistic" (p. 38).

Loose coupling in organizations has been characterized as difficult to coordinate, inefficient and wasteful. Indeed, academic organizations have not been incorrectly criticized for being "the least businesslike and well managed" (Keller, 1983, p.5). However, Birnbaum has argued that loose coupling in higher education institutions provides "significant benefits" because "partially independent and specialized organizational elements increases…sensitivity to the environment" (Birnbaum, 1988, p. 40). This occurs because subsystems of an academic organizational structure are not just linked by interaction to each other but are also linked by interactions to subsystems of the environment. Thus, in a system sensitive to its complex and often turbulent environment, loose coupling permits sub-units with apparently irreconcilable goals -- such as an honors program and an equal opportunity program -- to coexist (p. 41). Each sub-unit of the academic organization system flourishes by being especially responsive to its unique environmental subsystem (p.43). This situates a highly differentiated system that together processes a complex set of inputs and outputs.

Within the academic organization, sub-units interact in amplifying and stabilizing circular loops of mutual influence. This interactive complexity, palpably inefficient, makes it extremely difficult to identify singular cause and effect vectors (Birnbaum, 1988), a description that relates well to von Bertalanffy's (1950, 1968) expression of the design of open systems found in the biological and physical sciences.

The viewing of the higher education institution as cybernetic system results in obviating a number of assumptions normally made for tightly coupled Weberian organizations outside the academy such as rationality, cause and effect, and predictability. Since elements and subsystems processing exchanges with their environments affect each other in such complex ways, actions and decisions often defy a universal rationality, and it becomes extremely difficult to identify cause and effect chains or predict decisions and direction. This often results in decision-making that appears ambiguous and the meaning of which transforms over time, and easily invites criticisms of ineffectiveness.

If decisions at higher education institutions are not made linearly with goals and rationality in mind then leadership becomes a series of sophisticated tasks of optimization. In Birnbaum's description of the academic organization as a cybernetic system, the system's well being is pursued through "cybernetic controls" as sub-units of the system make corrections in their course based on "thermostat and feedback loops" (p. 181).

In a later study of presidential leadership, Birnbaum (1992) suggested that cybernetic leadership emphasizes select feedback along with constituent support; leveraging resources, and symbolic leadership to seek institutional changes. Such leadership is required because forms of more direct control are rarely available as viable strategies. The most effective presidents and leaders of academic organizations, according to Birnbaum, are those that help their institutions interpret their information (p. 69).

*Leadership and Ritualization*

Tambiah (1980) has described ritual as performance. This conception assists in the correspondence of leadership to ritual. The purpose of leadership and the purpose of ritual both fulfill deep need for creating meaning and orientation for the human experience. Ronald Heifetz (1994) suggested the purpose of leadership was rooted in human social arrangements of "authority, and its precursors, dominance and deference" (Heifetz, 1994, p. 49). According to Heifetz (1994), ubiquitous structures of dominance embedded in our organizations and communities furnish both the setting and mythology for leadership. The rich mythology of leadership has evolved beyond the "great man" (leadership by inheritance) and "trait" (leadership by natural abilities) approaches (Bass, 1981; Bass, 1990; Yukl, 1994). Leadership now emphasizes successful leadership practices (Kouzes & Posner, 1987). However, leaders are still viewed as symbolic representations of the community they lead, and hence symbolically responsible for the well being and success of followers. Followers count on their authority figures for *leadership* and *action*, disproportionately to their own efforts, and are easily disappointed when their situations do not visibly improve.

Kouzes and Posner (1987) have suggested five universal and "fundamental practices" of successful leadership, (a) challenging the process, (b) inspiring shared vision, (c) enabling others to act, (d) modeling the way, and (e) encouraging the heart (Kouzes & Posner, 1987, pp. 8-12). The ambient mythology of leadership provides for the necessary values, perspectives, and practices for successful leadership. Harrison Owen (1987) describes such a mythology as the "mythos...the likely story arising from the life experience of any group through which they come to experience their past, present and potential" (Owen, 1987, p. 16). For Owen, mythos embraces not just the words of the story – the myth, but also the enactments of the myth in "color, form, sound [non-verbal] and movement...[which]...is ritual" (p. 13). Therefore, for the research participants in this study, their everyday ritual mediates their mythos of leadership.

In a parallel to Van Gennep's (1960) classification of the structure of ritual, Heifetz (1994) proposed a structural paradigm for leadership. According to Heifetz (1994), successful leadership, both with and without formal authority, is a patterned and sequenced process of actions that seek to create a bounded and safe container for adaptive learning to occur (p. 138). Heifetz's (1994) fluid process of leadership includes (a) identifying the adaptive challenge and what needs to be learned, (b) regulating the level of disequilibrium to "bring it into a productive range," (c) allowing issues to ripen and focusing attention to them, (d) giving the work back to followers, and (e) nurturing and protecting emerging voices of leadership (pp. 138-144). Thus, Heifetz's (1994) description of the process of leadership parallels the constitutive features of a ritual journey.

The central purpose of leadership, according to Harrison Owen (1999), is to "liberate and focus Spirit" (Owen, 1999, p. 58). Owen suggested that Spirit, as a concept, illuminates the inadequacy of language to wrap around non-material but no less real phenomena. Organizational or community Spirit is expressed through the mythos of the organization or community. Individual Spirit is expressed in relationship to the organization or community. Both are transformed in relation to each other.

Drawing on Martin Buber's (1958) powerful claim that "I become I, only in significant relationship with an other, a thou," Owen suggested that "an individual becomes an individual in relationship to a group" (Owen, 1987, p. 56). Thus the organization or community becomes both the "ground and field" (p. 57) for the individual to actualize and find meaning and purpose. Therefore, according to Owen (1987, 1999), leadership that liberates individual and organizational Spirit fulfills the human need for points of reference. Like the human need to approach the sacred, Spirit fulfills the need for personal and community orientation.

What makes ritual theory accessible is the exploration of ritualization as secular ceremony (Moore & Myerhoff, 1977). Organizations as cultures (Schein, 1985 & Bergquist, 1992), and organizations as cybernetic systems (Birnbaum, 1991), while not the only models for viewing our academic organizations, more inclusively capture the complexity and "messiness" of colleges and universities as organizational structures. Faculty member reflections on peer colleagues' leadership will by definition explicate post-heroic constructions of leadership as process.

If leadership can be described with the same constitutive meaning-making features as with ritual, can an examination of self-narratives of research participants yield a grounded theory (Glaser & Strauss, 1967; Strauss & Corbin, 1998) explanation of the relationships between leadership and ritual? Since the premise of a naturalistic phenomenological study obviates a priori hypotheses, only time for study and the analysis of emegent data can yield an answer to this question.

# Chapter 3
# The Study

### Naturalistic Inquiry and Qualitative Research

Major theoretical constructions of leadership have been derived principally from a base in Western philosophy and in particular from research out of the positivistic research traditions of the social and behavioral sciences. The general doctrine of positivism advances the philosophy and methodology of the scientific method. The foundational assumptions to the scientific method are (1) determinism – that phenomena have causes, (2) empiricism – that theory about phenomena is verifiable, (3) parsimony – that theory is refined by way of economical explication, and (4) generality – that refined theory is readily generalizable toward prediction and control (Cohen and Manion, 1994, pp. 13-14). These assumptions of the positivistic inquiry paradigm have resulted in theoretical constructions of leadership that have been drawn largely from survey research and experimental observations. In the ardent pursuit of generalizability and validity, these studies have also decontextualized the data and explanation away from individual and personal domains of meaning making. This examination of leadership and ritual requires an alternative methodology.

*Why Qualitative Research?*

The aim of this study is to explore the relationship of ritual and leadership by examining ritualization in the narrative self-descriptions of research participants about their leadership work as faculty. Access to how faculty make meaning of their work is available only by examining their self-interpretations of leadership and ritualization as expressed in their interview narratives. A narrative analysis of these self-interpretations in the qualitative research tradition helps to generate beginning hypotheses on ritualization and leadership in faculty work, resulting in a possible grounded theory (Glaser & Strauss, 1967; Strauss & Corbin, 1998) that helps illuminate how faculty leadership work is performed outside roles of authority, and how faculty members make meaning of this leadership work through everyday secular ritualization.

At the heart of the question of how ritualization in faculty leadership might best be examined is the fundamental matter of objectivity. As Jerome Kirk and Marc Miller (1986) have suggested, qualitative researchers seek not so much to study objects as "much as report on their interaction with the objects" (p. 71). Such an interactionist and interpretive approach to research affords access to constructed realities such as faculty interpretations of their leadership work, but good qualitative research must necessarily abandon perfect validity and perfect reliability as attainable criteria for objectivity. Instead, the alternative is to develop criteria to ensure fidelity to an expanded vision of objectivity.

Lincoln and Guba (1985) have outlined five axioms that contrast the positivistic and naturalistic inquiry paradigms. The first axiom involves the nature of reality; the naturalistic inquiry paradigm advances the view that since multiple constructed realities exist, "inquiry into these multiple realities will inevitably diverge" (Lincoln & Guba, 1985, p. 37). The second axiom involves the relationship of knower to known; the naturalistic inquiry paradigm accepts that "the inquirer and the 'object' of the inquiry interact to influence one another" (p. 37). The third axiom concerns the possibility of generalization; the naturalistic inquiry paradigm forbears generalization in the positivistic sense, and instead proposes, "the aim of inquiry is to develop knowledge in the form of 'working hypotheses' that describe the individual case" (Lincoln & Guba, 1985, p. 38). The fourth axiom is about the possibility of causal linkages; the naturalistic inquiry paradigm refrains from drawing cause-effect connections, and instead claims, "all entities are in a state of mutual simultaneous shaping so that it is impossible to distinguish causes from effects" (p. 38). The fifth axiom involves the role of values in inquiry; the naturalistic inquiry paradigm accepts that "inquiry is value bound" (p. 38), suggesting the following corollaries:

> Corollary 1: Inquiries are influenced by *inquirer* values…;
> Corollary 2: Inquiry is influenced by the choice of the *paradigm*…;
> Corollary 3: Inquiry is influenced by the choice of *substantive theory*…;
> Corollary 4: Inquiry is influenced by the values that inhere in the *context*;
> Corollary 5: Inquiry is either *value-resonant* (reinforcing or congruent) or *value-dissonant* (conflicting)… (p. 38).

Within this paradigm, value-resonance between the problem, theory, and context generates the useful findings from the data. Clearly, this study was influenced by my values regarding leadership and my conceptions of ritual and ritualization. The context of faculty leadership work in a residential selective liberal arts setting also both influences and limits the findings to the research site I selected. These five axioms, therefore, result in significant implications for the actual operation of naturalistic inquiry.

Lincoln and Guba (1985) identified 14 characteristics of naturalistic inquiry. The first of these is that qualitative research, by definition, occurs in the *natural setting*. Second, the researcher is the data-gathering human *instrument*. Third, qualitative research results in the "legitimization of tacit (intuitive, felt) knowledge" (p. 40). Fourth, qualitative research utilizes a variety of methodologies to capture the multiple realities of the phenomenon being studied. Fifth, qualitative researchers favor selecting research participants for the sample purposely and deliberately in order to maximize and/or enrich the data. Sixth, the data analysis is conducted inductively because it is "more likely to describe fully the setting ... [and]... to identify the mutually shaping influences that interact" (p. 40). Seventh, qualitative researchers develop their grounded theory from the data in a particular context because "mutual shapings... may be explicable only in terms of the contextual elements found..." (p. 41). Eighth, qualitative research utilizes an emergent design because "what emerges as a function of the interaction between inquirer and phenomenon is largely unpredictable in advance" (p. 41). Ninth, data outcomes are negotiated with research participants because they "can best understand and interpret the influence of local value patterns" (p. 41). Tenth, qualitative research is reported in the form of a case study because it is more adaptable "to a description of the multiple realities encountered at any given site" (p. 41). Eleventh, research data is interpreted "idiographically (in terms of the particulars of the case) rather than nomothetically (in terms of lawlike generalizations" (p. 42), because data interpretation is so closely linked to local particulars of the research site. Twelfth, applications of findings are tentative and open-ended since data gathering processes are unique to the setting and cannot be duplicated. Thirteenth, the scope of the research project is determined as the inquiry continues, thus allowing the data gathering process and the researcher-participant interactions to focus the developing study. Finally, qualitative research utilizes alternative criteria for establishing *trustworthiness* of the data in place of the validity and reliability criteria of the positivistic research tradition (p. 43). In subsequent work, Guba & Lincoln (1989) expanded the considerations in the qualitative research paradigm to include additional criteria for *authenticity*.

Qualitative research approaches have only recently emerged as a rich source of new understanding on leadership. Elliot Eisner (1991) has condensed the 14 characteristics into six features of qualitative study that provide a framework for this study of ritualization and leadership.

Eisner (1991) suggested that qualitative studies are (1) field focused, (2) use the self as the instrument, (3) interpretive, (4) display the use of expressive language, (5) attend to particulars, and (6) are believable because of their "coherence, insight, and instrumental utility" (pp. 32-39).

The field of this study is the research site, Wilkinson College (a pseudonym) and the professional and personal lives of four faculty research participants. Since I was the collector of data, I was also the instrument for the study. The study was characteristically interpretive because I attempted to account for phenomena by interpreting the self-narrated accounts of participants. The principal forms of data were the interview narratives of research participants using expressive language to articulate their experiences and sensemaking of leadership and ritualization. Data analysis, largely in the form of analysis of narrative, attended to particulars of interpretation of their experience to develop theoretical observations to explicate ritualization in faculty leadership. The interpretation and analysis of data met the criteria of trustworthiness and authenticity, so I have confidence that the explication may be seen as making sense, insightful, and perhaps of some instrumental usefulness.

In particular, only qualitative research approaches can afford access to the research participants and their subjective interpretations of phenomena such as their faculty leadership work. In this study, I explored their self-reflective passage narratives describing their faculty leadership work for patterns of ritualization. In terms of the categories of major non-mutually exclusive approaches to qualitative inquiry, the case study, grounded theory, and the narrative analysis and inquiry approaches, all appeared the most appropriate to include. These approaches are based on a phenomenological point of view.

*Phenomenology*

One of the early scions of naturalistic inquiry, phenomenology has been defined as a qualitative research approach from the "theoretical point of view that advocates the study of direct experience taken at face value" (Cohen & Manion, 1994, p.29). Phenomenology springs from the earlier theoretical work of Edmund Husserl (1948/1973), often considered the founder of phenomenology, and the subsequent contributions of Alfred Schutz (1967). Husserl (1948/1973) emphasized the researcher "finding out how things appear directly...rather than through the media of cultural and symbolic structures" (Cohen & Manion, 1994, p. 30). This requires attending with particular focus, and results in a "consciousness of which there are three elements – the 'I' who thinks, the mental acts of this thinking subject, and the intentional objects of these mental acts" (p. 30). My pursuit in this process was to disassemble perceptual constructions of objects being studied so as to study the objects "in such a way as to free us from all preconceptions about the world" (p.30).

Schutz (1967) extended Husserl's (1948/1973) work by exploring how the everyday behavior of research participants can be studied for what they mean to them. Husserl (1948/1973) suggested that this could be accomplished by what he called the concept of *meaning reflexivity* (Cohen & Manion, 1994, p.30). Meaning reflexivity can be obtained only retroactively, through a process of stream of consciousness self-description. According to Schutz, external observations of behavior are "dependent on a process of *typification*... [where] ...the observer makes use of concepts resembling 'ideal types' to make sense of what people do" (Schutz, 1967, p. 30). Curtis (1978) has suggested the distinguishing features of a phenomenological point of view, which includes:

(1) a belief in the importance, and in a sense the primacy, of subjective consciousness;
(2) an understanding of consciousness as active, as meaning bestowing; and
(3) a claim that there are certain essential structures to consciousness of which we gain direct knowledge by a certain kind of reflection. (Cohen & Manion, 1994, p. 29)

This study of everyday lived experience with particular attention to the research participants' subjectivities, and what their experiences mean to them, attempts to access meaning making in the conceptual worlds of the research participants. The argument for phenomenology advances the view that since reality is "socially constructed" (Berger & Luckmann, 1967), multiple interpretations exist for experiences, largely depending on what meaning is attributed by the experiencer-participant. This makes a phenomenological point of view an excellent perspective to use to explore interpretations of ritualization in leadership from the narrative self-descriptions of faculty colleagues.

## Narrative Analysis and Inquiry

Narrative analysis and narrative inquiry methodologies can be located in Sipe and Constable's (1996) "interpretivist paradigm" – one of four categories of qualitative research methodologies they proposed. Rejecting the classification of research methodologies into "quantitative-qualitative" or "dominant-alternative," Sipe and Constable (1996) arrayed research methodologies into four arbitrary locations without using "rigid or unchanging differences/boundaries" – 1) positivist, 2) interpretivist, 3) critical theory, and 4) deconstructionist (p. 153). The methodologies in the interpretivist paradigm premise ontological assumptions about reality as subjective and constructed, with no distinction between the knower and the known. Thus "the world is constructed by each knower/observer according to a set of subject principles peculiar to that person" (p. 158). For interpretivists there are many truths, and "discourse is dialogic and creates the reality being studied" (p. 155-158). Since secular ceremony (Moore & Myerhoff, 1977) and ritualization (Driver, 1998) are, by definition, grounded in how meaning is constructed individually and socially, narrative analysis and inquiry presented viable methodologies for accessing how the research participants in this study ritualize and make meaning of their leadership work.

The qualitative research tradition is replete with examples of studies of oral and written narratives advancing towards building theory. Three personally inspiring examples are Paul Willis' (1977) classic study of how the institutional arrangements of a working class school reproduced class and social hierarchies, Valerie Walkerdine's (1997) study of how young girls are influenced by the popular culture media in their constructions of social and sexual identities, and Ellen Cushman's (1998) study of how inner city residents used oral, literate, and analytical tools in their daily resistance struggle against social welfare institutions. These studies served as admirable and inspiring examples for emulation in the design of this study.

*Narrative Analysis*

In the absence of direct access or observation of a phenomenon such as faculty leadership work, the study of representations of the phenomenon in the research participants' self-descriptions can be a rich source of interpretive findings. I utilized narrative analysis and narrative inquiry – the study of representations – to analyze the narratives I constructed from interviews with research participants. As Catherine Riessman (1993) has noted "all we have is talk and texts that represent reality partially, selectively, and imperfectly" (p. 15).

Riessman (1993) proposed an analytical framework for examining narrative that presumes "five levels or kinds of representation in the research process" (p. 8). At the first level is *attending to the experience* where a selection of experience is made to "construct reality in new ways... by thinking" (p. 9). At the second level is *telling about the experience* which is the "performance of a personal narrative" (p. 9), and where a second focus selection is made of the experience based on who is listening/reading. The interaction also generates a shared narrative. At the third level, *transcribing the experience* further selection and greater reduction occur so that they "ultimately create different worlds ... [and]... meaning is constituted in very different ways with alternative transcriptions" (p. 13).

At the fourth level, *analyzing experience*, typically conducted from written or audio transcriptions, "the analyst creates a metastory about what happened by telling what the interview narratives signify, editing and reshaping what was told, and turning it into a hybrid story... (p. 13). The fifth and final level, *reading experience*, opens the narrative to shifting interpretations contingent upon the reader's standpoint and what meanings the reader brings to the narrative.

Narrative analysis extends beyond content analysis. In traditional ethnographic study, narratives are considered "first-person accounts" that were "intended as realistic descriptions" (Riessman, 1993, p. 4). The narrative analysis methodology assumes that narrative text is more than form and structure, it is a living social construction, and can therefore only be explicated in terms of its interaction with a meaning context (Manning & Cullum-Swan, 1994). This meaning context, according to Riessman (1993), includes the layers of subjectivity embedded in successive representations.

Narratives derived from participant interview responses about faculty leadership work cannot by definition acquire Riessman's (1993) first representation -- the research participants' direct encounters with the phenomenon of faculty leadership work. Faculty interview narratives that were "told" to me as the interviewer-researcher acquired Riessman's (1993) second level of representation and generated a shared narrative interpreting faculty leadership work. Further meaning was constructed when I transcribed and reported on the shared narrative, in the form of narrative profiles in the subsequent chapters of this book, thus generating the third and fourth levels of representation. The fifth and final representation occurred when other readers read this book. Thus, Riessman's (1993) five levels of representation illuminated interpretation in terms of the research participants' contexts of meaning making, with additional subjectivity entering the research process of transcribing, analyzing, reporting, and reading of the narratives (Riessman, 1993).

In the autobiographical reflections of his experiences in the Fifties as a higher education faculty member and administrator, Alvin Kernan

(1999) recollected major "seismic changes" in the course of his years at Princeton and Yale Universities. He suggested that shifts had occurred in four of the "tectonic plates" of higher education – "demographic, cultural, technological … (and)… epistemological" (Kernan, 1999, pp. xvi). In one particular section of his narrative, Kernan wrote:

> Theory was really not what engaged our attention at the time, however, for we were far more likely to see our subject and our teaching in terms of their relationship to the social and personal problems of our time. Outside the academy, another world was taking shape in the fifties, prosperous, powerful, conformist, America the world power. Powerful but banal. Living in identical Levittown tract houses, manipulated by advertising, dominated increasingly by big business, exploited by cynical politicians, their thinking programmed by the media, more and more in debt on the installment plan to buy washing machines, cars and Frigidaires, the men in the gray flannel suits – Sloan Wilson's perfect image for his 1956 book about the trap – avoided emptiness by inhabiting without questions a culture that made illusion seem firm and sure. Sex was Marilyn Monroe, happiness was making money, government was General Eisenhower, fun was watching *I Love Lucy* on TV, and what was good for General Motors was good for the country. It was from this mindless conformity that we hoped to save our students (Kernan, 1998, p. 97).

While this narrative is available only at Riessman's (1993) fourth and fifth level of representation, it offers even richer glimpses of how the experience of teaching is interpreted in the context of time and place. In short, Alvin Kernan's (1998) narrative is explicated in its interaction with his interpretive context of teaching at Princeton University in the 1950s. The interview narratives of the research participants generated in the context of Wilkinson College in the early 2000s, and interpreted through the lens of narrative analysis are potentially just as thick and rich as Kernan's (1998) narrative. As we will see in the following chapters, these narratives did capture the times as research participants reflected on their experiences, commitments, and convictions.

*Narrative Inquiry*

Jean Clandinin and Michael Connelly (2000) have proposed another model, a "metaphorical three-dimensional narrative inquiry space," that outlines an analytical framework for narrative inquiry (Clandinin & Connelly, 2000, p. 50). Their framework locates narrative in terms of the three dimensions of "personal and social [interaction]; past, present, and future [continuity]; combined with the notion of place [situation]" (p. 50).

Along the first dimension of *interaction*, narrative inquiry explores participant interpretation of experience by first examining what the narrative reflects in terms of the themes of the personal and the interactive. In this study, research participants' narratives are mined for how ritualization and faculty leadership work are experienced and constructed personally and individually, as well as interpreted socially among their faculty peers. The second dimension of *continuity* explores how ritualization and leadership are experienced in temporal terms. Faculty participant narratives are examined for how past ritualization is remembered and how future ritualization is anticipated in the context of faculty leadership work. Finally, along the third dimension of *situation*, narrative inquiry explores how ritualization and leadership are experienced in terms of physical and social place and context. In this study, research participants' narratives were generally inspected for the Moore and Myerhoff's (1977) definitional properties of secular ceremony, such as repetition, deliberate and stylized action, style, and collective social meaning (Manning, 2000).

For the purposes of this study, I utilized modified procedures of narrative analysis (Riessman, 1993) to examine the research participants' narrative profiles, which I constructed from their interview transcripts. I then generally traced the procedures of narrative inquiry (Clandinin & Connelly, 2000). Both narrative analysis (Riessman, 1993) and narrative inquiry (Clandinin & Connelly, 2000) presented two intriguing qualitative research analytical frameworks for examining the narratives that I generated from participant interviews. In addition, they afforded the frameworks to explore the narratives in terms of how the narrators made meaning of their experiences in relationship to themselves, to their colleagues, and to their situations at Wilkinson College.

## *Participants*

The research participants in this study were a purposeful sample (Patton, 1989) of four faculty members selected from the faculty at Wilkinson College. Wilkinson's faculty, not unlike the faculty of other selective liberal arts colleges, comprises teachers and scholars who attend exclusively to the education of undergraduate students. At that time, ninety-six percent of the faculty at Wilkinson had earned terminal degrees in their academic disciplines. In addition to teaching, faculty at Wilkinson were expected to advise juniors in semester-long independent study theses, and seniors in year-long independent study theses, which provided rich opportunities for students as junior partners to help advance faculty research agendas.

<u>Selection of Site.</u> I selected Wilkinson College as a site for this study for a number of reasons. First, the faculty at Wilkinson were both geographically and socially accessible, in proximity to my home location, and due to my previously established relationships with many of the faculty and administrators at Wilkinson. Second, Wilkinson's rich and active tradition of faculty engagement in shared governance presented a potentially fertile site for exploring faculty leadership work. In addition, while aspirations for qualitative research do not include generalizability of the data to all settings, Wilkinson's characteristics as a "typical" traditional selective residential liberal arts college (Clark, 1992), and Wilkinson's faculty engagement with their students, the department, and the College, provided many opportunities for the research participants to reflect on their faculty leadership work.

<u>Selection of Sample.</u> The research participants in this study comprised a purposeful sample (Patton, 1989) of selected members of

the full-time faculty of Wilkinson College. Based on the responses I obtained from an introductory initial survey of interest that I sent to all 150 faculty members, I selected three to four respondents to the survey to participate in research interviews. In selecting the sample, my goal was to maximize dimensional range, to "obtain instances of all the important dissimilar forms present in the larger population" (Weiss, 1994, p. 23). I operationalized dimensional range of the sample through strategies that helped ensure that the sample for this study included research participants whose personal and professional backgrounds and experiences at Wilkinson displayed the widest significant variation in characteristics such as gender, academic discipline, and career seniority at Wilkinson College.

*The Researcher Role*

In the qualitative research tradition, the researcher is both the instrument of collecting data and the interpreter of data. This requires the researcher to attend to considerations that ensure the effectiveness and integrity of the research project. Lincoln and Guba (1985) have suggested that the "naturalistic inquirer" simultaneously attend to four activities, "making initial contact and gaining entrée to the site, negotiating consent, building and maintaining trust, and identifying and using informants" (p. 252).

I initially made initial contact with the Secretary of the College and the Dean of the Faculty of Wilkinson College, to discuss the general features of the proposed study. I secured verbal consent in principle to enlist faculty members at Wilkinson College to participate in this study. The Dean of the Faculty and I agreed to obtain final and formal approval from the Vice President of Academic Affairs as soon as a completed and approved dissertation research proposal was available. I subsequently obtained this approval.

Since the paradigm of qualitative research is essentially inductive, researcher subjectivity may affect the data (LeCompte, 1987). What successful qualitative researchers can do, however, is "objectively study the subjective states of their subjects" largely by becoming aware of their researcher biases and prejudices, and spending "considerable time in the empirical world laboriously collecting and reviewing piles of data" (Bogdan & Biklen, 1998, pp. 33-34). Therefore, identifying and making transparent biases and prejudices presents an effective strategy for managing researcher subjectivity. Indeed, Alan Peshkin (1985, 1988) has suggested that researcher subjectivity can be virtuous, and should be systematically sought and actively uncovered by the researcher during the data collection process, rather than accidentally encountered and retrospectively recovered at the end.

A principal source of researcher biases and prejudices and my subjectivity in this project emerged from my experiences with the selected site, Wilkinson College. Some relevant considerations from my background and relationship with the site include:

(1) I am an alumnus of Wilkinson. I have very fond memories of my five-year tenure at Wilkinson, which included four years as an undergraduate student, campus leader, and student employee, and a fifth year as an intern in both the Departments of Personnel (now Human Resources) and Student Affairs.

(2) I was awarded a special scholarship to Wilkinson, which furnished the only resource that made a selective liberal arts college education in the United States possible for an international student from a lower middle class family in a recently war-ravaged, developing country. I remain profoundly grateful for having been the recipient of this opportunity.

(3) I am personally acquainted with a number of now senior faculty members at Wilkinson, having enjoyed relationships with them as their student, advisee, and, in some instances, good friend and intellectual companion. These personal acquaintances did not include the four selected research participants in the study. In fact, only two of the research participants actually remembered me from my time as a campus student leader at Wilkinson.

(4) My academic experiences at Wilkinson, particularly the required senior year Independent Study Thesis, have influenced my perspectives on undergraduate education. In view of this experience, I consider a residential liberal arts college among the highest possible order of excellent undergraduate education for traditionally aged students.

(5) My experiences with campus employment and campus leadership have influenced my perspectives on campus governance and administration. In view of this experience, I remain very positively biased toward a consensual model of faculty self-governance as necessary and essential to advancing excellence in educational enterprise.

I was not able to identify any negative prejudices with regard to Wilkinson College.

## Procedures

*Survey of Interest*

This study commenced with a survey and accompanying letter from the researcher to all the faculty members at Wilkinson College, eliciting some initial information, and requesting confirmation of interest in participating in in-depth individual interviews. My letter was attended by a separate e-mail from the then Dean of the Faculty encouraging a response to my letter. The purpose of the campus survey sent to all faculty members was to introduce this study, and to obtain the basic demographic and response data which helped me identify and support rich qualitative research interviews with consenting research participants.

The survey accompanied a letter from me with supporting documents, and was designed to formally request interest as well as to elicit basic biographical and background information that would help me select a diverse sample of four research participants for in depth qualitative interviews. Individual faculty members who agreed to participate and were selected for the sample were then thoroughly briefed on the purpose and design of this study. I also obtain informed consent and described how the data generated would be both protected and used in the study.

*Interviews*

Robert Weiss (1994) suggested a number of research goals that indicate when the qualitative interview is the appropriate choice for gathering data. These include (1) developing detailed descriptions, (2) integrating multiple perspectives, (3) describing process, (4) developing holistic description, (5) learning how events are interpreted, (6) bridging intersubjectivities, and (7) identifying variables and framing hypotheses for quantitative research (pp. 9-11). The first six of these aims were readily applicable to this study.

The faculty members selected to be research participants were scheduled for a series of three separate interviews of 60 to 90 minutes in length in their Wilkinson College settings. This three-interview design was originally developed by Schuman (1982), and calls for the first interview to focus on the context of the faculty members' experiences, the second interview to describe their experiences of leadership and ritualization, and the third interview to reflect on the meaning of their experiences (Seidman, 1998). The interviews were deliberately divided to generate focus and reflection on the issues surrounding the topics being explored, or the "substantive frame" of this study (Weiss, 1994).

The questions for the research participants, as well as the diversity of the research participants, assisted in generating very dissimilar responses. I asked questions that were designed to elicit a diachronic telling of the story of how and why they entered the life of the academy, how and why they came to Wilkinson College, and how and why they engaged with their colleagues and the rest of the Wilkinson community. I asked opening questions and follow-up questions that were designed to ask research participants to describe and then reflect on their experiences and reflections on the processes of ritualization and leadership work. The frequency and sequence of interviews also facilitated reflections with shifting and fluid perspectives. I also began each second and third interview by inviting research participants to clarify and elaborate on their earlier responses, and all the research participants availed themselves of these opportunities.

Interview tapes were transcribed after completing the final interviews. I then selected and bracketed response passages from the interview transcripts to create narrative "profiles" (Seidman, 1998, p. 101) that captured major themes of meaning making. These profiles are reported in subsequent chapters of this book.

Drawing on the idea from Studs Terkel's *Working* (1972), Seidman (1998) has argued that the researcher-constructed narrative profile presents an effective strategy for "opening up one's interview material to analysis and interpretation" (Seidman, 1998, p. 102). This exercise would begin the steady climb of narrative analysis along Riessman's (1993) levels of representation, beginning with the second level of representation, *telling about the experience* (p. 9) to *transcribing the experience* (p. 13) and onward. It also created a ritual "passage narrative" (Grimes, 2000) that was now accessible to narrative inquiry (Clandinin & Connelly, 2000).

One of the aspirations of this study was to develop a model for how faculty leadership work was subjectively interpreted and ritualized by faculty members. Among other outcomes, I hoped that this aspiration would present a theoretical framework that integrated the subjectivities of research participants in terms of how they ritualized and made meaning of their professional and personal lives as faculty. My hesitant hope was that the theoretical framework that emerged would generate hypotheses for further research in the quantitative research tradition.

## Data Analysis

The process of building theory begins with mining the collected data for concepts and then "grouping concepts into categories" (Strauss

& Corbin, 1998, p. 113). These categories, or phenomena, developed in terms of their properties and dimensions are then related to the "research context" (p. 114), and categories and sub-categories are identified and named.

A tentative set of categories and sub-categories is then used to begin open coding, which entails a meticulous and comprehensive classification of the data in terms of the categories and sub-categories. These categories are then connected to each other in hypothetical relationship statements that then engender patterns for further exploration (p. 121).

Axial coding follows open coding and is the action of "relating categories to subcategories along the lines of their properties and dimensions (p. 124). In fact, axial coding is the search for "answers to questions such as why or how come, where, when, how, and with what results," in an attempt to "uncover relationships among categories" (p. 127). When the data are approached in terms of a research "paradigm" or "perspective on data" (p. 128), the beginnings of a theory can emerge. Once categories and subcategories have been integrated in a potential theoretical scheme, "selective coding" is used to integrate and refine categories, so that the research findings "take the form of theory" (p. 143).

My own strategy for coding the narrative profiles was much less formal. I approached the narratives as "passage narratives" (Grimes, 2000), seeking motifs of meaning making that attended to the general strategies for narrative inquiry (Clandinin & Connelly, 2000) and narrative analysis (Riessman, 1993).

## Trustworthiness and Authenticity

In qualitative research, the analog of reliability and validity is the notion of trustworthiness. Lincoln and Guba (1985) outlined four criteria for the trustworthiness of qualitative study, (1) credibility, (2) transferability, (3) dependability, and (4) confirmability. Later, Guba and Lincoln (1989) proposed additional criteria for considerations of authenticity and faithfulness in qualitative research, such as (1) fairness, (2) ontological authenticity, (3) educative authenticity, (4) catalytic authenticity, and (5) tactical authenticity.

*Trustworthiness.*

Credibility. As a criterion of trustworthiness, credibility is the likelihood that "credible findings and interpretations will be produced" (Lincoln & Guba, 1985, p. 301), and is operationalized by activities appropriate to this study that include prolonged engagement, persistent observation, triangulation, peer debriefing, negative case analysis, and member checking (p. 301). Prolonged engagement requires the researcher to invest sufficient time in the research site in order to learn the culture, test for distortions, and generate trust. My previous membership in the college community for five years and sustained connections with faculty and administrators over the past twenty years added to time I spent gathering data for this study, which sufficiently fulfilled the prolonged engagement criterion of credibility. Because of these same conditions, I was able to apply persistent observation, the goal of which was to develop the ability to identify salient factors of study in the research site.

Triangulation. The testing of emergent propositions from multiple sources, and peer debriefing, consultation with a disinterested peer, are two techniques that can also be readily applied by to increase trustworthiness. I asked research participants to review their previous interview responses and to respond with any additional reflections. Additionally, I used the responses and perspectives of the various research participants in the study to triangulate emerging propositions. Non-participating members of the college community such as the Dean of the Faculty, and Vice President for Academic Affairs, as well as members of the doctoral dissertation committee also assisted with their own reflections. Negative case analysis, the retrospective revision of working hypothesis, and member checks, the continuous sharing and discussion of data collected with the research participants, were part of the data collection and analysis procedures.

<u>Transferability</u>. Transferability entails ensuring "the widest possible range of information" through activities such as purposeful sampling, so that the data are as much as possible a "thick description" (Lincoln & Guba, 1985, p. 316). The provision of an initial survey of interest sent to all Wilkinson faculty members maximized opportunities to select a diverse sample of research participants. Single-site research case studies also offer opportunities for follow-up conversations with research participants, thus ensuring a large database for analysis. In the instance of this study, I was able to follow up with each participant at least two additional times during subsequent interviews.

<u>Dependability</u>. Dependability is the criterion that the research study be credible (Lincoln & Guba, 1985, p. 316), typically operationalized through an audit of procedures. The dependability of a qualitative research study is established by retaining raw data and records, thus leaving an audit trail for others to follow (p. 319). At appropriate points in the data collection, I consulted with my advisor and others to ensure an external dependability audit. In addition, I maintained all notes, transcripts, and other collected material in order to allow for the possibility of an audit trail of the data.

<u>Confirmability</u>. The criterion of confirmability attends to the same issues as those of dependability, but is addressed to research participants. The techniques of a confirmability audit include asking selected research participants to help review the data, and check and clarify the claims and categories developed as part of the analysis of data. I attended to confirmability in this study by asking research participants at each interview to reflect on their earlier responses, thus engaging them as partners in analyzing their narratives.

*Authenticity.*

The criteria for trustworthiness were developed as qualitative research parallels to the internal and external validity requirements of quantitative research (Lincoln & Guba, 1985). However, the criteria for authenticity – fairness, ontological authenticity, educative authenticity, catalytic authenticity, and tactical authenticity – were developed to determine the faithfulness of qualitative research, and are uniquely implicated in the naturalistic inquiry paradigm (Guba & Lincoln, 1989).

Fairness. Fairness addresses the question of whether the research study was conducted with integrity and respect for the dignity of research participants. A comprehensive introduction and explanation of the goals and procedures of this study was made to each participant before requesting and obtaining informed consent. These activities, along with the general ethical considerations discussed below helped to meet this criterion by ensuring that research participants were treated as partners in this study.

Ontological Authenticity. Activities related to this criterion help ensure that all the participating research participants and others who familiarized themselves with this study will be able to enlarge their consciousness through their participation. For research participants in this study, the activities that contributed to meeting this criterion included being interviewed and the emergent self-awareness that accompanied self-reflection, and the dialogue and discussion with me as the researcher. Also, the final question of the final interview asked research participants to reflect on the interview process itself and what it meant to them personally and professionally, further facilitating the conditions for ontological authenticity.

Educative Authenticity. The activities of this criterion lead to the sharing and improved understanding of others' constructions. Through a joint and participatory process of collecting and interpreting data, followed by a presentation in the form of this dissertation, readers of the dissertation were able to acquaint themselves to the diverse perspectives that led to the development of some explanatory observations. It was my hope that the readers of this study would be better able to understand the multiplicity of perspectives that led to how the research participants and I negotiated the joint construction of an explication of ritualization and faculty leadership.

Catalytic Authenticity. The activities associated with this criterion ensure that the outcome of this study is available to stimulate action and change. The explanatory observations of this examination of ritualization and faculty leadership hopefully raised new questions and considerations for the research participants of this study. At the conclusion of the study, I shared a copy of the final dissertation with each of the research participants. I would like to think that perhaps the observations of this study helped stimulate informal conversations.

Tactical Authenticity. Both the processes and the outcomes of the research study were designed, and subsequently executed to empower all those participating in the study. Openness and honesty about the data collection procedures, creating environments of comfort and choice for research participants, sharing data and tentative explanations, and soliciting interpretations were all activities that assisted in creating conditions of empowerment for the four research participants at Wilkinson College. I integrated various techniques and strategies to comply with the criteria for trustworthiness and authenticity outlined above. The outcome of these considerations resulted in research procedures and research observations that the research participants and I now own and remember with pride.

## Ethical Considerations

Ethical considerations are an important dimension in any research study. In the qualitative research tradition, Maurice Punch (1994) has outlined pothential issues of "harm, consent, deception, privacy, and confidentiality of data" (p. 89). At all points during the procedure of this study, my steadfast position of "do no harm" was embedded into the design and conduct of the study. I began this study with first obtaining a general institutional imprimatur by obtaining approvals from both the Dean of the Faculty and the Vice President for Academic Affairs. I then presented a comprehensive explanation of the goals of the study to all active research participants, after soliciting their informed consent for participation. I asked them to retrospectively reflect on their responses thus involving them in the interpretation of their narratives. These guidelines helped ensure against any intentional deception in the operation of this study's methodologies.

Every instance of my interaction with research participants included a thorough briefing for all research participants on how the data they helped generate would be utilized, and what information would be made publicly available in public in terms of publication. Research participants were assigned alternative names, with requisite masking of identity-related information, so that, as much as possible, no single research participant could be individually identifiable. This ensured research participants of their privacy, and reassured them safety from potential embarrassment and anxiety. I also masked the college with an alternative name (Wilkinson) in order to assist with protecting the anonymity of the research participants and the confidentiality of their narratives.

Ethical conduct in qualitative research is grounded in respect for the dignity of research participants who generously contributed their selves to further the study, and in my commitment to the integrity of the data. The ethical conduct of this study necessarily required that I adopt and maintain the position that research participants are partners in this study. I thoroughly briefed each participant on their rights and on the aims, risks, and benefits of this study. In addition, I asked each participant to document their informed consent. Additionally, I commenced the study only after obtaining either approval or a determination of exemption from full approval by the Ohio University Institutional Review Board for the Review of Research Involving Human Subjects.

This study was designed to utilize strategies of qualitative research inquiry, principally the methodologies of single-site case study, grounded theory, and narrative analysis and narrative inquiry, at Wilkinson College, to examine faculty leadership work for patterns of ritualization and meaning making. After a nominal survey of interest in participation, data collection procedures entailed a series of in-depth life history interviews. Interview responses were converted into narrative profiles, and these profiles were then examined for themes, motifs, and patterns. Interpretation and coding protocols related to the qualitative research methodologies were operationalized, and established criteria for trustworthiness were maintained. Always the goal was to ensure the effective application of data findings toward the construction of theory related to ritualization in faculty leadership at a small residential liberal arts college.

# Chapter 4

# The Narrative Profile

I constructed narrative portraits of four participants and conducted an oral and written review of the transcripts of my interviews to construct their narrative profiles. In constructing these narrative profiles, I attempted to capture and arrange a self-narrative of their early lives and their passage as teacher-scholars at Wilkinson College.

One of my inspirations for this project was Adriana Kezar's (1996) doctoral dissertation study of leadership in higher education, in which she used narrative portraits as a principal source of data. Excavating narrative "data" for significant themes has to be "interpreted "idiographically (in terms of the particulars of the case) rather than nomothetically (in terms of lawlike generalizations" (Lincoln & Guba, 1985, p. 42), because data interpretation is so closely linked to the researcher's familiarity with the research site, In this study, my own familiarity with Wilkinson College shaped my examination of the narratives. As was the methodology in Ken Bain's study of *What the Best College Teachers Do* (Bain, 2004), the goal of my interviews was to facilitate the conditions for participants to reflect on their teaching lives and the transitions of significance in their lives, so the "method was a lot like paddling a canoe downstream; [I] occasionally stuck [my] oar in the water to keep from running aground and to make sure [I] explored the main channels of interest" (Bain, 2004, pp. 186-187). The strategies

I used to explore the narratives emerged from the examination itself. As faithfully as possible I labored to follow their channels of meaning making.

At Riessman's (1993) fourth level, analyzing experience, typically conducted from written or audio transcriptions, a "metastory" is created by "editing and reshaping what was told, and turning it into a hybrid story" (p. 13). This methodology assumes that narrative is beyond form and structure, and that it is a living social construction (Manning & Cullum-Swan, 1994). These narrative profiles are therefore constructed as my metastories unique to my perspective and this time. Others may write different stories from these same transcripts. At another time I know I might construct these narratives differently.

The interview tapes were transcribed after completing the final interviews. I then selected and bracketed response passages from the transcripts to create narrative "profiles" (Seidman, 1998, p. 101), which captured major themes of meaning making. Drawing on the idea from Studs Terkel's *Working* (1972), Seidman (1998) has argued that the researcher-constructed narrative profile presents an effective strategy for "opening up one's interview material to analysis and interpretation" (Seidman, 1998, p. 102). This exercise would begin the steady climb of narrative analysis along Riessman's (1993) levels of representation, beginning with the second level of representation, *telling about the experience* (Riessman, 1993, p. 9) to *transcribing the experience* (p. 13) and upward. I proceeded through this process to develop the narrative profiles that were the research participants' *passage narratives* (Grimes, 2000).

## Figure, Ground and Sensemaking

Recall that Edmund Bolles (1991) connected meaning making to human perception, noting that in Gestalt psychology, "*figures* are the things we attend to; *ground* are the array of sensations we ignore" (p. 24). Therefore, what is meaningful can be accessed partly by understanding what research participants selected to reflect upon and attend to ("figures") in their interviews, and partly by discerning how and why they selected their "figures" and "ground" notions related to their faculty leadership work, and how they made sense of it.

For Rebecca, a faculty member in political science at Wilkinson, one "figure" was her emphasis on her "net" – her social network, reflecting on how important it was to her work as a faculty scholar:

> So this… net is sort of, you do what you're supposed to do, professionally, you meet people, you talk with them, you make a good impression or you don't, you do good things for other people and they do good things for you. And so then you can get established in that way. And… so… you have to have your own initiative, you have to work; you also have to rely on the help of other people. And that's one of the interesting things in… the discipline.

Although she was not the only one who described the value of her network of professional friends and colleagues, as we will see in her narrative profile later in this chapter, clearly Rebecca emphasized it the most. She described weaving together and utilizing her network to both construct and measure her accomplishments, and these were clearly the "figures" she chose to inflect in her reflections, to make sense of her experiences.

Sensemaking, Karl Weick (1995) suggested, is *grounded in the sensemaker* because it begins with a self that is shaped and identified in interaction with others (pp. 19-20). All the research participants articulated and made sense of their professional work in terms of their relationships with others. They reflected on teachers, mentors, and family members, and other early influencers in their lives, such as when another participant, Francesca, talked about the early peers who influenced her aspirations and ambitions: Francesca described her coterie of high school friends as

> an elite group in a way, but it wasn't just a matter of elitism; it was more of a matter of, these are the people we enjoy being together with. So we defined ourselves by what we were interested in, how we liked to spend our time and the kind

of things that we liked to talk about with each other. And also, I suppose, we defined ourselves by feeling good about who we were, happy about our accomplishments.

Relationships with adults early in life, such as teachers and mentors also helped shape their present identities of membership in the intellectual elite. Paula, a third research participant who teaches organic chemistry, remembered one early teacher:

> because… she was a pivotal person in… keeping me focused and out of trouble… Because she really took a personal interest in us. She really, if she didn't care, she surely acted like she cared. And… there were others, there was another teacher who had the same kind of impact, maybe not to the same extent. And he was… one of the science teachers, which may have kind of helped me feel a little more positive about science than that I would have otherwise. He did the same thing. He took a very personal interest, and cared about what he did. And I think that definitely reflects on what I do here [at Wilkinson College].

Sensemaking is *retrospective* as an "act of reflection" that corresponds to "a cone of light that spreads backward from a particular present" (Weick, 1995, p. 26). Specific events and phenomena are remembered and synthesized with meaning in terms of present values, priorities, and projects (p. 27). By definition, all the research participants' narratives were retrospective second level narratives (Riessman, 1993, p. 12) making sense of their present in terms of their past. In one resolute and compelling retrospective, Paula noted:

> I want to be remembered for my work on behalf of the students. I mean, whether it be teaching in my class, whether it be challenging them to think outside of the box, in terms of what are you going to do, what do you like to do, where are you gonna be. I think I want to be remembered for how I worked with the students.

The narratives of the participants in this study were not comprehensive descriptions or renditions. What they elected to emphasize ("figure"), by definition, also resulted in much information ("ground") that was left behind in the background, and left out of their self-narratives. So, sensemaking was an ongoing process of the self in relation to others and manifested in their narratives as attempts to explicate what appeared to them subjectively plausible – personally meaningful for them – rather than what may have been historically accurate testimony. In examining their narratives, I chose not to pursue coherence, or even to problematize incoherence. I sought instead motifs of ritualization that marked or greeted transitions that I could discern and describe in their narratives. The research participants I interviewed and write about in the following chapters used ritualization to represent their subjective constructions of significance, to embody their narratives with the meaning inscribed in their actions and decisions related to their faculty work. In their narrative profiles, we find their stories of meaning making.

# Chapter 5

# Francesca

Francesca is a professor of German and has been at Wilkinson College for over 25 years. During her time at Wilkinson, she also served in a number of administrative roles, culminating in her appointment as Dean of the Faculty, which she vacated only a year before the time I interviewed her. At Wilkinson, the Dean of the Faculty is an elected rotating position, which has historically been occupied by senior faculty members who have distinguished themselves in their service to the College at large. When I met Francesca, she had just left the Dean's office, and after a sabbatical, had returned to the faculty.

Francesca has been married to Fred, another faculty member in the German department. In fact, the couple originally came to Wilkinson because Francesca accompanied Fred, who had been given a tenure-track faculty position at the College. When I met Francesca, she and her husband Fred were sharing an office – a source of some anxiety for Francesca, as we will see later – and Francesca and I had to find alternative space to conduct two out of the three interviews. Except for the final interview, when we met in the office she shared with her husband, Francesca and I met for the first interview in an empty large closet that doubled as a student staff office, and for the second interview in an empty classroom.

These offices we interviewed in were all located in historic Kanter Hall, Wilkinson's signature academic building built in 1902. Located in the center of campus, Kanter resembles an old castle. At the center of this U-shaped building is a tower with flags of the College and the United States that can be seen from the highway nearly two miles away. Under this tower is an open arch that has served as the backdrop for Commencement ceremonies. A recently added ritual is for first-year students to be led on a march through the arch at Opening Convocation, and another march back through the arch at Commencement. Rebuilt in 1902 after a fire burned the original building, Kanter Hall is currently designated for total renovation as part of an ongoing capital campaign. Kanter Hall has housed academic department offices and classrooms since its opening, and housed the offices of the faculty in German. Generally, the faculty offices are located in department clusters, although rank and seniority occasionally disturbed this pattern when preferred offices (larger, in corners, and/or with windows) went to ranking members of the faculty. Three of the participants of this study were interviewed in Kanter, including Francesca.

I met Francesca for our first interview in a large corner office on the second floor of Kanter Hall. This was her husband Fred's office, which she moved into after leaving her Dean of the Faculty position. Since Fred was expecting to meet a student in the office shortly, Francesca and I went looking for a quiet place to meet, and walked down the large, airy, and thoroughly un-modern hallway. We found several classrooms but decided to rule out classrooms because we wanted uninterrupted privacy. We found a large closet with a tiny window crammed wall-to-wall with furniture for an office for occasional student staff. It was a locked room and Francesca had a key so we met in this "office." The room was bare, and sufficiently illuminated by an overhead light and the sunlight streaming through the narrow window. I remembered worrying about sound, our words seemed travel around in a hollow room.

## Early Influences

An early passage of significance for Francesca was her becoming a faculty member, a teacher, and a scholar in German. Francesca reported that this was a gradual drift and that as a child she grew up in the company of a reference group of bright and intellectually capable students, all of whom felt guided and inspired by teachers who served as encouraging mentors. This was a patter she experienced in high school.

> Well, I suppose in a way you find people who are somewhat like minded. You enjoy some of the same things. You think alike about some of the same things. And in some ways these groups of people are very different too because the people that I interacted with most in high school for example were Germans. I had some American friends who were close friends of mine too, but they were… it was a very mixed group of people. There were a number of young Germans living in my hometown because of industry that had imported German scientists after the end of World War II. And these were the children of those German scientists. So we have this kind of interesting interaction with people who experience with life is very different than mine. But they were smart, they were interested in school, and they wanted to go to college. And so in a sense they distinguished themselves from the bulk of the high school class. And it wasn't so much… I suppose we thought of ourselves as an elite group in a way, but it wasn't just a matter of elitism; it was more of a matter of, these are the people we enjoy being together with. So we defined ourselves by what we were interested in, how we liked to spend our time and the kind of things that we liked to talk about with each other. And also, I suppose, we defined ourselves by feeling good about who were were,.. happy about our accomplishments.

Francesca reported an appreciation of the role that teachers played in the lives of students, and Francesca identified this as an early influence in her future choice of career.

> Some of the faculty were just wonderful to us and inspired us. Again it was a little bit like some of the undergraduate faculty. You looked at their lives. You looked at the kind of things they were thinking about and doing, and you said to yourself, 'I would like to be, this is the kind of life I would like lead what these people are doing with students and in their own research, and writing, and so on, and this sort is the way I can imagine I would like to spend my life'.

For Francesca, the early years in school and then college at the University of California, and then graduate school at Stanford University as a Woodrow Wilson Fellow, were all passages of preparation for a career as a faculty member. Francesca reported this passage as significant in her life and career, as a passage that included learning from faculty mentors, who in turn encouraged her to apply and obtain a Fullbright to Germany. Francesca remembered this time in her life as one of immersion in a realm of intellectual curiosity and scholarship. She easily passed through the hurdles of graduate school, including oral and written examinations toward her Masters degree in 1966, and only much later obtained her doctorate in 1974. During the graduate school years at Stanford, Francesca and Fred decided to pursue careers teaching German in college.

*Coming to Wilkinson*

After they completed their doctorates, husband Fred and wife Francesca were offered a jointly shared position teaching at Wilkinson, and Francesca entered another identifiable passage in her life – coming to Wilkinson as a trailing wife and mother, sharing half of a position with her husband Fred.

While Francesca clearly aspired to become a full-time faculty scholar in her own right, her pathway was far less direct. She remembered the early years at Wilkinson as a faculty spouse, feeling isolated. She remembered that these were the early years of the women's movement and her own aroused consciousness. Francesca was able to obtain a series of leave replacement positions, which then facilitated the conditions for her husband's position to gradually increase to full-time. For Francesca, these were years of being busy and feeling fragmented:

> I learned that… I learned a little bit about how to deal with a sense of fragmentation in my life, because I felt very pulled in lots of different directions. I don't think that's changed for any of us. People with family commitments, whether they're men or women, people with small children, feel pulled. And I think the expectation for faculty have increased here since I started in the 1970's, increased considerably along many dimensions.

## *At Wilkinson*

Francesca began to get involved at the College, first as a volunteer on projects and committees, then obtained a part-time position as an assistant to the Dean of the Faculty. As she branched out, Francesca found herself drifting into academic administration:

> And I did a lot; I did other things for him [Dean of the Faculty]. And so I had my first real taste of doing more college wide administration. And I think that that being able to branch out, to get to know more aspects of the college and how they worked, how the pieces fitted together, and the sense that I had some influence over what was happening here. That was really very exciting for me. I did an awful of things like that. I also taught first year seminar, as you know, as everybody does. I was one of the first people to help design sophomore seminar inter disciplinary program. I taught three years in that program

Gradually, Francesca began to reframe the experience of feeling fragmented into an experience of feeling engaged in variety of different administrative opportunities across campus:

> a thread of experience for me at [Wilkinson] has been moving outside of the German department, you know, at regular intervals or almost consistently, and working here, and working there, and getting more and more of sense of how the pieces of the college and the curriculum so on fit together.

## Election to Dean of the Faculty

A series of search committee appointments, and other extra assignments, finally led Francesca to a nomination and election as the Dean of the Faculty:

> I think I was set… I set myself up for that. I mean everything I've been describing to you I think kind of led to that. So I would say there were two things that took me into that office. One of them was just the experience across the college and the fascination with how things fitted together at the college and the enjoyment I had had in doing, sort of, lower level administrative jobs. Pulling things together. Trying to make things work, trying to solve problems at a level beyond the classroom or beyond the department. That was one thread there. And the other thread was again the sort of mentorship that I was actually encouraged. I mean, when DH [Provost] left here to go to Bates, he said, you know, '[Francesca], I hope you stay at [Wilkinson].' And he had also had suggested at one point, you know, he said that you could be a Dean someday, maybe not at [Wilkinson], but at some other school. I think that sort of encouragement gave me kind of a, you know, the sense well I should really try this job because this job is about… it's another level of building skills, and another… It's a risk, but it's another level of stepping out and seeing how the whole College works, and

looking for a chance to pull some things together and make them more coherent. So I think that was the road into the Deans office.

Francesca's various assignments and activities then led her to join a community of colleagues and friends outside her department, particularly women faculty friends:

> Over the years I've developed relationships with people outside of the department who are, who may have been working, teaching in the same area that I was, or someone that I have worked with on committees consistently over time. I mean, I for an example would say that I had a continuing relationship with JF [faculty], with DH [faculty], and really, simply because we saw, we felt compatible about many of the ways that we thought. I came out of the Deans office with relationships with a couple of people in Gardner [administration building] that I continue to, to be, that I see regularly, that feel to me like good and important relationships. But I think a certain number of people that I related to, I lost when I went into the Deans office, and I haven't really recovered those. And I also think that while I was there I formed new relationships. I've always enjoyed knowing some younger faculty, newer faculty, as well as the people who are more in my own rank, or in my own age bracket. But it would be colleagues, not necessarily just in the department, that I've worked together with on a project, or where we'd undertaken an initiative together to, to try to get something new established.

Francesca reported that as her circle of relationships expanded and changed both the nature and texture of the relationships, and what was expected also began to transform. She described the relationships as:

> the sort of relationships where you don't get together every day or even every week, but you can, sort of, pick up the threads when you do see each other. So the content of your

conversation is likely to be both professional and it could also be personal at some level or other. But it's not as though these are people that I see every single day. But they are, in a sense, they're people that get in touch with each other because they want to discuss an issue that's arisen or a problem they're trying to solve, or mean that we can do that together. So they're not just kind of getting together to talk, but more a matter of well, here's where I am, and this is something I'm thinking about, you know, or dealing with, and what do you think. [They were], I suppose in a sense consultants and support, a support network basically. But I think that's how a lot of these relationships function. As a support network and kind of consultants, yeah, or people that you collaborate with on certain things. And then there are two or three people who, that I just feel close to as an ongoing part of their lives, but not a large number. I mean, one of those people is now, is retired, but she and I are still very much in touch with each other, and see each other fairly frequently. But it's real friendship, I mean; it's support and consulting. But those are real friendships. A couple, two or three people like that.

When asked about how these friends influenced her, Francesca reflected that:

> How… I don't know, I… that's a hard question to answer because I'm that sure they have [influenced me]. And I, I suppose to some extent I've adopted their ways of thinking, but I think that's kind of mutual and interactive. And I think that, and there've been times when, I think, you know, I've been able to learn something from them, not because I would have done what they did or thought the same way that they did, but I, I learned something by watching them deal with an issue in their context and realizing how I would have dealt with that in mine. So what have I learned from them? Well, I suppose something about just the ongoing importance of having close friends and people that you stay in contact with. Because basically I'm a person who, sort of,

withdraws, and I need to be reminded that it's important to foster, to keep relationships alive, because that's part of being a whole human being.

Reflecting on what she thought she had contributed to this circle of friends, Francesca suggested that:

> Well I think, and this probably has worked both ways, I think, one of the major things that I've, other people have done for me, and that sometimes I've been able to do for them, is encourage them to go forward with something, to take a risk, to, to move to the next stage. I think that's an important part of these friendships and relationships. I think it's, it's becomes then a kind of mentoring relationship even if you are peers. You're, you're supporting each other in stepping out, and moving into a new role, or taking on a new responsibility, and taking a certain amount of risk in doing that. And I think that that would be true for all of the relationships that I would count as important ones. They've all functioned that way, both, in both directions. I wouldn't want to claim that I ever supported JF in that way, but, but maybe I have in ways that I'm not aware of. Certainly I know that that's true with some other people. And certainly that would be my prime… one of my main experiences out of all these relationships, that I was encouraged to think that I could do something beyond what I might have thought I could do.

This significant passage for Francesca was a passage from trailing spouse and part-time faculty member to Dean of the Faculty, from the experience of feeling fragmented to the experience of being a campus-wide contributor, from feeling intellectually isolated to being a member of an enlarged community of friends mutually shaping their lives at Wilkinson.

## From Dean Back to Faculty

After completing her term as Dean of the Faculty, Francesca took a year-long sabbatical, and returned to the faculty, re-immersing herself in the department of German. Francesca left the Dean's position in the middle of a somewhat controversial curricular revision. She reported being glad to return to an almost exclusive faculty teaching and research role, having reconstituted some of her perspectives from her decanal experience:

> Well when I came out of the [Dean's] office I didn't particularly want to get involved in many major issues. I just wanted to be on the sidelines for a while, because I'd been so involved in so many issues. And I did have a year of leave. And when I came back I was, I was simply, I was, I was just very focused on going back into the classroom. That's where I wanted to put my time. I wanted to try to see how I could manage that, and how I could do the best job that I could, in teaching. And I, that's what I really wanted to focus on, and try to resurrect some sort of a research program. I wanted to do that far more than I wanted to serve on any elective committee, or become engaged in, in some of the debates that were going on the faculty at the time. I think that, I think that one thing that I've learned increasingly over time is, and maybe this is a change, is trying to understand why people do the things that they do and from what perspective, and trying to see some integrity in that, or appreciate it. And certainly trying to understand motives for behavior before I start condemning the behavior whether it's a colleague or an administrator. And maybe that's just is because I wished people had done more of that for me.

## Senior Faculty Member

In her new role as senior faculty member and former Dean of the Faculty, Francesca found herself sought out by others for consultation and advice, and to play roles that required a special credibility or experience, and Francesca almost appeared a little surprised by this new kind of attentiveness from others:

> I don't know, in general, I think people who were in the Deans office are accorded a certain amount of respect simply because they were known to have worked very hard. And so there's, you know, there's that component of things. I think it's very much of a generational thing. I think the younger faculty members are more inclined to see someone who had that role as a potential leader, at least, or at least as someone who, whose opinion on things they might respect, maybe more than the person's own rank and age colleagues would. But I think I've been called on to do some things that were, that required a certain kind of credibility. I chaired a tenure and evaluation committee for someone who wasn't in an actual department, or at least the department couldn't function that way. And I know I've done a few other things where it was not a bad thing to have a person with some long-term perspective and experience involved. I think it's more a matter of that, you know, that maybe I have a longer-term perspective on things and, and a kind of accumulated experience. So people occasionally consult me. I've had people talk to me about what should I do in this situation or how should I think about this thing that got said to me. From time to time I have people talk to me about things like that, but not on any really regular basis.

## *Looking Back*

Francesca reflected on her years at Wilkinson and identified a continuing motif of being a mentor and connector to her colleagues, both in her role as an administrator, and as a faculty member. Francesca suggested that she had indeed influenced and shaped the experiences of colleagues and friends at the College:

It seems to me one of the roles I did play as a faculty member when I was not yet in administration, was, was to try to share information and make contacts between and among people who wouldn't otherwise have been touch with each other. And I think because I worked on so many different committees, and in different programs, and even in different parts of the institution that weren't necessarily strictly academic, I knew more about what was going on around the College. And I, and I tended try to make contacts between people in departments or just sort share information around, build connection. And I think that that was maybe one of the things that I liked to do best. And I think that that was one of the things that sent me into administration. And I still, I find myself doing that, you know, maybe all faculty do this, I'm sure they do, but for me it's just almost like an automatic response. If someone tells me about something they're working on and I know somebody else who's working on something that connects in some way or other then I'm immediately gonna try to get those people together. Or alert someone in a department to something another department is doing that is related. I think I did a lot of that, and it was a, before the Deans office, I was doing this sort of thing. And I think it was a, it was partly a translation thing; you kind of translate from one group to another, but also just in making connections. So I would say that was one of the things that I did as a faculty member, that at least that I saw myself as doing this at various points. And another thing, another role that I think I played, we talked a little bit about mentoring yesterday, and you were asking me did I think, you know, had I had an impact on other people or influenced some decision or something that they made, and I honestly can't answer that. I don't know really if I did or not. But I, I do think that one of the things that I try to do, and I had a friend I was talking to last night who talked about her own leadership in an administrative context, and it suddenly occurred to me, yes I think I did that as a faculty member as well as an administrator. I was always trying to prompt people, to, well to, to congratulate them on something they'd done, or be, push them, help think about themselves as moving into another, into a next stage. So it was a sort of a mentoring, I suppose, but it was kind of in the background or sort of low key. I wasn't trying to become a mentor to someone, I was just saying, 'you know you did so well on this'. It didn't matter what it was, something I'd read that they'd written, something they said in a faculty meeting, or some performance on a committee. It was just, like that was automatic to me, that I would, that I would encourage them to now go on with this or have you thought about that.

At this stage of her career at Wilkinson, Francesca was beginning to think about her legacy at Wilkinson, and what she would like to be remembered for by students and by colleagues. This was a difficult conversation, with some moments of soft crying, as Francesca reflected about her nearing retirement at Wilkinson:

I was trying to think what would I like to be remembered for by students. And I think, maybe, you know, for the things that I said yesterday, that they got, they were challenged but they got a certain level of encouragement. Or that they, you know, thought about something in a different way or, or that they had the feeling I can do this, I can learn beginning German or whatever it is. It's those kinds of things, I mean, just learning a foreign language, that's a huge hurdle for a lot of people. It's a, it's a very frightening thing. It's a real phobia thing for some people, but those kinds of things. And then as far as colleagues are concerned, one of the things that I've learned about [Wilkinson] over the years, and I have no illusions about this, as I watch people retire, the college moves on very, very quickly. And you find yourself, I think, as a retired person, how ever much of a leader you were at the time that you were on campus. You find yourself as a retired person, someone that people really have to rush by, because they, you know they have so many other things they need to deal with, the daily urgencies. And bit-by-bit you lose contact with what's going on at the school, and so you're, you're more and more on the outside. And I think it's sad for people to kind of hang around and want to be on the inside when they've retired. And so I have to illusions about that. I think the college has to move on, and can't spend a lot of time remembering the people, who even made major, sort of, contributions to things. But, I think, I, I just simply don't expect that there be some sort of institutional memory about people, because that fades as personnel change, unless you got your name on a building, you know, something like that. And even then nobody knows who Kanter was or Berry, or these people. But it would be, I think, I think it's, it's, it's very great when your colleagues remember you well, you know, we have this going on, and these are the people who were involved in initiating it, or in fostering it, whatever 'it' is, at least for the time that those colleagues who would have any reason to remember those things or think about them. But otherwise, you know, I don't expect… that there's much memory about people as they leave an institution. So, you know, what would one want to be remembered for? Well, the very things that I tried to describe that I think, you know, that I've maybe done for people.

At first, Francesca talked about the experience of retirement in the abstract, but then seemed to struggle back to her own feelings about retirement. She appeared to grow more pensive, and reflected on feelings of loss, feelings of perhaps fading out of significance as she neared the twilight of her career at Wilkinson:

> I think, I mean, in a sense, that these are things that I've been dealing with, and thinking about myself. And so it's kind of close to the, close to the nerve I guess. But, I think that's sort of specific to me, and who I am, and how I process things, much more than a kind of general faculty approach. I mean I don't think that I'm representative in some ways, but I do think that people who are, and I know, I know a

couple of colleagues who are sort of processing, you know, what have I done over the last twenty-five years. It's a, it's, it's a kind of, a self-evaluation. It's difficult. It's not so easy, cause you, you, you want to claim good things, and you want to see some, you want to see some kind of coherence and consistency, and some meaning to what you've done. But I think that's why we construct narrative, because we're looking for meaning. And so that's a very important thing to be doing.

The narratives of Francesca's early passages share many motifs, among them, a community of friends who share intellectual habits and purpose, and who shape each other's lives, a mutual mentoring and shaping of each other's experiences and perspectives. These passages also share distinct phases of struggle for significance, followed by commitment to a place and to others, and emerging in a renewal of meaning making. Later in her career, Francesca reflected on her campus role as a prompter and connector of opportunities, and as noticer and chelebrant of the accomplishments of her more junior colleagues.

# Chapter 6

## Paula

I met with Paula in Sealy Hall, which has been known for a long time as the Chemistry Building. Decades ago, Sealy Hall was a dilapidated building with creaky wooden floors, with ill-lit hallways punctuated by dark ornate doors that opened into offices and outdated laboratories. The Sealy Hall that housed Paula's office was a very different place.

Originally built in 1902, and remodeled in 1960, Sealy Hall was then completely gutted, expanded, and renovated in 1999. It now houses the departments of chemistry, biochemistry, and molecular biology. This Sealy Hall I entered in the early 2000s was clean and airy, spacious and full of artificial and natural light, and with much of the woodwork restored. I passed by laboratories with people in white coats and protective glasses and found Paula's office on the second floor in a corner cluster of offices. Her office was spacious, two walls of large windows faced the campus and one wall of shelves was cluttered with books, among them Gerald Gibson's *Good Start* (1992), a book Paula would refer to several times during our interviews.

Leaving her desk, Paula invited me to sit with her in a small round conference table with the two chairs in the corner of her office, and this is where we conducted all our interviews. Transcribing and re-checking Paula's interviews required listening to the tape in very slow speed; her transcripts were almost twice as long as any of the other participants' transcripts. Paula talked very very quickly, and we covered more ground. She had so much she wanted to talk about, that she frequently interrupted her own sentences to start a new thought.

Our interviews occurred in the spring of her sixth year at Wilkinson, about three weeks before Commencement. Paula had just been awarded tenure this year, a process and a passage that she noted as very meaningful and significant in her narrative about her time at Wilkinson College.

## On The Way to Teaching

Paula remembered her inspiration for teaching as having emerged early in her life. Like the other research participants in this study, Paula's aspirations for teaching and scholarly work came from early experiences with teachers who inspired her. Like the other research participants in this study, Paula was helped to feel that she was especially intellectually capable:

> I went to large inner city school south of Cincinnati, on the Kentucky side. Discipline was an issue and academic excellence. I was bored in high school. It was easy, and I found it a little boring. And I think to compensate that boring, I got over involved. So I was involved in things like student council, and I was president one year. And then I was involved in band, and worked forty hours a week at a job outside of high school. And I graduated valedictorian without a whole lot of effort. So when I think back to high school, I think if I would have gone to a more challenging school I could have gotten a lot more out of it. But I think I also feel like I got a lot out of it because, because of my student council involvement. And, and it wasn't so much what I did in student council, as it was the advisor for student council. Because she was a, she was a pivotal person in keeping me, keeping me focused and out of trouble... Because she really took a personal interest in us. She really, if she didn't care, she surely acted like she cared. And I think that, there were others, there was another teacher who had

the same kind of impact, maybe not to the same extent. And he was, he was one of the science teachers, which may have kind of helped me feel a little more positive about science than that I would have otherwise. He did the same thing. He took a very personal interest, and cared about what he did. And I think that definitely reflects on what I do here.

Paula went to Georgetown College for a B.S. in chemistry. She described Georgetown as very similar to Wilkinson. This description was also very similar to how she would later describe her own role as a faculty member at Wilkinson and her relationships with, and aspirations for, her students:

> The faculty take a personal interest in you. They really help you not only in terms of classroom, but they also help you in terms of what are you doing this summer and what are you going to do when you're done here. I remember my professor being particularly, my key advisor being particularly intent on trying to get me to balance work and socializing, cause he thought all I did was work. So it was a, it was a good experience. By the time I, by the time I was a senior, well I guess it was my junior year, I knew that, I knew that I had a pretty good idea that I wanted to teach at college like that. But I wasn't sure if I wanted to do that just because that was what I knew, or because that was really what I wanted to do. And so when I went to graduate school I was really open minded about, maybe I wanted to teach, maybe I don't want to teach, but either way I've got to get a Ph.D.

After Georgetown, Paula went on to the University of North Carolina, Chapel Hill for her Ph.D. Like many of the decisions in her life, Paula selected UNC over Vanderbilt and Emory, largely on instinct:

> I just kind of go with that instinct; does it feel like it's the right thing that I should do? I do make pro and cons list. But often I just ignore the list and just do, do what I want

to do. When it was time, when I had decided that Ph.D. was what I needed, I went to my advisor and I told him, "How do I pick a graduate school?" and he told me "Where do you want to live?" And I actually told him "You're crazy, that, that cannot be the criteria," you know, "Tell me, tell me the real..." And he said, "No I'm telling you," he said, "Where do you want to live?" He said, "If I had it to do over, I would go to the University of Hawaii." And, and I told him, I said "Well, I'm thinking more along the lines of, I would like a big institution, with lots of money, but in a small town, because I don't want to live in a big city somewhere." And he suggested a few institutions. And I went down to visit UNC, and on the drive in I thought, this is the place. And then when I met with the various faculty and the students that I met with that day, I accepted the next day. I mean, I went back and we had some little form we had to fill out. So I did. One of things that was a real pet peeve for me is that I don't like the arrogance that you find in academia sometimes, and I certainly don't like the arrogance you find in male scientists. And none of that, none of that in that entire visit, whether it was a male graduate student, or a female graduate student, or a male professor, or a female professor, I didn't get any of that sense of, kind of an elitism, and had I gotten any of that I wouldn't have been there, because that, that was something that was particularly important to me. And I guess I'm kind of headstrong.

At UNC as a Teaching Assistant (TA), Paula began to discern a preference for teaching and working directly with students, even as it threatened to affect her graduate work as a scholar:

> I think the things that I enjoyed the most when I was in graduate, I mean I liked my research project, I mean I liked, I mean, I took great satisfaction in the successes when they happened. But I got much more satisfaction out of the tutoring that I did, and then early in my time at UNC, once I was trained to use a certain piece of equipment,

that the facility operator had decided that he was tired training people, and recruited me to be the trainer. And, I enjoyed that. And my first, my first semester, because the first semester you have to take classes and you also teach as part of your teaching assistantship, and I wanted to be super TA, and so here I spent hours making comments on the lab report and having office meetings. And on my first graduate school exam, out of a 100 points I got a single digit. And that was a rude awaking that I was going to have to work a little harder than I had been working, and that I needed to balance my time.

As happened to Charles, the other science faculty esearch participant in this study, Paula was encouraged to proceed to a research institution after her Ph.D. so that she could continue to do the research work of a scholar. As was also true for Charles, Paula was actively discouraged from teaching at a liberal arts school after completing her doctorate:

At a Research One institution like NC Chapel Hill, some people had the attitude that if all you're going to do is teach, don't waste space in my lab. And so you kept it kind of quiet, so that you were taken seriously. And so that by my, when it came time to start thinking about finishing up, so by the beginning of my fourth year, I started talking to my advisor about, I want to teach in a small liberal college, and got absolutely no mentoring about, you know, what should you do to get ready to do that, because you didn't know, and that's when the story started with don't sell yourself short, don't go to a liberal arts college, they'll saddle you with teaching, you won't get to do research. And I'm just sitting there thinking, hmmm, they'll saddle me with teaching, it's what I want to do, so I guess, I'm thinking, it's a good thing to be saddled with.

Although her heart was set on finding a teaching position, Paula elected to take a two-year post-doctoral research position in Baltimore, Maryland:

> When I was coming out of UNC, and trying to decide about career decisions, a trusted mentor there told me that "I think you would be better off if you went and did a post-doc first." He said, "You don't have to do a post doc even, but I think that, if you'll do the post-doc, it'll give you a wider experience, it, it will potentially give you more confidence. And then in the long run, your research at whatever institution you end up with will benefit from that." And so I did a post-doc for two years in Baltimore Maryland. Outstanding science. Very driven by the science. And then when it came time to do a job search I applied at ten different institutions like [Wilkinson].

## Coming to Wilkinson

As the post-doctoral research position in Baltimore, Maryland, came to an end, Paula began a search for teaching positions, but she was unable to secure a position, because she had no formal teaching experience. Frustrated, that "doing what felt right wasn't really going to work," she applied for a research position in the corporate sector, getting her out of Baltimore, and bringing her back to Kentucky. Before long, she realized that and she applied for teaching positions again, and found Wilkinson College:

> I ended up with three interviews and was turned down on all three interviews because I didn't have the teaching experience. And I very clearly remember talking to one of the chairs and saying to them verbatim, "And when the hell was I supposed to get this teaching experience." And she let me know. She said, "I'm angry about this, I think they're ridiculous. And they don't know what they're talking about, and they can do their own search next time, because I'm not

> doing it." So, that experience was pretty, it made me realize that maybe just doing what felt right wasn't really going to work. So I ended up taking, and, and I had to get out of Baltimore, I, I needed to be out of there. And so I took a year with a company, in a research and development section of a contract company. And I thought that this would be good. It'll be good money. It'll be good experience. I can, I can do this.

A few months later she called her faculty advisor at Georgetown College to reconnect with him.

> I said, "I'm going to be in town, you want to get together for lunch?" And his first answer was, "Oh you're going to give a seminar?" I was like, "I knew I shouldn't have called you!" And, so I had been at the company about three months, and went and gave a seminar. And then I realized that day, I was in the wrong place; I've got to go back and try again. And that afternoon I went and bought a printer, so that I could print resumes without my bosses knowin' it, and bought the book called, *Do What You Aren* (Tieger & Barron, 1992), which was a career guide based on personality types. And sent out about thirty resume packages to both liberal arts and Ph.D. programs... I mean I really enjoy the research. I've got some work done. I thought that well, I'll just send the resumes out, and wherever I get interviews, and continue with what seems to be the best fit, that's where I'll go.

## *Early Years at Wilkinson*

Paula's search yielded several job offers on the east and west coasts. She waited to hear from somewhere in the middle of the country. Then Wilkinson called.

> And I came up here, and knew instantly, that this is the place, that I needed to be. The students that I met with, the position that the department was in, the thought that

> renovations were going to begin within a couple of years, the fact that there were going to be lots of retirements in the department, and so there was going to be the opportunity to make a significant difference in a fairly short period of time. So I came here. And I decided, okay, I am a single female. I'm moving off the face of the earth socially, so I'll just marry my job, and I'll be, I'll be the best professor I can be. Here I am, and have never once regretting coming here. There've been times I've questioned the sanity of teaching at a liberal arts college because of the workload, and the magic balancing act that you're supposed to try to do. But I have never once regretted choosing [Wilkinson]. And my husband is a [Wilkinson] alum. He graduated in '89. We met within two weeks of me being here.

Paula remembered her first few years at Wilkinson as marked by the intensity of a challenging workload and driven by her own self-expectations for being an excellent faculty member. In the first year, a faculty colleague went on medical leave just as the semester began and his load was distributed to others. In her second year, all the chemistry faculty members were displaced as offices and laboratories were spread all over campus when Sealy Hall closed for renovation.

> It was awful. I worked fourteen fifteen hours a day. I didn't know which way was up, because I had very little teaching experiences. The week before school started, my senior colleague in organic chemistry, who since then has retired, got hit by car, who made a dramatic recovery, thank God. But the way things were set up, I mean, I had no problem teaching a class, because, I mean, I can read the book. I can certainly, I can remember what I learned, and I can, at least, wing it in the beginning. But the labs, and he was supposed to take the lead lab, and I was going to go to the lead lab, and then do the other two labs, based on what I learned. And the week before school he's not here. So I had a lot of learning to do very quickly. And it really, it was difficult.

> That first year was very difficult. Burning the candle at both ends. Trying to be super teacher. Wanting to do a good job in all areas simultaneously, but not recognizing that it takes a while. You have to learn these things, and then practice these things, and make mistakes, and it takes a while. And, we had a lot of additional departmental responsibilities because of preparing for the renovation.

At the end of her second year at Wilkinson, Paula realized that in an effort to please her senior faculty colleagues she had assumed far too many responsibilities. Something had to change.

> I was pretty overloaded. I did not have a perspective to recognize that I'm inappropriately overloaded. But then end of my second year, fortunately [Wilkinson] has a review hearing your second year, and for the, when I did my review my second year, the committee that reviews that, basically told me "You are overloaded, you are doing too much, you need to get some perspective on this." And once I realized that I overloaded, and my department had helped me become overloaded, I went outside of the department. I went and got a mentor outside of the department, and asked him, okay, is this reasonable? And he would help me balance things, and so that by my third year, things were still crazy because we moved out of the building. And being a chemist for seventeen months. Being a homeless chemist for seventeen months was challenging. And so by your third year, my understanding, that things should be starting to calm down, because you'll be doing repeat classes and you can focus more on the research… And I appreciate that because I feel like I have a much better sense of the overall picture of our curriculum… For the first five years, every semester, I had at least one new preparation. So there, so I was repeating classes in addition to getting new classes.… It's given me a better sense of the big picture, and because of that, I mean, I've done extensive work this year completely revising the organic chemistry course and lab. And I'm very

happy with the early results that we are seeing. So, so I guess I kind of paid it forward. The first five years, or four years, whatever it was, very difficult. And I know in hindsight that I created a good deal of that on my own. But then some of it is just the nature of the beast in terms of, you're supposed to be excellent in teaching, and in scholarship, and research, and service to the community. And it's a tall order to fill.

## *Learning from Senior Colleagues*

Paula remembered the first few years as years of learning and being mentored by her faculty colleagues. She came to an academic department that had been stable for nearly twenty years. While her colleagues were role models of tremendous learning, she also thought "there was some part of me that kind of helped them." Paula now acknowledges drawing on this early experience of exchange "because now I have four faculty that are more junior than me. And I want to be a good role model for them."

> One of things that I think was kind of unusual about my situation is, I was the most junior faculty member in twenty years. Which means there hadn't been whole lot turnover in that position. And the last person that had gotten tenure in this department had been fourteen years prior to that. And so it left a huge gap in experience level and in perspective, because the kinds of things that I needed to be doing and thinking about, at my level, were very different from the kinds of things that they needed to be doing and thinking about at their level.

Paula sensed the wealth of teaching experience in the department that she could draw upon, and she identified what she could learn from them, but she also sensed that she had brought something to the department as well.

> I don't think I would have gotten as much out of it, if they hadn't been so senior to me. Because I think, there was some part of me that kind of helped them, kind of helped them up, and really was impressed by, I mean, when you've got someone that's been here forty-two years, and thirty-eight years, and thirty-six years, I mean that's quite a track record. In my time here, I have sat in on classes by two of them because, my first semester, I wanted to learn how to teach. And so I would sit in on their classes to not necessarily learn the chemistry, but to watch how they did things.
>
> … I think it was both a seeing things to do and seeing things not to do, and giving yourself permission to make mistakes in classes. And it's okay. That even after thirty-two years, you can still make mistakes in class. And that's okay. So I think that, it was good perspective. I also got to know them better. It helped me to know my colleagues faster than I would have without that interaction, because it's very easy to just stay, to cluster in your own little office, in your little lab, and your little workload. And, I mean, I can go days and not even say anything but good morning to my two-office mate people right here. And so I think it was a, I think it put me on the fast track to getting to know my department. And I recognized very quickly that all of my colleagues were very different, and they all have different things to offer. And that they weren't all the same, and that we shouldn't expect each other to all be the same.

Paula reflected on these early years as replete with valuable lessons, and helping to change her perspective, and as an investment in the future of the department as more and more senior faculty members retired:

> I think I've made some mistakes along the way that could have been avoided. I think that I could have been more efficient with some things along the way had I been given some direction. And I can guarantee you I wouldn't have been quite as tired along the way, had I been a little more

efficient with some of things that I did. And some of it you have to learn on your own. I know that. But I think that there's some of it that, I mean I can, I can put the passing article in their mailbox. I can ask them how is their day. How is class going? And I'm not, I'm not as intimidating because I've only have been here few years more than them, not thirty years. And I just, I just feel like it's important to, and I, I think quite honestly I'm paying it forward again, because I think that it will foster collegiality. Because we, we're on the, I mean, we've had four very senior faculty members recently retire. We've got another one retiring this year. There are three senior faculty members that are left. Two of them will be on research leave next year. So that next year I will be the second most senior faculty member in the department. And for the, these junior faculty are the future. And if we can foster collegiality and respect, now, among ourselves, then that will extend to the students. And it will just make us a stronger, healthier department.

## *Giving Back*

Paula was now an active contributor to the department and to the college, engaged in activities that were focused on serving her students and her junior faculty colleagues. In her descriptions of the many sources of involvement, Paula also saw herself in an emerging role as a faculty spokesperson, articulating concerns to the administration, empowered by her own experiences and emboldened by having received tenure. As an informal leader, she thought, "we could do better. And now I'm saying it a little more strongly because I believe it a little more strongly." Paula articulated her specific commitments:

> In the beginning, like I said, I didn't know how to say no. And so one of the consistent, consistently I tried to prioritize my outside involvement, by who does it benefit. And so one of the major commitments I've made is I'm on the pre-health advising committee, which completely makes sense, since

> I'm an organic chemist, and organic chemistry is kind of the gateway to any of those health professionals. So I've made a commitment to that. And I, and I'm committed to that because I think it benefits the students. Then, I've also been involved with some faculty mentoring kinds of initiatives. I belong to Project Kaleidoscope, which is a group for young faculty who are interested in leadership issues. And when I came back from one of those meetings, when I was there, and I think the one that I went to was in my second year, and asking people, you know, "How do things work at your college? How are decisions made? And you know what kind of resources do you have?"

Paula collected this information on improving the quality of work life for faculty, and she developed some recommendations. She took them to the Vice President for Academic Affairs who encouraged her to pursue them. And although she outlined some plans for acquiring the resources she wanted, her efforts stalled when she could not give enough time to lead the projects. Now she appears to have found a more assertive voice.

> And I didn't use to say it quite as strongly as that before; I used to say, I think we could do better. And now I'm saying it a little more strongly because I believe it a little more strongly. We have to do a good job. There are too many junior faculty that leave this institution. I don't know the statistics nationally and there's no way you would ever get those kinds of numbers about how many leave and why did they leave. I mean, because you could probably get the numbers on how many left, but the why did they leave would be ambiguous. So that's one major pet project, is not only the faculty mentoring within my own department, but campus wide. I mean, there needs to be, there needs to be a communication. And again it comes back to community. Because it's very easy on this campus… it's very easy to become very isolated.

Paula listed a number of projects that she led, and these projects allowed her the opportunity to advance her commitments to encouraging girls to study the sciences, just as she herself was encouraged into the sciences in school and college.

> I've done some random committee service. I'm big in to outreach… one of the big outreach programs that we just finished, we bring about 120 sixth grade girls to campus. And they spend the day going to different workshops, and that is focused on women in science. And in another one of my more recent endeavors is bringing summer workshop to [Wilkinson] for chemistry high school teachers, with the idea of, if you can teach the teachers then you can impact a lot more students for a longer period of time. And for [Wilkinson] this is the second year, it's every other year, this is the second year that [Wilkinson] is the host site. I've put a lot of time and energy into that. And that's kind of, kind of departmental, but its kind of campus, because certainly if you bring thirty-five chemistry high school teachers to an absolute wonderful facility like this. And then they've got seniors that need to figure out where they're going to for school. We'll be fresh in their mind.

Paula reflected on her reasons for her engagement in the department, and in the campus. She appeared to be deservedly proud of having arrived and survived, listing numerous accomplishments from graduate student to faculty member at Wilkinson. She noted more balance in her life, and Paula was now able took back at all her accomplishments, including most significantly the earning of tenure.

> I guess one of things that's probably one of my biggest accomplishments is that I just finally got tenure. But I don't really know what difference that's going to make. You know, you work the same. I do think that I'm going to speak out more. Because I did I notice, I had noticed at a few meetings recently that I'm more willing to take the unpopular side, or

to speak a little more clearly, because I think I am, I am very diplomatic about how I speak, but I think I have noticed in the last few weeks that I don't have to quite as diplomatic. I can be more clear and so that my message isn't missed.

## *Restoring Balance*

The earning of tenure allowed Paula to begin restoring more balance in the professional and personal dimensions of her life.

> I think I am getting better at balancing my professional life and personal life. And that's something that's been really important in the last couple of years. Because I think that one of things that can happen to you at an institution like this, is that you can become so consumed by the institution that you don't have anything outside of the institution. And you don't benefit from that. The people that are close to you don't benefit from that. And the students don't benefit from that. When I had a student tell me a couple of years ago that there's no way she would ever go teach because you can't have a life and teach. That was a real wake up call. Because when I sat and looked at it I didn't have a life. I was working around the clock. My husband was picking up the slack in every way shape and form. So, so I am getting better at balancing. I am proud of that. And I'm an advocate of balance. But I'm also an advocate I mean you can tell that I'm also not a slacker. You know, I'm not somebody that, I am very committed to the students, and to the success of [Wilkinson]… I also think… one of our components of success has to be balance.

## *About Student Success*

Paula noted that the principal recipients of her work were students. Students and their accomplishments provided Paula with a measure for her success at Wilkinson.

> I am proud that my first senior IS student just got her Ph.D. She is a rock star. She is, the amount of work that she published as a graduate student, the people that are clamoring to get her to come work for them. She's a nice genuine person, and, and it just, I had only a small role in that but I am proud, I am proud of that. And I'm also proud of my other student from that year who is the director of a reading program down in Athens.

In tracing her emerging leadership at Wilkinson, Paula identified herself first as a member of the chemistry department and then a member of the Wilkinson campus community.

*The Faculty Administrative Role*

Now that she had earned tenure and was no longer the junior member of the faculty, she sensed her voice getting stronger in engaging her colleagues and the College administration to help make changes for the better.

> I think I am first and foremost a member of the chemistry department. I think I feel a stronger allegiance to my responsibilities in the chemistry department, and maybe that's because we are in such transition. But then I also feel a strong responsibility to the colleagues, something as trivial as, I've only missed one faculty meeting in six years. I feel responsible. I feel the need to be a responsible member of the community and to try to be one of the level headed voices. I don't, I don't see my role as a go along to get along person. But I also am not constantly complaining, and griping, and confrontational. I mean, so I think I'm, one of my roles is try to give the administration feedback when I think things need improvement. And I also try to make it a point to give them feedback when I think things have gone well. So, I think, I guess, that's kind of my faculty administrative role. And, and I, I think part of the reason I feel a stronger

allegiance to my department is cause that's where I have more of a direct connection with the students. And so I take my role as advisor very seriously. I like to know the students. And I like to try to help them be creative about what they want to do. They don't just take courses because we need to get that, check that box on the, on the distribution page, but take courses because it might be something that you enjoy. It might be something that complements what you want to do. And so I take that role very seriously. It's fun. Time consuming, but its fun. So I think that, and I try to be involved in the campus community outside of my department, but it's tough. And so I have been very selective. I mean, I, each year I work on the [Wilkinson] Volunteer Network program selection committee, because I feel like that that's something that's important. So I try to be involved, but I just physically cannot be everywhere at all times. So I try to be selective in trying to be a member of the campus community outside of that administrative role, but in the fun kind of role.

Much more comfortable now with her responsibilities as a scholar and teacher, Paula is now, especially after receiving tenure, ready to come out and engage the Wilkinson faculty community outside the department of chemistry.

> I don't know much about those people. And so I find it intriguing to get to go, and I guess we have faculty discussions, or if there are seminars, and sometimes I'll just randomly show up at a seminar that has absolute nothing to do with anything that I know about, in my field, just because I'm curious about, what do they do? So I do try to, so I am gradually trying to go visit other people's homerooms. I haven't done as much of that in the last, this last year has, with coming up for review, it's been very and, but I've had to, I've had to be very self focused, and I think I'm just now starting to redirect my attention to people and things outside of me, in my, in my situation.

Paula would not have acquainted as many people had it not been for the experience of being "homeless" and temporarily displaced during the Sealy Hall renovation, and working out of several other buildings. This led to her suggesting more opportunities for interaction between faculty from different departments. But Paula also acknowledged being challenged by the insufficiency of the precious resource of time, and she seems to want the College to help her find a balance to be able to engage other Wilkinson faculty members and fulfill her many responsibilities; "every year the only thing I can think of that the College can do for me is give me more time."

> And the only reason that I know as many outside, as many people outside of my department that I do, is that I spent seventeen months, my office is between, my office was in Geology, and I taught classes and labs in Tenet, and I had equipment in Mayfield. And so I had to be in all those different places. And it was one of those situations where I was a guest in their, in their building, so I feel the need be sure that, you know I accommodated them. That I didn't take advantage of their, of their...Yeah. So, so I, so I got to know people during that seventeen months. I think I can, I tell you very candidly that there's no way I would have gotten to know that many people, and as well if I, if I had just stayed in my own building. In Sanders, you've got Geology and Philosophy, and then Publication Services are down there... I wouldn't even have known what Publication Services was, had I been, had I always been in chemistry. So I think geography is a huge, and there aren't, there aren't a lot of opportunities on this campus for faculty to get together for just casual conversation.

Paula went to the Vice President of Academic Affairs and asked to have more opportunities for faculty gatherings on campus. The College responded with Friday afternoon gatherings but this did not quite meet Paula's needs for engaging faculty colleagues across campus in extemporaneous conversations.

We started these Friday afternoon things. And I've gone a few times, but they're very, they're formalized and they're very stilted, and they're very, I mean, I don't want to go and have an agenda. I just want to go, and walk up to somebody and say, you know I've seen you in faculty meetings, but I don't think we've ever met. But we don't have a lot of opportunities like that. I mean, I guess I could just go randomly cruise Kanter, and knock on people doors, but that's just, it just not right by me. And we stay so busy. Every year when I fill out my report there's, there's the last part you're supposed to talk about your goals and what can the college do for you. And every year the only thing I can think of that the College can do for me is give me more time. I don't want more money; I just want more time. And every year I write the same thing. And what would… (I)… do with all that additional time? Take a walk on campus. Go read some journal articles. Maybe even sit out on a bench, and just randomly accost students as they walk by, just talk with them. And, I could just think of any number of things I would do, keep up with my professional current job, I mean periodically even call a friend at another institution to say hi, think about course development, just to be able to just relax and sit and think. I don't think, there just doesn't seem to be time for that. I mean there's no time to think. You gotta rush to the summer if you want to have time to think. So, so time is what the College can give me. And I always give them suggestions on how they can give me time too, teaching load and committee responsibilities. So I always give them suggestions, I never just leave them hanging on, gee, I wonder how we can give her time. So time.

## *Challenging Students and Colleagues*

Paula reported intentionally working to influence two groups of people on campus, students in her classes and laboratories and colleagues in her department. Paula's influencing of students is implied in her role as a teacher who challenges and inspires learning and actions of authenticity, "encouraging people to do what they really want to do," a role that Paula's own teachers played with her when she was a student.

> I think that I really push the students. If I really want them to get the most out of their college experience. And when I say I push them I don't think I push them in terms of learning the material from my class, I think I push them in terms of encouraging them to think about options, encouraging them to think about what do they want to do. And I think I try to encourage the students to do what they want, and to do what they'll be good at. And I think some of the most important advising I do in organic chemistry, is essentially giving students permission to drop the class. And to go on and do something different with clear conscience, and not feeling like they should take organic chemistry, and they should be a chemistry major, or whatever. So I think that some of the best influence I've had is encouraging people to do what they really want to do rather than what they feel will make the most money or will be the most prestigious, or whatever. And then also the students that do stay in chemistry, or in another science, trying to help them think about what are different, what are different things I could do, I mean, do I, do I, do I wanna just go be a clone of me, which I don't want them to do. I mean, I want them to do what's good for them, but sometimes I think it's comfortable for them just to follow the example that we set, rather than, you know, look into being some bioengineer, or look into being a congressional representative. So I, so I really try to challenge the students to get outside of the box.

Paula reported challenging her faculty colleagues to facilitate questioning and stimulate action "constantly pushing and poking, are, are we doing the best we can do."

> I'm the one that's always asking the questions, "Why do we do it that way?" "Do we do it that way because that's the way we've always done it, or do we do it that way because

it's the best way?" "How do these things fit together?" "I know about my little part of the curriculum, but I don't know much about the rest of the curriculum, can we, can we talk about this?" So really, I think that I'm the one that constantly pushing and poking, are, are we doing the best we can do. And if we are great, I'll sit back and relax and feel good about it, but if we aren't, and there are things we could do better, without killing ourselves. And one of my major motives has been, in talking with, especially the chair and then the others is, I don't think we need to work harder, I think we need to work smarter. And if time is such a major issue for all of us, and the administration either is not, or cannot give us that time, then we need to figure it out on our own.

## *A Stronger Voice*

Paula was now emerging as a leading agent of change in the department. She was no longer responding to her senior faculty colleagues as much as initiating a re-imagining of her department and the chemistry program.

> And we need to be trying to look at our own situation, because we know our situation best. And if there are things that we can do to reorganize the curriculum, to reorganize our departmental infrastructure so that we can make it a more supportive, thriving environment for the faculty, then everybody will benefit, because if we have a more thriving supportive environment for the faculty then, I think that will trickle down very quickly. So, I don't remember what your question was, but I'm always asking why. I think I am the one pushing. We have staff meetings every week. And I get that opportunity every week. And with my lovely little PDA, all week long as I think of things, I have little staff meeting note, I keep a running list, and then when we're done the business on the agenda, then I can pull out my PDA and say, "Okay, this week, I want to ask about..." And so I'm pretty

> regular about it. And, and the thing that's nice though is that when you bring these questions up, there's always, there's always one or other two people that are like "Oh, you know, that's a, that's a good question! We should look at that." And so that we've got quite a docket of things that we will be discussing over the summer, and into the fall semester. But it's, it's good conversation, and a lot of times, I think, those conversations are lacking because we're so busy taking care of the routine business, and so busy taking care of the, you know, putting out the fires, that, that we don't really have time to step back from the micro issues to the bigger issues of, you know, are we, are we doing the best that we can do, are there smarter things that we could do. And what are we doing well? And I, and I think that, I think that's where my energy goes.

Paula now felt a more confident voice emerging out of her now six years of experience.

> I've learned a lot in terms of, I mean, when I first, I'm the kind of person that, I like to have data and information before I form an opinion. And I've been here long enough now, that for some of the bigger issues, I'm starting to have opinions. I feel like I have enough data, and enough personal experience to start having opinions about whether I think this policy is good, or whether I think this administrator is doing a good job, or this faculty member is a good colleague. And maybe this faculty member is not such a good colleague. I mean, so I've been here long enough that I'm, I'm starting to have some opinions. And for me that's a big deal. I mean, cause I don't, I don't form opinions quickly. And once I have an opinion, once I have a commitment about, you know, I, I think this program needs to be changed. Or I think this, this, this aspect needs to be improved, then I'm, then I'm willing to do that. But I, I make those decisions slowly. And that is going to play a big role when it comes time for me to take a leadership role in the department. Being deliberate

about my decisions and my opinions. And I try to be, I mean there are some people on campus, they just seem to get all worked up and just angry, and spew stuff. And you just sit there and think do you really mean what you're saying? Do you even know what you're saying? And I'm, and I'm more the kind of person I think, I'm very deliberate about what I say, I'm conservative about what I say. But if I say it then you know I mean it. So I think that having been here long enough to learn, to learn about higher education, to learn about the [Wilkinson College], to learn a little more about what does it mean to be a professor. So I think that's gonna be, I don't know, I'll continue to change, I'm sure. But that's been big part of the process. I'm not quite as naive as I was six years ago.

## *Rhythms of the Year*

Reflecting on her six years at Wilkinson, Paula can now identify predictable rhythms that she can count on during the academic year, an unstoppable "roller coaster" ride punctuated by markers, and with a stop for the summer when "you can expect a more leisurely pace… and it's a vacation. You have time to think. You have time to work really one on one, with maybe one or two students, rejuvenate yourself, and start thinking about getting those classes ready for the fall."

> You can count on it being a roller coaster. You can count on that when the semester begins get on the roller coaster and every four weeks the intensity just because it's exam time. And then you kind of slow down a little bit when it is exam time. And so that right now, at he end of the semester, you can count on things being very frenetic. And then specific to [Wilkinson], you can count on the first six weeks [before] spring break being in fast forward, because you've got seniors that are trying to finish up. And then immediately following spring break, things are kind of crazy and hairy because we've got orals that you're scheduling. So you can count

on the fall being a little more controlled. The spring being completely fast-forward. And then summer comes, and summer as I have learned, means very different things for different disciplines. I just had taken for granted that one week after graduation, your students show up and you start doing research, and you do that for ten weeks. And then you get about a week and half off for vacation, and you come back and you get ready for the fall semester. And I realized that in other disciplines, that that's not the norm. And that's not what's expected. So that I think that the summer slows down and you can expect a more leisurely pace. I mean, you work forty hours a week and it's a vacation. You have time to think. You have time to work really one on one, with maybe one or two students, rejuvenate yourself, and start thinking about getting those classes ready for the fall. And then the week before school starts it kind of ramps back up. And it's time to go again. And so that that's, I think that's a pretty fair, and then the thing that's unique about [Wilkinson] is that the spring semester is much more intense. And I think it really is intense for all the students. I don't think it's just the seniors. Because I know that the week before spring break, my poor sophomores just look, I mean, they just look like, one more thing, and they just weren't going to make it. And I try to let them know, that you know, "Hey folks, I see what, I hear ya, I see ya, and I'm right there with ya. We can hang in there, we get two weeks of break". So I think that the roller coaster analogy, and then so at the end of the semester you can get off of the roller coaster for four weeks in the winter break and for two or three months in the summer break. And then you get back right on. And as you know with roller coasters you can't get off in the middle of the ride. You just gotta, you gotta hang in there no matter how high or low it gets. I think that's probably the best description for rhythms in campus. And it happens everywhere. I mean, I think everyone feels the effects of that cycling kind of effect that we get, cycling kind of effect.

The academic year roller coaster at Wilkinson, noted Paula, has a number of significant markers, campus events and ceremonies that stand out, such as Opening Convocation in the first week of the fall semester, the Passing, a march by seniors who have turned in their Independent Study theses on the first Monday after Spring Break, Baccalaureate, a church service on the Sunday before Graduation, and Commencement.

> I mean, the big, the big institutional ones are like Opening Convocation. And each semester, that's kind of the mark of, okay, it's time to begin again. And then of course here, the Passing in the IS. I mean, that's, that's huge. And then Baccalaureate, kind of going, and sitting for about hour an half, two hours, thinking you know, I don't have a to do list. I don't have anything on my desk I need to grade. I can just sit here and relax and tomorrow Commencement. I can just call, and I can show up in my little gown, and just relax. And that's kind of the beginning. It's like, you know, spring is evidenced by the first robin showing up, or summer is evidenced by coming and putting your gown on the, on the hook. And then it's time to begin summer. And I think the thing that marks the beginning of the school year is all the first-year students unpacking their belongings, and I don't think all faculty are as in tune with the beginning of the school year as the faculty that in the first year seminar courses. Because we get the firsts, I mean, two or three days of encounter with the first year students on a more personal, individual kind of basis.

## *Academic Ceremony Reflections*

Opening Convocation, besides marking the beginning of another roller coaster, also offers Paula a tangible sign of her advance at Wilkinson. Seating for the faculty at Convocation is by seniority, and for Paula, moving up the row was not so much a matter of advancing status as much as an observable mark of her increasing engagement in the Wilkinson community.

> I, I like the opportunity to, to kind of take a breath and think about, you know, it's time for another semester. And I like the opportunity to see the seniors there, and just kind of think about: Boy I, I really hope that they will take advantage of this, that they really will, that they'll realize that this is my last chance in college, and really give themselves the opportunity to do something with it. So it's kind of, I guess maybe nostalgic is the word. You kind of, and you sit there and you think about your own, and you sit there and you look at all of the faculty and you think, oh my gosh, you know, every year I move a little further up in the ranks. So before I was like, you know, the last one in the row, and watching all the people in the front row. Now I'm up a row or so, so it's kind of. I think it, and, and, and some people choose not to go. I go every year because it's, I think it does mark, you know, it's kind of a defined time for beginning. I think, I look behind me and I think, wow, I've come so far. And then I look ahead of me and I think, wow, there's much further that you can go. And I'm still the, and I think it will be, I, I wonder how it will be now that I'm, I've crossed that line from non-tenure to tenure, because your role really, in my mind, becomes very different.

Commencement offers another opportunity for Paula to mark her place at the College, as well as to see a visible transition of her students moving on. Place in the faculty line is determined by seniority and Paula has seen herself move up the line every year. In her sixth year now, Commencement also offered Paula the opportunity to see two full cycles of students – from first-year to seniors – graduate.

> I like it. I mean, it's kind of fun to see everybody in their, in their little gowns, you know, the kind of pomp and circumstance of the event. And quite honestly it's the only

time I get to see some of my colleagues. They line us up by the year you came in, and so that my little year started out as fourteen, and I think we're down to two. And so I like to get to see those colleagues, and I'm, I'm also aware of the people that are immediately ahead of me now, and before I wasn't so much. I was more aware of the people who were right there with me, and then the people that came in immediately behind me. But now I am, I guess I'm starting to notice other, other people around me. But I like that, and I like seeing the students. I like to see them, they line us all up here, and they have the students, because they have faculty on both sides of the walk, and they have the students come down the middle, and it's just... And I, and I first, I've, I've gone through my first two full cycles of students now, so I've seen them as first-years, and then seen them as seniors. And so having them walk by, and you just think, boy you've come a long way. You really have come a long way.

Commencement is also a sad experience for its finality. Paula arranges to meet her students at a designated place to meet their families and to say "goodbye" and "good luck." After Commencement, Paula reports feeling a "sense of gosh they're gone," an emptiness that a scheduled faculty lunch helps fill.

It's always kind of sad to see your seniors go. I have learned enough now that I tell my seniors now, if there are people that are important to you, you've gotta make sure, that you set a place that you're gonna meet, because if you don't, then after graduation, after commencement you're gonna wander around looking like you're lost. And, and, you're gonna feel that even a greater sense of, of emptiness. I said, you want to make sure, and I said, between now and then, I said, I'll tell you where I'll be standing, and I'll stand there for about thirty minutes or so, if you want to come by, come by. And if you get busy, I won't be there. So, and, and I didn't do that my first few years. And your seniors go and graduate and you never managed to hook up with them, and you just feel that sense of gosh, they're gone. And then we have this faculty lunch after commencement, and I've, I've learned that that's a nice way to go and, kind of, kind of, fill that void of, of those students being gone. It's a nice opportunity to go, see some people you haven't seen. I usually try to make it a point to sit at tables with people I don't, either I don't know or people I haven't, haven't gotten to talk to very much. It's a nice closure kind of, kind of experience. Some people view it as, why do you keep giving us all these free meals, I'd rather have more money in my paycheck. But I think I like that social opportunity. And then we leave the lunch and you just kind of stroll back across campus. And you don't have to rush because you don't have anything to grade, and you don't have anything that has to be done that afternoon. Yeah, so I just kind of mosey back.

## *Post-Tenure Reflections*

A very significant and personally meaningful transition that was not accompanied by public ceremony was Paula crossing over to becoming a tenured faculty member. While pleased with the accomplishment of attaining "a sense of permanency," Paula also wondered what her future at Wilkinson might be and "where would I like to see things go." Tenure afforded her a perspective informed by the experience of having survived, and a perspective that allowed her to begin thinking long-range about her future.

> It's kind of anticlimactic. You're like great, now what. But it also brings some sense of responsibility with it, I mean, you kind of feel like oh well, now. And there's a sense of permanency because you feel like okay now I'm going to get to stay. And so I really should be looking, rather than looking a year ahead, two years ahead, maybe I should think about five years and ten years, where do I want to see myself, in respect to the department and to the campus. Where would I like to see things go, because I, I suspect that I, I don't want

to, I don't want to go into a holding pattern because I think I'll get bored, and feel stagnant. So that I think that, I'm taking, I feel like I'm kind of time off right now, and that I'm just kind of catching my breath, and, and just getting through the semester. And then this summer, that week in between graduation and when my students start, I'll sit down and think about, you know, what have I done? What kind of things that I've done that have been, that have been good? And where would I like to see things go, five years, ten years? What's the five-year game plan? What's the ten-year game plan? But I, but I, I, I do need to take that time… I do recognize that some parts of my job are getting easier. And since those, I, cause I've got more experience. I've got better perspective. And I, and I, it doesn't take as much effort anymore. And I can do a good job without as much effort. And so that now it's time to start thinking about, well now that I've got this extra time… energy that can be reallocated, where am I going to put it?

Paula reflected on available options she could spend her time and energy on. She could focus more on her research, she could get more involved in her professional associations, she could engage in the administration of the College so that she could help "affect the situation of the faculty here."

> Yeah, I definitely would say that, (I'm in) that in-between place right now. On the one hand it feels good because they've given me a vote of confidence that says, okay, you get to stay. And then on the other hand it feels little intimidating because now I get to stay a next time. What, what, what will be my legacy? What will be said about me in thirty years? I hope it is positive… The perspective that I had as a first year faculty, as a second year faculty, now the perspective that I have as a six-year faculty member, the students don't look at me as new anymore. I'm, I am not a new kid on the block. I'm the middle of the pack. And my perspective has changed… I mean if you, if you feel overwhelmed and

burdened, and threatened, then your perspective gets a little shaky. But if you feel like you are managing what you're supposed to be doing, and you're doing a good job at it, and you're not threatened. Then your perspective is much more positive.

As Paula looked back, she reflected on how she had changed at Wilkinson, how she seemed to have arrived at a place of her own making, combining "my passion about what I do, and my commitment to what I do" with a calm that came with the experience of, among other things, managing her time and her tasks more effectively.

> And, and I think that, when I think back through the folks that I've stayed in closest contact with, I would think that my passion about my work, my passion about them doing well, my passion just about, just about everything. I, and I think that passion comes across in a very personal way. And it hasn't always been that way. My first year or two, I felt so much pressure and anxiety I guess about, you know, what if I make a mistake in class, what if I give up too much control in the classroom. And so that I think some of that was kind of, kind of hidden. And once I got to the point that I realized, you know, I can do a pretty good job. And it's okay to make mistakes. And just having the confidence to say, to say, I don't know the answer to that question, but if you write it down I'll get back to you. And, and making sure that I got back to them. So I think that, that gave me the freedom to just be me.... I think I've gotten more focused. One of things in the beginning that was overwhelming is, you can be nickeled and dimed to death with your time in the course of the day between the e-mail, and the paper mail, and the committee meetings. I mean, you can totally run yourself like a Tasmanian devil and get nothing done. And I think that one of the best professional advances I have made is, is focusing. And I think the research thing helped with that. Time to be away, and to think about, how am I going to use every day? So that being more efficient, so that you can

get more things done in the day, and then, some of it too is being more responsible for me, in terms of, I think, the best advice out of the *Good Start* (1992) book is, don't be a victim. You're not a victim. No one is telling you, you have to work a hundred hours a week. No one is telling you, you have to grade those papers by ten o'clock tomorrow… And now there are boundaries. And I make it clearer to the student, to my colleagues, to the college, you know, I will make time for you, but I can't give all of my time to you. And I've been very clear, more so with my colleagues and the college, that there's only so much I can give and still maintain me. And so I think I'm getting better professionally about doing that. And it just makes you happy and, happier and healthier. And you get more done in each of the areas that you're supposed to be getting something done. So I think that's probably my best professional change.

As Paula began to feel more confidently in control of her time and her energy by erecting boundaries that helped her restore more balance in her life she improved the quality of her contributions to her students and her colleagues, and began to talk with administrators about faculty time and workloads.

The analogy I think about in my mind, the analogy the high-strung puppy versus a basset hound on the porch. I am calming down a little bit in terms of this is a marathon it's not a sprint… So I do feel like I'm a little calmer, maybe a little wiser, with a lot more room to go. But I'm claming down some. And it doesn't necessarily mean slowing down. It just means calming down. And I, and I don't, the tenure helped, but I really think this started happening about a year half, two years ago, about the same time as the research leave. You know, just taking a breath, stepping back, and figuring out, okay how do you, how do you realistically do this. And it, it's been a continuing motif in my conversation with the administration and with colleagues, in terms of, you cannot be a healthy productive faculty member if you're working a hundred hours a week, because that doesn't leave any time for anything else. And if there's not time for anything else then you're imbalanced, and it's, it's gonna catch up with you. And so now I'm pretty.., I mean I know I have this much time that I'm going to devote to my job this week, and everything needs to get done. And maybe sometimes done is good enough and it doesn't have to be perfect.

## *Leaving a Legacy*

Paula reported being animated by both curiosity and adrenaline. Her passionate curiosity motivates her work with her research, and her pursuit of the adrenaline high comes from tracing her "best contribution," in the visible impact on the lives and learning of her students, and from "the opportunity to make a difference for those people who go make a difference for somebody else."

> I want to know, I want to know the answer. I want to know, cause, cause I'm working on a model system. I want to know if it'll work… So, so I do it because the curiosity of is it going to work? And it may not. And we may.., we may find out that after all this time, and get this molecule, and it doesn't do what we want it to do… So part of it is curiosity, and part of it is adrenaline. I mean, the adrenaline that you get from a student… that comes in and says to you, thanks… I'm glad I got to do IS with you. And I'm glad we went to the IS dinner last night, I didn't want the dinner to end. Part of it is, a student contacted me the other day, and he's been accepted to a Masters of Health Administration program, a joint Ph.D./MD program. And he's gotten a, he's gonna get a fellowship that will cover most of his costs. And he says thank you. And then it just, so you feel like you're really, you really have the opportunity to make a difference for those people who go make a difference for somebody else… so, it's just, it's the adrenaline. Seeing things happen that make some small positive difference somewhere. I would like to be

> remembered for my integrity and for my equitable treatment of the students. I, I want to be remembered for my work on behalf of the students. I mean, whether it be teaching in my class, whether it be challenging them to think outside of the box, in terms of what are you going to do, what do you like to do, where are you gonna be? I think I want to be remembered for how I worked with the students… The research is important, but I'm not gonna solve the world's problems. The departmental activities are important because, you know, we've gotta have a good department for the future students. The college activities are important cause you've gotta have a college that's sound for the future students. But the students themselves, they're what's most important to me. What, what kind of foundation I give them both as a person and as a scholar, intellectually and socially, so they can go and do what ever they go and do. I feel like that's my, my best contribution. Because, I think, that's one of my main responsibilities, I mean, as an organic chemist. I mean, from the teaching side of things that's almost how I am defined.

One legacy that Paula would like to leave is a revised and greatly improved curriculum in organic chemistry "is as good as it can be," because it's the gateway course where people decide whether they like science or not.

> If the course is the best, the course and lab is the best it can be, then it gives the students the opportunity, a genuine opportunity to make that decision. I mean, do I want to go forward with this? Or do I want to do something different? And for the pre-med students, I mean, there are fundamental concepts in organic chemistry that really do relate to what you end up doing as a doctor, those problem solving skills and those logic, logical connections. And maybe not so much the details of all the minutia, but the bigger picture, and it really is important for them. And sometimes I think

they get so busy trying to get the A, that they lose sight of the fact that the bigger things are actually more important. That's why it's important. So I want it to be the best that it can be so the students have a fair chance.

# Chapter 7

# Charles

I met Charles for our interviews in his corner office in the basement of Kanter Hall. As I waited a few minutes for our first interview while Charles returned from class, I surveyed the names on other faculty office doors and the faculty pictures and profiles that were posted on the department's bulletin board in the hallway. It appeared that the psychology faculty occupied all the offices in this corner.

Charles rushed back, introduced himself to me, and ushered me into his office. An unremarkable faculty office in many ways, windows on two sides illuminated an office with a desk, chairs and shelves full of books. He noted to me later that he had been unusually fortunate as a new faculty member to have been assigned a corner office. Apparently no senior faculty members wanted to move since all of the psychology faculty would soon be moving within a few months into their newly constructed psychology building.

Charles grew up with aspirations of becoming a lawyer. He is the second oldest of four sons born to an engineer father and homemaker mother. Although one of his brothers was in business, two of the four brothers were practicing attorneys.

> That was a family profession and... I [thought I] would end up there eventually. And in fact I remember talking to one

of those school guidance counselors about before taking the SATs and things and asking about various professions. I had said law and actually I had also said, oddly enough, psychology, and I remember very clearly her saying, 'well' the various profiles, I forget what sort of test we'd taken, 'don't indicate that you would be particularly good at that area,' and I always remember seeing how ironic that this where I end up. At the time, I didn't think much of it because I thought of going to law school because that's what we all do. But, that's not how it ended to be. Perhaps maybe her comments unconsciously motivated me to prove her wrong.

## *Early Influences*

After high school, Charles went to Oakland University and Western Michigan University, and then transferred to Michigan State University, majoring in English. And although going to graduate school in psychology came much later, Charles remembered an early indication that he wanted to be an academic:

> I was a good student. I had a good grade point average. But I was not overly focused on academics. Even in college I had no real intention of going on to graduate school and getting a Ph.D. Except, in my last semester, which was a summer semester, I went over the summer to finish because I transferred so much I needed to make up credits. And I remember taking a course in the philosophy of law or philosophy of social sciences. And I remember, one of the few professors… I actually remembered his name, Dr. K, and politically we were completely opposites. He was… [a] socialist, and a theosophist, or at least more conservative than that. But it was such a great course and I even remember very clearly a day after class walking back to, we lived off campus in an apartment, walking back, I remember crossing the bridge over the Red Cedar River thinking I want to be a Ph.D., I want to be an academic. This would be the life. And it was really the first time that I thought about it and it was

> such a sort of definitive experience. I can't even remember what the class was about. I remember thinking this is what I want to do. And I didn't actually didn't go back to graduate school for about eight years after that. But I remember very clearly that was the point that I decided that this is what I want to do. I hadn't decided on psychology at the time. Then I was thinking I'd go back and get a PhD. in philosophy and do this. After I graduated I spoke with some people at the University of Michigan, where I thought to go to take some classes. I realized at the time that philosophy wasn't really the area that I was interested in. So when I graduated I went and got a job, I went to business.

After graduating from Michigan State, Charles began working full-time at the store where he had worked during college, making what he felt was a natural transition.

> I started out at B Dalton. I actually worked through college, so I was the Assistant Manager through my last few years in college as an undergrad. And then when I graduated I just went in and worked full time as a manager. I think that it might have been a year and half, two years after I graduated. Then I went to work for Toys R Us… Let's see, I graduated in 82 and I started, it was about six years before I started graduate work. And between that time I decided I wanted to work with psychology specifically working in development.

Over time Charles flourished in his new career, and he recalled feeling uneasy about his work, and eventually elected to resign his position rather than accept a significant promotion.

> I hated every single day that I worked there. I worked in Detroit, Washington, and Los Angeles. It was finally after I had been asked to go to the opening in the Las Vegas market. That would have been a big career promotion for me at the time. The next step would have been in the corporate offices. But I decided that I didn't want to do this anymore, that

> I couldn't. I essentially quit in the management program, although I stayed working for the company and started graduate school and eventually just quit all together. I focused on my graduate work instead.

After talking with "some people at the University of Michigan where I thought to go to take some classes," he realized that philosophy was not for him. So he went on to work as a full-time manager at B. Daltons, where he had already been working as an assistant manager during his college years. Two years later he went to work for Toys R Us. It would be eight years after college graduation before Charles returned to graduate school to pursue a Ph.D. in psychology.

Charles remembered some memorable "observations about what I perceived as very serious problems in childrearing factors" that gradually pointed him to psychology. Living in Northern Virginia at the time, and intrigued by the psychology of the interactions he observed at Toys R Us, Charles decided to learn more about psychology.

> I worked at Toys R Us…Seeing so many bad things, problematic things. I was in Northern Virginia and decided that well I needed to take courses in psychology, if I'm going to go to graduate school I got to get a background in it. So I started taking undergraduate courses at George Mason University, which is the closest school. I formed a bond with one of the professors there. She was a developmentalist and she had studied attachment with Mary Ainsworth, a big figure in attachment. And she was also an important influence on me in terms of the interest I have now in attachment relationships. Of course I work with animals. I try to look at similar models and things. I finished taking undergraduate courses and then I began the graduate program for Masters. So I went through that and they didn't have a terminal Ph.D. in the area that I was interested in. So when I was finished there I applied to Virginia Tech.

Virginia Tech was not an easy selection. Charles looked for a school where he thought faculty were engaged with their graduate students, declining even to go to the University of Virginia "for many reasons a better school, certainly more well known." In the end Charles selected Virginia Tech for the opportunity to work with a faculty member he admired – RL.

> RL had been teaching at Virginia Tech, although he is not there anymore. I wanted to work with him. I liked his work. I liked the idea; he'd been looking at early prenatal influences on development. Looking sort of at non-genetic factors… arguing against genetic models of development, and arguing for early prenatal influences shaping development. It would be very difficult to tease them apart if you were only looking at postnatal work. You really need to focus on the earliest forms of development before we can make conclusions on genetic influences and things like that. So I was very attracted to his work.

At the time Charles thought he wanted to get a Ph.D. in philosophy. In retrospect, Charles said he was happy that he elected to spend some time between college and graduate school working. He noted that "five years might have made a big difference… I was much better prepared for the stress." Additionally, it allowed him to obtain a higher position while a graduate student: "I occupied a position that had previously been a faculty position." Now he advises his students to "work a couple of years, and then you'll know if you really want to become an academic."

## Coming To Wilkinson

Charles came to Wilkinson not without a great deal of deliberation, and after exploring his prospects at his previous institution, particularly St. Mary's College in Maryland. He reported feeling content as a visiting professor at St. Mary's, but he knew that future opportunity for advancement was foreclosed. St. Mary's was a

Maryland's honors college. And I was a visiting professor for five years. And I got to the point where I could have stayed there probably indefinitely. But, I was one of four of the developmentalists, and so there wasn't going to be any tenure track position available. So I eventually decided that career-wise, as much as I loved being there, it was on the Chesapeake Bay, it was beautiful, it's a really good school, I needed to think of my career as well. And so I began applying to other jobs.

His applications yielded two offers, one from Wilkinson College and another from Randolph Macon College. He recalled feeling torn between his love for living in Virginia where he had settled and enjoyed a quality of life. Virginia was a special place for Charles, but he could also see new opportunities at Wilkinson.

[Wilkinson College], I think, is a better school, but quality of life... living outside of Richmond [the nearest major city]... there's just no comparison. They've had summer there for two or three months already; we're still leaving winter at the end of April... I very much wanted to life near Williamsburg. That part of Virginia was very important to me. I'd worked essentially through beginning of graduate school and this is also where I settled in Virginia. This is where I... sort of in my own mind when I began graduate school, it's almost that's where I would have ended up, that's where I wanted to be.

In the end, Charles accepted the Wilkinson position because he could live closer to his parents and brothers in Michigan, and because Wilkinson advanced his professional interests in teaching and research. When Charles came to interview at Wilkinson, he remembered he was

very impressed by the other faculty. I liked them much. I liked the school. I liked the look of the school, it's a beautiful campus. It has a very strong academic reputation. Those

> were significant factors in my decision. Although ultimately I believe the ultimate decision to come here had nothing to do with that. My parents are in Michigan, and two of my brothers are in Michigan, which is only about 3 ½ hours away. And my niece and nephew are there. That I think was the decisive factor. It made my parents happy that I would be closer to home. So that is why I took this job over the Randolph-Macon job.

Since Charles has been at Wilkinson, he reported feeling gratified about the professional opportunities available to him. He was soon going to move into a new building, where he would build his own research laboratory and begin to define and advance his research agenda.

> Now with our new building, serendipitously I suppose, having taken the job, [Wilkinson College] is now going to have a new psych building, with vastly expanded research facilities, for my research and others. We will have sort of the ideal. So if I look in retrospect it was the right thing to do. I could not have anywhere near these sorts of resources at Randolph-Macon. It would have been a heavier teaching load, less emphasis on research. So while… quality of life would have been better, professionally this was the right thing to do. Even though I didn't make the decision for pure professional reasons it had the effect of working out that way.

## *First Years at Wilkinson*

Charles' glad entry to Wilkinson came initially with an experience of some shock. While he was elated to be at Wilkinson, he noted, "It was rough. It was a rough first year for me." Arriving at Wilkinson, Charles was heartened with his new department's collegiality:

> My colleagues are great. This is one of the best departments, in terms of really getting along, having sort of a shared idea of the direction of the department. Sort of a shared theoretical

orientations so we were all sort of on the same page on virtually everything. Which I think is sort of unusual in a lot of academic departments… It's more unusual to find a department of any kind where everyone sort of gets along… and look there really isn't any politics here. I mean there's college politics, but there aren't too many department politics. And that I am significantly grateful, profoundly grateful for that… that we get along. And the work environment is so important, you want to be able to be happy, at least in that. So that part [I am] very happy about.

What appeared to surprise and distress Charles about Wilkinson were a series of quality of life factors, ranging from the benefits package to the rural location of Wilkinson:

Several months actually after I got here that I found out that I was completely incredulous to the benefits, 'cause I've been very used to the kinds of benefits that includes dental and optical, the very generous medical benefits. Suddenly realizing that that wasn't the case everywhere shocked me. That was hard. Also I left behind all of my friends. This is a very rural, remote… I missed living near DC. So the first year was rough.

Near the end of his first year, Charles came to reconcile the tension between his attraction to the academic community of Wilkinson and his disappointment with the quality of life.

It wasn't until last semester, and towards the end of last semester, and as the new building has been coming close to being finished, that I've become more than reconciled to being here. I'm actually sort of happy, I'm happy that I am here, but it took a while. It was a rough first year. It wasn't academics, but again, it was more of a personal thing. Academics, the students are great here. They are different though, I have to say, that [Wilkinson College] and St. Mary's show a lot of similarities. They both have senior projects. They both have strong research emphasis, a lot of writing emphasis, strong academics. Honors College was, I think, by and large very similar. But there are differences in students.

In the end, what made Charles happy were the collegial academic community, the new building with his psychology research laboratory, and the students he worked with. Charles noted some differences between students at his previous and current institutions:

The students at St. Mary's were more engaged with the faculty. They were more likely to drop by just to talk. And in fact there were days where I would have to take: this is a no chatting day. I have no time just to sit and talk. But at the time people would just drop in, and they would stay, and it would be long. I would have trouble getting my work done. But now I find that that doesn't happen very often, that some students will stop by, but most of the time people don't stop by just to talk. And I find that I miss that now. Academically they are great students and they are engaged they are involved. But, they don't get as involved in research either. That may be that we don't really have the facilities at the moment. Perhaps with the new building that will change. But I did find at St. Mary's, that students were more likely just to come in and say I want to do this research project, that they're more likely to do independent studies… There's more of a distance between faculty and students. I don't know why. But academically they're about the same, all very strong students.

## The Academic Good Life

Charles' experiences working at Toys R Us was ultimately what led him to decide that psychology was what we he wanted to study. He reflected on his motivations for working at Wilkinson College.

> I guess my most basic motivation is I like this job. I like being part of academia. I like teaching. I like working with students. I like working with colleagues on interesting ideas. I like having four months off in the summer. I like having a month off in the winter during the Christmas break, two-week spring break. I like, from my perspective, working less than two hours a day in terms of teaching, and then having time to read or even if I'm just reading papers. I find that more enjoyable than my previous life in working at Toys R Us, things like that. So I guess I would have to say that's what my... it's perhaps not a, you know, noble goal searching for absolute truth or something like that. I enjoy this life! And that's what motivates me to keep going. I think that's probably true of many of my colleagues. While many are probably motivated for higher ideals than I am, I think we like this life and it's the best life possible... This is a wonderful life. That's probably my deepest motivation. It's sort of, I don't think it makes me happy, because I wouldn't list this is as purely an emotional reason. It is a very fulfilling experience. Probably not for any abstract reasoning, it's for a very practical reason... It's the practical reasons that are the important ones for me. I enjoy being able to sit in the afternoon with students. I had a couple of students in yesterday and we just sat around and talked about their senior year, their IS experiences, and what they're going to do next.

Reflecting on his passage to the academy and his first two years at Wilkinson, Charles described what he had grown to value:

> I think if I had gone right on to school I probably wouldn't be here. Those years out of school changed my perspective. It made me realize how much... just how serious academics were. I think, as an undergraduate, you don't really see the seriousness of it, the importance of it. But if you go out and do something else before then you... oh well. And just the leisure, the ability to sit and talk about something rather

than working thirteen hours, coming back the next day, maybe get two weeks off for vacation. This is a much, much better life, and I appreciate it profoundly more having done the other world.

As hard as it was to live away from the East coast that he loved, Charles reported enjoying the academic life at Wilkinson. When he compared notes on career experiences with his brothers who were attorneys, Charles clearly felt he had chosen the better life.

They are envious of what I do. Envious primarily because of the vast amount of free time that they perceive that I have. And in fact, I have four months in summer, a month off at Christmas, two weeks at least in the spring and then at least a week if not more in the fall. Whereas they work constantly, six days a week at least, long hours. They don't perceive or feel that (inaudible) what I do is work. They are correct about that. I get to interact with interesting people. We talk about what we want to talk about. I teach the courses that I want to teach. I do research that I find interesting, whereas they deal with the cases they get and they have to do it. So they are somewhat envious. Although they make vastly more amounts of money than I do. I think both of them, my two that are attorneys, if they could do it over again I think they might be more likely would choose an academic career.

Charles described three components of teaching, scholarship and service to the College in his role as a faculty member at Wilkinson.

Teaching, which is some combination of course work, and then supervising independent study, junior independent study and senior independent study; research and scholarly activities, our own particular empirical research; and then engagement and involvement in a broader discipline be it APA, American Psychological Society. I am a developmental psychobiologist and our main professional organization is the ISDP, or International Society of Developmental

> Psychobiology, so I tend to be more engaged with that. So we have of our research and scholarly activities. And then a third component would be service to the College. Service on committees, attending… tomorrow is registration so I'm going to be there tomorrow to work the registration… giving guest lectures, talks on campus. There's a lot of others things that we do. Prospective students, they'll come and sit in our classes or we'll talk to them, or call them, or various things. I supervise a couple of clubs, a faculty advisor to several of the clubs, one is a fraternity. So that's it, essentially.

Charles also believed that the role of the faculty was central and most important to the work of Wilkinson College.

> We have, I think, very well defined jobs… Faculty matter the most. People don't come here because of who cuts the lawn, or who is the president of the college, or who the food preparer is. They come here to be educated. It matters who the faculty are. It doesn't matter who anybody else is. … And that means that there are differences in terms of importance to the college, for the life of the institution. I think it has to be recognized we are held to different standards, in our work we have to publish, we have to do major research. We have to do many things that non-faculty members do not have to do. It makes a difference.

Charles' understanding of the centrality of the faculty role also included a sense of faculty prerogative. He believed that the faculty, in the form of perhaps a faculty senate should be co-equal partners with the administration.

> From my own point of view, I would like to see a faculty senate. I would like to see the faculty viewed as almost a co-equal branch with the administration, with the Board of Trustees, sort of, supervising the College. I think that's a model that's in place in other schools, where there's a faculty senate that, in fact, has authority, that certain things

simply cannot be dealt without their agreement. Well, of course, that's not the case here. The administration, the Board of Trustees, can essentially do what they want without consulting the faculty. But they do, but, they do make decisions that there's nothing that faculty can do about it. I don't particularly care for that. I do recognize their arguments at times, but it would be nice to have a relatively independent faculty. I think that would be a healthier way of running things… The Board will do what the Board wants. They don't have to consult the faculty. Sometimes they become, they can be acrimonious. They get worked up about their positions. But, I think, from my point of view, that's sort of pointless. It doesn't make sense to raise your blood pressure to get upset about these things…Voicing opinion is important, but the Board doesn't want to hear… or they only hear what they want to hear. That's the way that it is. And I don't particularly care for that, but I recognize that that is the situation.

## *Rhythms and Conversations*

One dimension of the academic life that Charles reported he liked was the order and stability of his life as an academic.

> I like a routine. I don't mind being in rut. I do things very much the same way. I come in. I try to get in by 8:30 every morning. I get my coffee. Hopefully there is a doughnut left over at the faculty lounge. There weren't any today, which is sort of annoying. I got there too late. And I start, I do my email…. I either have meetings or appointments before class. So I do my class prep and teach at noon. Come in do prep class prep for 2:00 class. Perhaps see another student. About 4:00 I go home. My day is Tuesdays and Thursdays. I call my parents every afternoon on Tuesday and Thursday. Friday afternoon usually I talk to my brother. At least once a week I talk to my friend over at George Mason, an old colleague. I have a very predictable day. And I like

that. Thursday at 11:00 o'clock we have faculty meeting. Tuesdays and Thursdays at noon we go to have lunch with students. Invite students over to the school cafeteria. I like well ordered.

This orderliness is punctuated by scheduled gatherings of faculty colleagues and students, times to talk and shared ideas.

> Every noon, every Thursday at 12:00. Others go. Gary [department chair] usually goes. I go. CT started going. JN used to go. He teaches a class now at noon so it's harder for him to get over there. MA who's a visiting faculty member, SC, she'll very often go over. So we will go over and many of the psych… students and psych majors will come and join us for lunch. It's al lot of fun. We laugh, we sort of talk about the department. Talk about directions. Talk of the new building. Some students talk about their IS's, other projects they're doing. It's a nice relaxed environment for 30 – 45 minutes we're over there. Get a free lunch. We get to meet… I enjoy it very much. I'm glad we do it… And I wish more students availed themselves of it. The ones that do, I think, enjoy it. I think that as a faculty member I do too. It's really important that they see us outside of the classroom. Because in their junior and senior year we have to work so closely with them on their junior independent study, the senior independent study, I think it's a good idea that they see us outside of class, just to get an idea of working more one on one in a more casual environment. It just makes everything work better together.

Another weekly gathering that Charles reported that he looked forward to was the department faculty meeting.

> Sometimes they last long, and sometimes they're shorter. It's just a nice idea that we all get together. We sort go over everything, Gary sort of tells us what's been going on about the new building. What problems we've encountered. How

close they are to finishing. What we need to do for the curriculum review this year. There's just a lot so we've met for longer periods going over the new curriculum. How the changes we've made appear more to be based on research methods. People actually have more opportunities to the labs, we've added developmental. So I enjoy that. I think that's an important aspect of the week. Gary usually has an agenda, a few items that we need to go over... Also, like at the beginning of the year we will discuss the IS assignments. How many each person will do, [and] try to make it equitable in that if someone is doing a large number of tutorials or they're teaching a lab course, if they have high enrollments, somebody may have say one fewer IS student and somebody else perhaps will have one more.

## *The Senior Faculty*

As one of the most junior members of the psychology faculty at Wilkinson, Charles reported how very grateful he was for the mentoring and advice he received from his senior faculty colleagues. He described the specific ways that the senior faculty have helped him.

> The College is pretty good about letting you sort of determine your own kinds of things that you'll be engaged in... SC is not here this year, she was here last year. She was very helpful in sort of telling me how to prepare annual reports, and things like that. Of course... the department chair is also very supportive. And Bill and CT, as well, have always been like, do you need help with this? And this is how things are done here. They've been extremely supportive and I rely on them greatly... I think it's been in very practical ways...
> 
> What would be the way to frame my faculty evaluation? Or what committees are the good committees to be on? The ones that you might want to avoid as junior faculty. They may come with a great deal of work. It is better perhaps to be on committees that are less work... So you stick to the ones that aren't going to disturb your level of progression

to tenure. In terms of... about the distribution of Junior IS, or Senior IS, and getting involved in that. In terms of matching student interest to faculty interest, they've been very helpful with that as well. They have been very good at helping [me] get acclimatized to the [Wilkinson] culture. And I am grateful to that.

Charles grew more comfortable at Wilkinson as he found a tone of collegiality and values that he shared with his department faculty. He also sought opportunities to contribute to the department.

> We have, as they say, a real good rapport in this department, and so people are back and forth just popping into an office and talking for a few minutes, just checking the hall to see if everything is going okay and stuff. So we have a very sort of casual relationship, which I think is good. Again it builds some solidarity in the department... They are very concerned about students [and] they spend a lot time with them here. We're faculty, when we're here we keep our doors open... If I'm here I leave my door open. So if anyone needs to talk to me they can do it whenever it's open. If I'm busy with someone else often they wait. I think that the open door policy is very important. I admire that of everyone here. That we sort of engage to the human. If we're very busy we still take a few minutes for the student or for a fellow colleague. I think that we always have generally agreed that we were redoing the curriculum, we had a curriculum review, and that was one of the suggestions that I made. I thought it was necessary [for] the development of a major area in experimental psychology. It should be represented as one of the laboratory courses. Fortunately with the new building we will actually have the kind of facilities to do real developmental work - both child development and my own animal work, we will be able to do that actually.

## Comparing Academic and Business Worlds

Charles reflected on his experiences in the worlds of business and the academy and he noted the differences in how departments were run and people were led. The department chair's role, in particular, managing the department had many differences and similarities to his previous experiences in retail management.

> The chair at Virginia Tech was an IO psychologist. I think he tended to run the department in ways that are similar to the way business is run. Lot of delegation that may have been just the model the University imposed. But he certainly used that, different committees and things. [He] delegated a lot of authority, which is basically the model that I've been used to, as well. A lot of delegation to store levels from the corporate level… The structure in many ways is similar. The focus, however, is very different, that when you're in business you're motivated by a bottom line. That we are there not to help people, we are not there to worry about the employees, except beyond what they can do for the company. And the corporate view was everyone is expendable and everyone is replaceable. And it's not a bad idea to replace people periodically, just to keep everyone aware of the fact that they are expendable… We had a recent incident here at [Wilkinson], 30 people were let go…. There should have been greater consultation with faculty. No faculty were let ago in this role, just staff. School is not a business and we're all a community… You can worry about your employees to a limited extent, but the ultimate bottom line is the profitability of the company… stockholders… that's what matters, not whether you've hurt some employee's feelings. And they are very different models; academia is not run typically under that model.

Charles seemed glad that he had had the business world experiences. He believed it was important to note the distinctions between the two worlds of the academy and business because most of his students will graduate and work in the business world.

> Because most students are not going into academics, the vast majority are going to go on and do something else entirely than what their major was. So that they need know that, that it's okay if you're not going on to graduate school in psychology. That if you're going to go work in retail or you're going to do something else entirely different, that a psychology major still is as applicable, and we shouldn't, you know, ignore the students that are not going to go on and become graduate students. We don't need that many more graduate students. We need to educate people that aren't going on. The ability to have done something else really shakes you loose in that academic mindset, going to graduate school, get a Ph.D., and go on to doing what I am doing. Most people aren't going to do that. You need to focus on those kids too. I think that was the critical… doing something else makes a big difference.

## *The Department Chair*

Charles described an unstructured style of leadership in the psychology department at Wilkinson, and attributed it to the department chair

> [He] carries a great deal of the work. And he does a really excellent job. He's a great department chair. We just received our curricular review and comments by the Vice President saying how well it went and how the department is perceived by our fellow colleagues throughout the College in a very a positive light. It is well run. I think that reflects his leadership that he presents the department in a strong light… I think he really represents us very well. He gets across our needs and what significance we have to the college. But within the department I think it is a very democratic basically process, that we all have regular faculty meetings every Tuesday we

get together. We discuss everything. We usually arrive at a consensus. Fortunately we all think the same way about the direction of the department… I think it is more of a low-key kind of approach to leadership… It works well for us… For us we all get along well enough. It's… not a purely hierarchical position; he is sort of our representative. And he consults us on everything. And we get feedback. And it's assumed, well most of the time, I trust your judgment, whatever is best I know you'll make the right decision. It would be very unusual if I didn't agree with that. So I like it. I think there are seven of us. He keeps us all on track. It's not at all, I wouldn't even say it is not even assertive, and it's more of a consensus. It is very egalitarian. I appreciate that. Even coming from a business prospective where it was rigidly hierarchical, and everyone knew their place… You knew whether you were not supposed to talk up. Here that is not is at all the case… I would say that it's a quiet sort of leadership. We all sort of realized that there's these bureaucratic things we have to do, forms that we have to send in. Many times they're an onerous burden and grateful that he is sort of the conduit through which we have to do that. But it is never "get this done" or "we need to do this." It's more, "let's all do this." That's the way that it works. Everyone here sort of does their thing. It's a subtle leadership, but it is a very good one.

## *Academic Ceremonies*

Another dimension of the academic life that Charles liked and thought important were the College academic ceremonies and public occasions in the department.

> There's a few that are sort of College wide that we participate in. Graduation, obviously, is a big deal. There's Convocation at the beginning of the year, which we all attend. We also have for the graduating seniors coming up, there'll be sort of a department party. We get together. We often do that at the beginning of the year. Or at the end we'll have a sort of

department picnic. Those would be the main things… I like graduation. Well, part of it, we get to wear our regalia. I love to wear the regalia, only one of the few people that do… I think it's important. I think the rituals that are attendant on a college matter greatly.

College ceremonies and rituals are important because they bring rhythmic opportunities for people to gather. Charles believed that academic rituals allow students and faculty to commemorate and celebrate their life in the academy.

> Academia has an historical… [aspect]. I think we need ties to that past over the last couple of thousand of years, the growing nature of academic schools, colleges and universities in the last few hundred years, they've developed. We can't cut ourselves off from that. It's important that we remember those. I think the way that we do that is by ritualized institutions, the robes, commencement, everyone lining up, marching through an arch, or marching into an auditorium… And it's those experiences… people don't remember any individual lecture, I imagine that many of my students won't even remember who I am many years from now. I have a hard time remembering any of my faculty, I couldn't even tell you my advisors name. But I remember the events. I remember my graduation ceremony. I remember those collective experiences. Those stand out in mind. And it reframes your understanding. To me that's what's important. And I like that. I don't know why. It's my sense of historical tradition. It's nice to together to celebrate academia. It's an important part of humanity… There's a very long historical tradition of academia. And I think we need to continue that… It matters, the kind of engagement. And… [Opening] Convocation where we get to get together at the beginning of the year, everyone is in their robes. Of course, like I said, I like to wear my robe… This is the beginning of the year, and let's take this seriously. We're about very serious work. And we should look at it that way. I think it's brought forth

> by putting on the regalia, marching into the Convocation, the President addressing the college, the graduating seniors, and the incoming class.

At the time of this interview, Charles had been serving on a "first year experience committee," and one of their recommendations included changing the location of the Opening Convocation from the Chapel to the side of the Kanter Hall arch opposite to the side where Commencement is held annually. When the new location of Opening Convocation is combined with the ceremonial Passing, the annual march of seniors through the Kanter archway on the first day after Spring Break after they have turned in their independent study theses, Charles thought a ritual "symmetry" was achieved.

> The idea would be that the incoming class, the Convocation will be on this side of the arch, where the president speaks. Then of course graduation is on the other side of the arch. And there's a march through the arch, as you know through IS. We were thinking that symbolically, that would be a nice symmetry that at the beginning and the end of your career, that you start out facing Kanter with the sun rising (inaudible) and then leave from the other side where we have the Commencement address. And I think that's a good idea... A crossing over that you have made the complete move through the arch. And you've completed your education. And now it's time for you to go out into the world and leave the College.

Charles believed that academic ceremonies and ritual were important because they met a fundamental human need for marking significant transitions.

> I think in general, for humans in general, rituals make a difference.... its important, in terms of transitions, that we have graduation ceremonies and wedding ceremonies, major transitions in life across human cultures going back tens of

thousands of years. There have been institutionalized ways of marking those events. And I think it makes people, one, recognize them as important, but also as a shared experience. And for the College life, when we talked about this in terms of the health, the financial health of the College before, in a very practical way, doing those things in the immediate sense might seem kind of silly and maybe stupid. But thirty years from now when people look back on their experiences here, at least it's been my experience, even the bad ones you forget and you just look at these four years or five years are the best years of your life. Thirty years from now you will look back, and you will almost uniformly agree that these were the good years. That you had the most freedom, even though many students think oh there was so much work. When you get out in the real world and have a job, family, and responsibilities, you will look back and say these were good years. And for the health of the College, those sorts of experiences, the Commencement, the Graduations, the march through the arch at the end of IS, just the whole sort of, the [numbered] buttons that you get [from the Registrar's Office] for IS, the tootsie roll that you get at the end [also from the Registrar's Office]. Those matter… I am sure most people, if not all students, have those buttons, because that was important. It signals, it symbolizes a lot of work that you put into it. It's a capstone experience. Maybe it is a stupid little piece of plastic. But, you remember your number. And you remember that part of the tradition of being here, the Independent Study. So I think humans have this general need for institutionalized, ritualized experiences that, sort of, group celebrations, that later on you remember.

These rituals were also important for practical reasons related to the future health of the College.

> I look at it through a practical sense, that, we need that two years from now, people they look back on it and think that was a big deal. But when you look back across your life,

your fifties, and your sixties, making decisions about where to send your children to school, you'll look back and you'll remember those experiences. And I think if it's been a positive experience, positive life, and it's when alumni start writing checks, when alumni start to send some of their children here, it all perpetuates the health of the institution.... What we do now as faculty members, and as administrators, and anybody going here, not just affects the immediate lives of our students. It affects the lives of faculty that will want to work on. Every faculty member here thirty years from now probably won't be here. Many people unfortunately won't even be alive. But, the students that we have taught will be in their fifties and sixties. And they'll be in good jobs, good professions... the big donors that come up with million-dollar grants to the College. So what we do ensures the health of the College thirty, fifty years from now... So it does matter what we do in the long term. I talked about the life of the institution is more important than any individual here. That's what we have to keep in mind. The rituals that we have set a structure, that several decades from now, will payoff, that ensure the life of the College.

## Helping Students Succeed

Charles wanted to be remembered by his students for having helped them succeed beyond their initial expectations. He was particularly proud of his work at his previous institution, St. Mary's, where he hoped he helped students elevate their expectations.

> When they come back for their fiftieth reunion I will probably be dead be then. I doubt any individual will remember... I hope, someone remembers. A few students that I think maybe I have made a difference in their lives. C students, first generation college [students]... I hope that I made a difference. And their lives ended up differentially. That they didn't drop out and leave school. They started out C students and ended up A and B students... In particular

two students ended up getting married at St. Mary's. I was the best man in their wedding. I remember very clearly the first day of my intro psych class, right out of graduate school at St. Mary's. It was an even class and they were both in the class. They were both first generations. Both parents had gotten divorced and things like that... We started working together on research projects and I hate to talk about it like I mentored them... [They] graduated as valedictorian and she graduated not as valedictorian but with a very high GPA. She had gotten a faculty senate award. They had gone to conference and published a couple of paper. Tara had been approached to do some Internet research and two publishing companies to review books by Ph.Ds using the Internet to collect data. I had to tell them that you know she is just an undergrad. They said that was fine they were so impressed with the work she had done. She reviewed the books and gave her comment. They paid her for it. I like to think that I had a hand in that... They have jobs that they are very happy with. I like to think that would what I would be remembered for.

Charles' reported finding it most satisfying to work with "C students." He wants his legacy to be about making a marked difference in the lives of his students, and this was most likely working with students who were not as academically prepared.

> The ones that you don't expect to turn out well. Sort of slips by and no one knows. You get to know them and if you take a C student and they graduate with honors. That would be the legacy that I would want. Not a room or a building, or you don't need to remember me. I made those kids lives different. Hopefully I had a hand in that. That made a difference. That is going to get me out of purgatory... Often faculty... want to work with the best students, the A students. You don't notice the C students. Or the students that don't do that well and sit in the back and don't talk. You have to notice them. You have to... You can

> make the biggest difference with them. The A students they are going to do well no matter what you do with them. They may develop personal bonds with you. You may work with them. I have worked with many A students as well. But they are going to do well regardless of who their teachers are… They are smart. They are motivated. Their lives have sort of worked out well. They are going to go on and do well. You can't forget the C students… I hope that is one thing that people will look back at, those students that I worked with and I was most concerned about. I enjoyed being around them. I remember one student, Charley who as being a good C student and didn't do very well. At graduation his dad pulled aside and said that you made the difference that he was not headed for anything but down. Charley is working in psychology now. He is married. He is very happy with his job. That made me feel real good when the dad came by and said you know we really thank you for what you did. I had to… do bad things at Toys R US, selling those lousy toys to all of these kids, thrusting them with cheap materials and cheap toys that they really don't need. I think perhaps this is sort of making up for those bad years… I hope as the years go by the more similar experiences like that will happen. Those are the kids that I like working with the best.

Charles reflected on his future at Wilkinson and thought about the kinds of commitments he would like to fulfill someday.

> I would also like to think I played a role in helping the psych department as move into the new building, develop new curriculum, and focus on the neurosciences. I hope people remember… that I played a part in that. Of course all of us played a role in that. So fortunately we all had sort of a shared dream of where we would like for the psych department to go in the next couple of decades. I hope people remember that that's a role that I played, as well. We got into the new building. We established greater ties with the bio department. Then people will begin to recognize.

On campus there is a little view that the psych department is not as a real science. I don't care for that attitude. I think hopefully we can lay that to rest by the next few years with the new facilities that we have. Forming closer bonds with biology, creating this sort of science quad here at the south part of campus. People have a new respect for the psych department. I hope to be involved in that. Someday maybe administration. When I was in graduate school I wanted to be an administrator. I wanted to be a department chair.

# Chapter 8

# Rebecca

I met with Rebecca in her office in Kanter Hall in late April, during the last week of the Spring Semester. Rebecca's office was located in the basement of Kanter, along with the clustered offices of other faculty in political science.

When I arrived for the first interview, I waited for a few minutes outside and sat on a chair in the hallway outside Rebecca's office. Her office door was open and I could hear voices, presumably of students, talking together in her office. Minutes later, Rebecca walked down the hallway and invited me in to her office and three students who were lounging in her office excused themselves. This scene would be repeated at subsequent interview appointments, and I learned that Rebecca allowed her office to also serve as a lounge for some select students, mainly political science seniors. Indeed, Rebecca's methodical thought and work on her relationships with students and colleagues appeared as a signature theme in her narrative.

Rebecca's office, like other basement level offices in Kanter Hall, had high and open windows that looked out into the grassy courtyard. The office was illuminated by the light from the window, accented by a couple of lamps. The inside walls were full of shelves packed with books. It was a warm, inviting room that needed a fireplace to fulfill the ambiance. Rebecca sat behind her desk against a wall and invited me to sit in a deep chair to her right.

## *Preparing for the Academy*

Rebecca began by explaining how her experience as a faculty scholar in political science was shaped by making choices between what she was interested in doing and the decisional circumstances she encountered. The birth of a child was an early crossroad, which led her to resolve to proceed to the academy.

> I have often said that being a scholar and a teacher, being a political activist and being a parent share some dreadful characteristics, which is you can always see how you can do better. You never achieve that high standard and there is no end to the work. There's no end to being a parent. I have a child who's in college and... I'm still parenting this child. And there's no end to what you can do as the teacher. You can always do better, you can always read one more book you can always tweak that lecture one more time. There's no point at which you can feel authorized unless you do it yourself. You say, ok, this is, this is great! This is enough. And the same is in political activism. There's always something wrong with it. You can't do all those three all together. It's hard enough to do two. So, that's the tension between political activism and political scholarship. It ended when I had my first child. I, I made it very clear to everyone, when this child is born I'm out of here. So, since then my focus has really been on the academic side.

Rebecca remembered her early years in school as academically enriched. Her academic ambition was encouraged more by her teachers than by her family. Her teachers encouraged her early interest in politics and social justice, and this encouragement combined with Rebecca's own developing ambition to excel academically led her to win awards in politics and related activities.

> I was in the same school from the time I was in second grade all the way through eighth grade, and then went on to the University school, which was believed to be… a school that had a real commitment to academic achievement, innovative teaching, progressive teaching, and producing students who would go on to college and, and who would do well. So that, that was the climate I was in. I came out of eighth grade I think it's probably fair to say, having won almost every prize in my school in my grade. I remember my mother remarking that people have remarked to her that it wasn't fair that I had won all these prizes and that other students hadn't been recognized.

Rebecca then proceeded to high school where she reported continuing to be nourished by encouraging teachers

> particularly a history teacher and a speech teacher, who really had championed me and really pushed me. Looking back… I have always had a strong interest in politics, I'm not quite sure where it came from. There's no trace in my family of, of people having been elected to office, or a lot of conversation at the dinner table about politics. That just wasn't there. But I have always had a strong interest, and a strong interest in issues of social justice. Again, I'm not sure where that comes from either. But in any case, when I was in high school, I did a lot of history, I did a lot of English, and I wrote a lot of poetry, I won the American Legion Government Prize. It was an exam that you took and there was another similarly related prize that I won at the time that involved government and politics. I remember studying for that exam, I remember being in my bedroom reading the booklets that defined the differences between villages and townships in the State of Ohio. I came in, in the top five in the State of Ohio, and then I was nominated by my faculty members and sent to Buckeye Girls State, which is the mock legislative, political, and government of the, of the state. I was also encouraged by my history teacher to take

the United Nations Exam. They thought I would do so well. And I remember resisting that, and I did not take it because something else was also going on. I was also in debate during this time, and, and doing a lot of that. There were also some negative things that happened. In my first year at high school, the National Honor Society inducted people and they inducted first-year students for the first time, which was a surprise. And they inducted a lot of athletes who weren't very smart. And I remember my speech teacher, Mr. Brubaker, coming to me and saying, "How do you feel about this?" And I first thought, why well this is the kind of school this was. You know, those who were rich and those who are athletes, and those who were popular got rewards, and those who were smart, if they didn't have all those other things, it didn't make any difference. And... looking back that was a real recasting. Even though in my junior and senior years I went on winning all these prizes and all this stuff, and also, I think it's fair to say, I don't know that my parents would agree with this, I didn't get much support at home. I didn't get much encouragement. My parents used to tease me about being a debater, and you know, to there, to be just to them, I would argue with them. And I'm sure that was obnoxious. And so though I was a debater, this is a debater. But I think one of the reasons I didn't do the United Nations test, my teacher just about broke my arm over there, but he was right, I should have taken it. But, I just didn't see much point because I wasn't getting much encouragement... And looking back, the past looks clearer than it was. Because I also had a strong interest in English, I was writing poetry, I was writing stories. In eighth grade, I wrote a, you know, a 150-page novel which somehow I've lost or destroyed. You know, I have, I have a lot of, you know, so there's that trace, as well, and I think it wasn't until after my children were born that I finally reconciled, not for interest in literature and interest in politics, but an interest in political activism versus in an interest in the truly academic.

The absence of enthusiastic family support was more clearly manifested in what she remembered as their "inattentiveness" to her college search, which she attributed to their own incomplete college experiences. Although she aspired to attend a private school, she eventually found her way to the University of Kentucky.

> My parents did not have college degrees, although they went to college. They dropped out, I think, it was somewhere in the middle of their junior year when they got married. And so, I was, I was ranked ninth or tenth in my high school class. We didn't have good guidance counselors. I didn't have much idea about what I wanted to do except I wanted to go to Ohio Wesleyan College. I'm from, from Kent, Ohio... And mostly, the university had a big impact. Of course, I went to the university school, too. So we were doing language lab at the university, and we were doing, you know, swimming at the university pool, and using the library, all of that stuff. It was really lovely. Our graduation was held at the university. In any case, there wasn't much vision about what I should do, and my parents believed despite what I was telling them, and what was even known at the time, that private schools will provide financial aid for those in need. And I didn't get my act together; I didn't take the PSATs, for example, and from this, kind of, comes National Merit. No one ever made it clear to me that was an important thing to do. My parents were absolutely inattentive to this. And so when it came to it, I applied to Ohio Wesleyan, the University of Rochester, and the University of Kentucky. Ohio Wesleyan, by choice. University of Rochester because that's where the family doctor had gone and my mother thought well maybe that would be one place. They seem to think it's a good school. Oh, I applied to Kent State University, as well. And I applied to the University of Kentucky because my father and his work would travel in and out of the state, and they thought would be convenient. And I knew that I would not stay in the State of Ohio. That was just out of the question. My family has been there since the early 1800's. It is a big

huge family. My name was, my last name was known; I knew I would have no anonymity, I would have no privacy. I was wait-listed at Ohio Wesleyan and the University of Rochester because I applied late. I don't even think I applied until right after the deadline. I was admitted at Kentucky and Kent State, both in the honors program. I chose to go to Kentucky in Lexington.

The University of Kentucky and the "South" were a cultural shock to Rebecca. She was appalled at the openly visible racism and she found herself disappointed at the "general intellectual climate" of the undergraduate experience. She responded by engaging in "self-marginalization" from the undergraduate student experience.

> It was really interesting. It was both awful and terrific. It was good for me to be in another culture, and it was another culture. I didn't realize what a Yankee Northerner I was until I went to school in Kentucky… you know, Kentucky is a border-state, it wasn't a state in the old Confederacy. But I was just appalled at the racism, I couldn't believe it, and so, that immediately, it not only set me apart, I engaged in self-marginalization from the mainstream… of that campus. This was an institution… [where] the fraternities used to have the Confederacy Ball. And they would dress up in Confederate uniforms. I found that morally reprehensible, and I still do. I don't know if they still do that. They use to play Dixie at the football games and the black students would stay seated with their fists in the air. And no manner of persuasion could get that university to stop that at that time. The first black basketball player didn't join that team until my first year in college, coming from northeast Ohio that was just so not happening. So, that part was a real shock. And it was, it was a state school that admitted every student who graduated from high school in the State of Kentucky who applied. And that's very democratic and very generous. But, it also meant it's a group of hard drinking wit-less clods

who flunked out after first semester. The general intellectual climate was not good.

While Rebecca did not find the University of Kentucky undergraduate experience very fulfilling, she was able to find intellectual inspiration in the sub-community of graduate students and faculty in the political science department. In a pattern that she would repeat throughout her career, Rebecca found mentors among graduate students and faculty who now comprise a network of accomplished professionals in her discipline and in higher education.

> Having said that, there're some wonderful things about it. First of all, the University of Kentucky has graduate students, and I got fairly into my political science major. I had a great teacher, AF, who didn't stay after my first year. But, I had him for an Introductory US National Politics course. He was absolutely terrific. He just grabbed me. He made sure I talked to him; he made sure I was networked with people… He got me an internship at PBS in New York City in 1970, working doing survey research… in advance of the '72 election. My parents wouldn't let me go do that. I remember my dad screaming and yelling, "Oh, those hippie professors!"… He left to be an administrator after two years… He gave me good advice. He was just absolutely wonderful. In fact, when I went to graduate school, he was an administrator at Syracuse University, which is where I got my Ph.D. And he arranged for me to visit and talk to people, and he arranged for me a place to stay. He was really great about that. When he left, he put me touch with MB, at the time a junior faculty member at the University of Kentucky. I've known MB ever since, I got e-mail from him, you know, two weeks ago; he's now a senior vice president at the American Council on Education. Before that he was the provost or vice president at Northeastern University. He has always, sort of, kept his eye out for me. He was also absolutely terrific. I wrote my senior thesis with him. He was great. And so they were wonderful,

wonderful graduate students, they were wonderful professors, a powerhouse political science department at the time... And even now when I go to APSA meetings, I will cross paths with those people and their graduate students who are now professors all over the country. I don't have any remaining close friends from my undergraduate years, who were undergraduates with me; there's still some I keep in touch with. But my close, you know life long friends, are those graduate students... So there are, you know, people like DK, and BD, and MJ, and DI and others are the ones who, you know they just really helped me be serious about political science, and helped socialize me, to become a professor. That was, that was such a strong political science department, terrific graduate students, key professors, and then a really good supportive radical political intellectual community, a small group. But there's something about that larger dreadful climate that really create the wonderful indigenous radical democratic progressive group... And that was, that was the role I stayed with.

## *Building an Academic Network*

Rebecca also found courses and people at the University of Kentucky outside political science who inspired her incipient interest in women' issues, an interest that later became a signature theme of her own research in her discipline. The women students she met were later to become accomplished professionals and members of her academic network.

> When I look back, I took courses outside that department, and I had some really good, really good courses. I was in the honors program there, and I had, I did a seminar in the first year that was required with JD, who's [now] just retiring from the University of New Hampshire. She was a key pioneer in Women Studies internationally, but nationally certainly, but also internationally. She taught two key courses, one was

Women Writers of the 20th Century. I think that was the first Women's Studies courses at the University of Kentucky. And she also taught Feminist Political Thought. And there were a key group of us: DG, who's on the international relations board with SK, who I think is, general counsel for American Energy Incorporated, AEP here in Ohio. And DG who I think, she was, she went to graduate school at the University of Pennsylvania in History. DG and SK went to law school. That was a really good group of very smart young women in these courses. And, and that also, absolutely key. But it really is the case, there was a, there was a small group. And, and maybe, looking back, you know, I'm so political science now, that looking back I can make the, you know, the connections with all those people.

Rebecca's search and for graduate school eventually led her to Syracuse, but it took her a while to get there as she deferred her admission for two years. She married a junior and chose to wait for her husband to graduate. Then, after he graduated, her husband enrolled at a graduate program that began with a year in Bologna, Italy. So after waiting a year for him to graduate, Rebecca went to Italy for another year, which added Italian and European politics to her intellectual interests.

I applied to Syracuse University, SUNY Buffalo, I, I, again, got not the world's best advice. I was encouraged by MB to apply to Emory, but Emory was in the south, and I knew that was not, not for me anymore. I was definitely not gonna go south. Syracuse, SUNY Buffalo, University of Wisconsin at Madison, George Washington University, University of Oregon which is where MB got his Ph.D. So again, not real clear advising and not real clear thinking on my part, and, and not very, in fact, I can't really remember how I got my act together to make those applications. I don't even remember if my parents gave me the application fee, did I pay that myself? How did I manage that? But, what I do remember is that the choices came down to Syracuse and George Washington University.

I got married the summer after I graduated, in August, after I graduated from college, to someone who was a junior, and so I came back to Kentucky and worked for a year, waiting for him to graduate. And I deferred admission to both Syracuse and George Washington. And then John applied to graduate school. And he applied to a range of, of schools that offered Master Degrees in Foreign Policy and International Affairs. And he got accepted to a variety of schools, one of which was Johns Hopkins University, and you spend the first year in Bologna, Italy, in that program. And so I deferred for another year and went with John, and we lived in Italy for a year. And I learned to speak Italian and I took a course, and worked in the library at the Johns Hopkins School for Advanced International Studies. And it was a perfectly wonderful time to be in Italy. And in fact, that put me on a trajectory of studying not only women and politics, which I knew I was going to do anyway, my senior thesis was a Women's Studies thesis in part… It focused me on Italian politics, European politics, and that, that really got me directed in a particular way. And so I deferred again. And at the end of that first year, John had decided to leave graduate school, and now all the decisions, not only where I was going to go to school, if he had stayed at Johns Hopkins, I would have gone to George Washington University because the Hopkins school was in DC.

When she finally arrived at Syracuse, she wasn't sure it was the right choice, indeed she still regrets it as a mistake.

So I went to Syracuse, which in many ways was a mistake. The department was not good. The school did not have a whole lot of money. It didn't have a student center, it didn't have a very good library. There was no orientation for graduate students. There was a lot wrong with that program. I was admitted in a fairly small class of about a dozen. Only four of us made it through the program with Ph.Ds. The dropout rate, in fact, I think of that first class only four of us even remained, and the class ahead of us only two made it through. So, something was seriously wrong there. And I don't have real fond memories of Syracuse.

And yet, even as she sometimes regrets her decision to go to Syracuse, Rebecca talked about her experiences at Syracuse with pride in deepening and enlarging her community of fellow scholars and friends. It sounded as if what were really important in her reflections about her accomplishments were not so much what she had achieved, but all the communities and all the people who she knew. The relationships that were formed were very important because it seemed to be the dominant way she explained Syracuse and her other school experiences.

But in any case there were some good things about that, I did make, again you know, some really core friends who are really life long friends. My friend JC is now at SUNY Buffalo now, he's a Republican, he's a major advisor right now to the Bush campaign, widely published, just a great guy..., and then my friend SO, who is... vice president for faculty. She had some high-ranking administrative position, I think she's been in it two years at the University of Utah. Those are really, you know sort of key people that I keep in contact with, and then MG, who graduated with us, is a key spokesperson for the Israeli Army. And so we get to hear him on NPR... he's doing some interesting things. And then I had a couple of really key faculty in political science who were really good to me. MP, who's now at Arizona State University, I lived with, with her family for a month after I'd taken my first job and still finishing my dissertation. I came back to Syracuse, lived with them and finished up my dissertation. TP, who's now at the Kennedy School, was my dissertation advisor, again really good, you know, good academic advisement and real good personal support. I just got an e-mail from him the other day, you know, just really

> terrific, and, and also BM, who was a, someone I had a lot of coursework with. And then a lot of these courses, in particular, I was in class with JC and I know both of those fellows, you know, cling to each other, thank God you were there, you know that made that seminar worth it, that, that small group was really good. And I, I see those people at the academy meeting.

Rebecca's husband transferred to Cornell, and Rebecca was able to meet yet another set of mentors and friends at Cornell, including two very close women friends. She seemed to have wished she had gone to Cornell instead of Syracuse.

> Another important thing happened to me when I was still in graduate school. John went back to graduate school. He went to the International Relations Program at Cornell, which is sixty miles south of Syracuse. And so after I had done dissertation research abroad so I came back, to live with him in Ithaca, and to a connection from GM, who was the director of legislative research in the Italian province, and SK, I met ST at Cornell, and ST and MK just immediately turned me in to the Cornell environment. And they have been phenomenal mentors to me, every step. It's really remarkable. I was never their student, I don't shed glory on them from being a Cornell Ph.D., I'm not, but they're absolutely wonderful to me. And through them I met MG and CR, who again, just, and KM, as a matter of fact, who's now at the College, really, really good friends. Every Friday evening, at the APSA meetings, this must be twenty years now, KM, MG, and I go to dinner. No one else is allowed to come, not Vick, who was MG's dissertation advisor, not husbands, not boyfriends, nobody, it's just the three of us, it's our protected space. So that connection at Cornell were really, really, intellectually important to me, and that, they were people who shared my interests more closely, was the better program even though I wasn't in it, I got to work with people that wrote letters for me. That was really important…

> These are people whose names I remember, with whom I'm still in contact, for the most part. And part of it is, you know, when you have shared intellectual interests and opportunities to continue to cross paths with people, then that begins to develop and sustain a friendship. And there is something about knowing people across a long period of time... And so, you know, I want to keep... friends not only for the loveliness of the friendship and because I feel so close to them, but because they carry part of my history.

## *Network as Nourishment*

In addition to the nourishment of friendships, Rebecca reported that her friends provided her the benefits of an outside world of social capital. For Rebecca, the connection with the outside helped her work as a teacher and scholar at a small liberal arts institution.

> If you don't go outside, I think it's much harder to stay intellectually engaged and harder to stay up on. Your, your teaching even, and I think a real danger at a liberal arts college is that you're always with people who are younger than twenty-two. But you age and develop and expand, and get better at some things. And if you don't go outside, I think there is some kind of juvenile mindset that sets in, a kind of provincialism, a kind of dysfunctionality that's really dangerous. And, and so I think that people, consciously or unconsciously, recognize that this is a danger and, and go outside for intellectual satisfaction...

Rebecca's various circles of friends and colleagues have helped her access opportunities for professional advancement, including memberships in elite professional groups, professional association offices, and opportunities to edit and publish. While she self-described herself as "smart," Rebecca suggests that her opportunities have been the result of what she called "realistic political considerations."

I'm part of a group of people, who does research on Italy, does research on Britain, and does research on women and politics, and over the years, because I've had good mentors, and because I've been connected, and because I have white-skin privilege, and because I'm not hideously ugly, and not terrifically overweight, and because I'm fairly articulate, I've had things open up to me. And, and I recognize those advantages. I sometimes say, why me, I'm not smarter than some of these other people. But I realize that that's not all there is, it's just not all there is, in terms of public perception. In any case, I began taking advantage of opportunities that were presented to me… I've been elected to executive committees of organizations and appointed to editorial boards. I know many of those appointments came because people I have met through conferences, who were sufficiently impressed with me, that when they put together a slate, they knew it couldn't be only men, it couldn't be only people doing certain areas, and, and so they put my name forward. I know that that happened to me, and I know it happens to other people, I know it happens for men as well. And I don't want to downplay, I am a smart person, I've been active… I've initiated things at a certain level of energy. And, and so I know that those are valuable things I bring, but I also know that it's not only that, it's, it's not thoroughly meritocratic, there are other considerations, and… realistic political considerations. But I did get to play in a wider network, and at one point then I became program chair, and I've turned down a lot of these things, but I became program chair for the Women of Politics section of the American Political Sciences Association for the 1998 APSA meeting. And I put together the program of all the panels for that section. And at the same time, a person that I had recruited to follow me in that line, an officer-ship at the Kennedy School at Harvard, she and I put together a conference called Frontiers of Women in Politics Research, and we held a one-day conference at the Kennedy School. And boy did that draw attention to me, I was getting e-mails

> from everywhere, including people trying to bully me, or to, to lever me to include them. That was a big opening up. And I was going to conferences and presenting papers, and I was doing that in Europe as well, and so JL, he and I were becoming friends and sharing research stuff, and as a result, JL asked if I would be willing to propose to Oxford University Press a series of books on gender and politics; we would co-edit and we would close the manuscripts from scholars. And so we've done that. And so that again opens up that network, connecting me with more people.

Rebecca suggested, that while the social capital gains were valuable to her career, she needed a sustenance that she could get only from a "larger intellectual pool" than was available at Wilkinson.

> I was, yes, I mean, there's, there's no denying that there's absolutely that kind of social capital gain. But I will say that two things, one is that what really drives this for me is that I'm in education, easily bored person, and so, and I can't get all that I need intellectually from the [Wilkinson College], or even from my close friends in the neighborhood, and, and, and people I see, you know, sort of on a weekly basis. I need to be in a bigger, I need to be in a bigger pool, it doesn't have to be a bigger teaching pool, but it, it does need to be a bigger intellectual pool. And so that's really been driving now. But at the same, and the other thing that's so, here's the intellectual part, one does get social capital, but I'm not really doing it for that. I'm doing it for the other.

Rebecca described her various networks, many of them defined by sub-disciplines and research interest areas, as communities in concentric circles starting from the smallest community, the teaching community at Wilkinson. Each community then folded into others as part of a much larger community of political sciences scholars.

> That community, sort of larger community of political sciences and scholars, it's one where I'm primarily known as a scholar, and someone who does research and publishes. Because one doesn't normally teach at in a wider world, I have taught once in summer school at Cornell University in the Government department, since I've been on the [Wilkinson] faculty. But primarily, I'm, I'm known as a scholar. And my role in that larger community is, is one that I have made myself because you're not hired or recruited or formally installed some place, you have to more entrepreneurial, more, you have to initiate things, to have a role in that wider community. And it's, it's not that one does that all by oneself, … but that's something that you have to create, as compared to one's role at [Wilkinson] where there's already a structure for understanding what your role should be. There's already a platform. In the wider-community, again my role is someone who's known as a scholar, who does a particular arena of work that's in Women and Politics, someone who, in a sub-fields that I work in, has been working here, in the United States.

Rebecca reports that entry into the various networks she has was not automatic. She has had to work to get in.

> So this, this net is sort of, you do what you're supposed to do, professionally, you meet people, you talk with them, you make a good impression or you don't, you do good things for other people and they do good things for you. And so then you can get established in that way. And, and so this is combination, you have to have your own initiative, you have to work, you also have to rely on the help of other people. And that's one of the interesting things in the, in the discipline.

In this social capital view of her world, Rebecca evaluates her accomplishments in terms of the many joint products (publications, editorships, etc) that she was able to develop, and the exchanges of favors and advantages she is able to facilitate for herself and for others, including students at Wilkinson. In this sense, she discerns a difference in the quality of her network based on the graduate school she attended. Clearly, Syracuse was not the best school to get her Ph.D. when it came to having the most advantageous network. Still, she suggested she had made the best of her connections, for example from the people she met at Cornell.

> I mean there's no doubt, you know, the connections I made at Cornell have been really, really helpful. But it's also interesting that there are some advantages I don't have. I don't have, I don't have a good graduate degree, as it were. Syracuse is alright. And it was certainly a, you know, have some good graduate students who've done a lot of good things, and, and I'm still in contact with those people. And you know that network has also been really helpful. But you can see a big difference between those who have Ivy League connections and those who don't. And to the extent that I have the Cornell connections and some connections at Harvard, that's a huge difference. And that's a reality of academic life. That's something that I certainly can't change that larger overall picture, except in so far as, as, you know, in doing some nice things for somebody who's at Mississippi State right now. She's talented and smart doing interesting work, and you know, circulating that and getting her name out and things like that. But I can't really change that, that larger part of the academic world. And I certainly can't change it for myself. I can't go back and change my graduate degree.

## *The Fairy Godmother*

The connections Rebecca has so carefully developed are most gratifying to utilize in the role of a "fairy god-mother" with her teaching and advising, when she is helping her students at Wilkinson with their intellectual work and with finding direction.

> So, here the role is, is primarily that of teacher, and to add to that, because I am so networked out in the wider world, the role of advisor is a really important one, and I can do some of that for first-year students and non-majors, but I can really do good helpful things for a student when they begin to major in political science. There's, there's just tons of stuff I can do and I love doing that, and I, one of the things I really like is talking to undergraduates seriously about their intellectual lives, and where they're going to go from here. And trying really hard to encourage them, as they're doing well in school, or doing alright in school, but getting more serious about it, to think not about being here, but think where they're going now. What are they learning? And what are they preparing them for? And, and what opportunities should they be looking for now. I really like that part of the advising, and find that really satisfying. And sometimes it's almost, what I would call my fairy godmother role, sometimes I can go [snaps fingers] and make something happen for the student, and that is so wonderful. It's, it's just great.

Rebecca's network of connections has served her well as a scholar and teacher at Wilkinson. The connections brought her opportunities to advance her own research agenda and to assist political science students at Wilkinson with making connections to others in the discipline.

## Faculty Administrative Work

In addition to the role of teacher and scholar, Rebecca noted that faculty at Wilkinson have another role, an administrative role that is unfortunately not shared equally by her faculty colleagues. Some faculty members gravitate to the administrative roles easily, and some avoided any involvement at all.

> The role in terms of administrative work… is not shared equally at the College, and that, for a couple of reasons. One

is that some people really, really like to be administratively involved. They liked to be close to the administrative action of the College, and, and though they, you know, run for lots of offices and serve on lots of committees and volunteer for things, and are really, really wired for, for doing that administrative work at the College. And then there are [those] that could probably take it or leave it, but they do a good job and they get elected and appointed to committees because the permanent administrators and the faculty who often are selected people want to have good people in these positions. And so the same people get called on over and over again. And there's another group that's administratively just absent from the College, that you never see them, they never are on committees, you might not ever know them even if they've been here ten years. So that's not shared equally.

Rebecca identified herself as being one of the faculty members at Wilkinson who involve themselves in campus governance and administrative matters, a role she considers herself aptly prepared for.

And I think probably those of us who do a lot of that kind of work or get elected to that are seen as having certain leadership responsibilities. I'm really outspoken at faculty meetings. I've… seen circumstances, including in committee meetings, where people let me take the burden. I'm impatient. I have a pretty good command of parliamentary procedure. I have a lot of experience with meetings, and if I want to move something along I could pretty much move it. And so then people count on me to do that.

Often this role of faculty leadership means that Rebecca is asking questions as a tenured senior faculty member that junior faculty members may hesitate to ask. She sees her questions as providing a critical countervailing balance to the work of the administration.

To stand up to the administration, this is the virtue of being tenured. And I'm maybe not as responsible in as I should

> be but there are some things that I will just say publicly that junior faculty members won't say. And so yesterday in the faculty meeting we had a series of reports that are, you know, there's some strengths to them and there's some weaknesses but they're all going to just pile work on the faculty, and I kept raising questions. This will increase the course load, who will teach the courses that we're teaching now, if we leave those to teach other courses. We have proposed a reduction in faculty teaching load, how did this new proposal sit with achieving a reduction in workload. I mean those are things that I'm real straightforward, I mean I hope I'm not nasty, I'm sure I can be, but even just the straightforward question seems to take a lot of guts to ask. And so, I think that's another role of I'm seen as someone who will, who will stand up to administrators.

Rebecca saw her role as a faculty leader as also including paying attention to the particular experiences of junior faculty members, by continuing to emphasize their scholarship, and by being "decent" to them. This role also furnished her with another opportunity to use her network to assist and advise others.

> I think I've been pretty decent to the junior faculty in my own department. When I was chair I didn't give them dreadful teaching loads. I put helpful things their way, publication opportunities or information about money. I'd write letters of recommendations for them. I'd review their review files before they're submitted to make sure nothing's missing... I think I've been decent, not just to junior faculty in my department, but also junior women, which I think is really important. Really supportive in regard to things like resolving maternity leave policy and stuff like that. And then, I think my other role is, is to be a fierce defender of our role as scholars, and in absolute terms of this time... I think it's really important that I don't see how, at a college of this caliber, one can teach and not be a productive scholar. I just, I don't see how teaching is possible. And so I feel pretty fierce

about insisting that this is part of our job. It's not an extra, it's not just for our pleasure, it's absolutely a necessity. And then I think it's also been a good thing for junior faculty.

## *About Women and Being Scary*

Rebecca's role of leadership includes a special sensitivity to the experience of women faculty, acknowledging that Wilkinson is especially hard on women. This perspective is also informed by her personal experiences and her scholarship in women's studies and politics.

> I think it's really important to talk about the difficulties of being a woman in this job at this institution, because that is a real important issue. And although, the college in many ways is… receptive and positive in regards to gender. In other ways, it… creates what has been called a chilly climate. And it has made things, I think, very difficult for female faculty, especially female faculty who increase in power across time, and most particularly for those who are head administrators… We go after administrators, and I think a piece is [that] senior men collude intentionally or even unintentionally, unawaredly, to set women against each other, to keep women from achieving things. There's a high level of jealousy among some senior men for successful senior women. A lot of men who've been, not a lot, many men who've been involved in mentoring women, can't get past that next point… And I don't think there are many men on this campus who've dealt with that very well. The level of gossip among men is really high, they're closed, they're coherent, so what you hear is, you know, not the whole picture. So there's that. And I don't want to diminish this, I mean this is all the stuff that's really important.

Over the years Rebecca has developed a set of strategies to respond to the "chilly climate" for herself and other women in the faculty. She described a stance of now "being scary" in her role as a senior faculty leader, a posture based on strategies that draw on her early experiences growing up with ambition, a self-developed "internal fortitude," and a large reservoir of nurtured connections in an academic network.

> I'm the oldest of seven children. I have four younger brothers. I've been in a male dominated discipline, you know, since I was seventeen years old, and so I'm sort of used to this stuff. And I have some, you know, internal fortitude, or whatever you call it, but, a sort of, who cares? You know, I basically get to do what I want, I really enjoy my teaching, good students seek me out. You know, what could be better than that? … I'm not sure this is the best strategy, but for a long time I've had the strategy of being scary. And by being scary, I mean I publish a lot, and I let people know it. You know… when something comes out, I send it over to the VPAA. I list it in the *[Wilkinson Reports]*. I let people know, …I'm out-spoken, and in many ways, right. And other faculty see that, and that's a resource that, and that's a actually a strategy that is, that is very helpful to them. Another strategy, I don't know how good this has been, is the one I talked about before, which is so much of my intellectual work is off-campus. I found another community to sustain me there.

# Chapter 9

# Crossings And Rites

In this chapter I offer the themes and motifs that I identified in the narratives of research participants. At all times possible, I have privileged their narratives to give voice to the findings and their stories. The review of research participant narratives as a means of obtaining access to meaning making is grounded in Bolles' (1991) and Weick's (1995) notions of sensemaking. The narrative profiles of participants as constructed were developed from the transcripts of interviews with research participants. Their reflections furnished the ore that I mined for the meaning they constructed about their teaching lives, and about their sensemaking of their work of leadership.

## Interpreting Narrative

When asked to reflect on the process of the interviews themselves, Francesca identified the connection between constructing narrative and constructing meaning:

> Well, obviously you set up the questions, and you were paying attention to the answers because you followed through on the answers in certain ways… You have a very clear general outline… you prompted the thinking without specifically trying to guide it in a particular direction… You know you

provided a general framework for a narrative to emerge. And I assume that's what you were trying to do. I mean, I certainly recognized the sort of returning to certain points and trying to get at them in different ways. And to look… for some, I don't know, consistent responses or common responses, or patterns. Patterns. But not patterns that aren't, aren't there. But, I mean, just in terms of… just creating a framework for a… kind narrative to emerge.

In developing and examining the narrative profiles, I remained mindful of Clandinin and Connelly's (2000) notions of *narrative inquiry* in my approach to the narrative profiles. In *narrative inquiry* the narrative is examined along three dimensions. The first dimension is *interaction*, which is the exploration of participant interpretation of experience by first examining what the narrative reflects in terms of the themes of the personal and the interactive. In approaching the narrative profiles, I attended to how ritualization and leadership were experienced and constructed personally and individually, and how research participants reported they were interpreted by their faculty colleagues. The second dimension is continuity. In this study I explored how ritualization and leadership were experienced in temporal terms. I examined the narrative profiles for how past ritualization was remembered and how present and future ritualization was explained and anticipated in the context of their leadership work. The final dimension is *situation*. In this study I explored how ritualization and leadership were experienced in terms of place and context. I inspected the narrative profiles for Driver's (1998) notion of ritualization and Moore and Myerhoff's (1977) definitional properties of secular ceremony. I also examined the research participants' representations of Wilkinson College in terms of Grimes' (2000) consideration of the research site as a *passage* system. The narrative profiles in the context of this system served as the research participants' *passage narratives*.

The research participants' ritualization described, marked and greeted transitions in their lives, and these rites were locatable on a continuum between the ends of formal and institutional ceremonies and highly personal ritualization. These rituals were supported by ambient ellipses of significance and meaning making, inflected with values that guided their transitions. Their transformative rites were often attended by, as one participant described, memorable "pivotal persons," people who often opened the gateway for their transitions, and guided them through their transformations.

Their work of leadership as faculty members could be arrayed along a continuum between formal roles and informal and personal commitments. Formal roles of leadership were institutionally sanctioned and came with authority and status vested in the positions, while informal assignments, commitments and roles of mentoring were often local to their academic discipline, department, and their personal aspirations. When both the continua of ritualization and leadership are intersected, a scheme describing how faculty members utilized ritualization to make meaning of their work of leadership emerges with interesting implications.

## The Sacred and the Non-Sacred

Eliade (1957) argued that the spiritual or meaning-making need that is fulfilled by the juxtaposition of the sacred and the non-sacred (profane) space is implicated in a human need to punctuate and orient ourselves in reference to an otherwise infinite, intractable, and unmarked universe. Sacred space is found in "privileged places, qualitatively different from all others" (Eliade, 1957, p. 24). For Charles, a certain bridge in Virginia will always be marked as a privileged place because

> I remember crossing the bridge over the Red Cedar River thinking I want to be a Ph.D. I want to be an academic. This would be my life. And it was really the first time that I thought about it and it was such a sort of definitive experience.

For Charles the bridge over the Red Cedar River is marked like no other, it is qualitatively different from all other spaces, and generates a profound construction of significant meaning for him. This "sacred space" (Eliade, 1957) of the bridge over the Red Cedar River uniquely punctuates the experience with all other spaces in his life and all other bridges Charles has crossed in his life. At the same time that this bridge crossing marks, as well, a significant transition for Charles.

Eliade (1957) also theorized that we catalog time into sacred and non-sacred (profane) time. Sacred time is "reversible and recoverable, a sort of eternal mythical present that is periodically reintegrated by means of rites" (Eliade, 1957, p. 70). For Charles, remembering the anniversary of the day he crossed the bridge over the Red Cedar River would be for him like entering a sacred time. Each remembered anniversary is punctuated time, a return to a peak in a stratified temporality that engenders special and significant personal meaning for him.

My search for ritualization in the "passage narratives" (Grimes, 2000) of my research participants was a search for contours of self-inscribed meaning and self-described experiences that served as transition markers, lighthouses of subjective, often deeply personal, and not always communal significance. Charles' reflection about indulging in pomp and circumstance, and wearing his academic regalia at commencement marked communal significance shared by many others in the Wilkinson community. Paula's personal reflection about how far she has moved up in the faculty line at commencement marked a transition with far less communal significance. This transition had meaning for her and many of her colleagues in the highly personal and local context of a department that had seen a number of faculty members retire, Paula's recent tenure decision, and her passage from an identity as junior faculty to now a member of the senior faculty.

Additionally, not all ritualization was locatable as distinct bounded actions or times. As Grimes (1995) noted, ritualization is often undifferentiated and diffuse in a "ritual entailment" that occurs "whereby one rite piggybacks on, evokes, or bleeds into another" (Grimes, 1995, p. 12). So ritualizations, like clouds, while often discretely identifiable and marked were also bounded with and enmeshed inside other ritualizations. What identified ritualization essentially was their function of transformation in transition, their marking the sacred in a life and world.

## Ritual and Ritualization

In examining the narratives of my research participants I located self-described ritualization along a continuum between one end of rituals and ceremonies that were public and communal, and on the other end ritualization and greeting experiences that were personal and subjective on the other end. (See Figure 1 below).

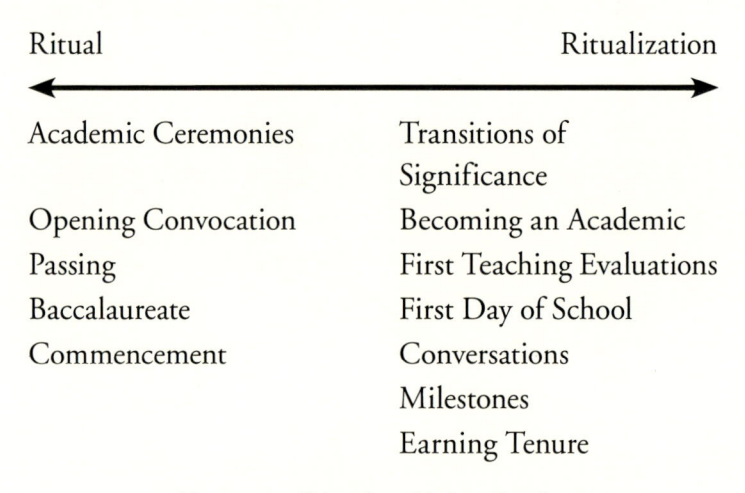

| Ritual | Ritualization |
|---|---|
| ←————————————————→ | |
| Academic Ceremonies | Transitions of Significance |
| Opening Convocation | Becoming an Academic |
| Passing | First Teaching Evaluations |
| Baccalaureate | First Day of School |
| Commencement | Conversations |
| | Milestones |
| | Earning Tenure |

Figure 1 – Ritual and Ritualization

Public and communal ceremonies were enacted in the context of a "passage system" (Grimes, 2000) that entailed a public and larger perimeter of shared significance: the ambient values and commitments that inscribed the ceremonies. At Wilkinson College, academic ceremonies such as Opening Convocation, the Passing, Baccalaureate, and commencement marked transitions in a public, stylized, communal space for ritualization. Personal and subjective ritualization experiences were implicated in a more individual "passage system" (Grimes, 2000) with a smaller perimeter of significance. Paula's highly charged transition from a non-tenured assistant professor to a tenured associate professor was marked in a more personal and private space. Driver (1998) has offered ritual, for example, (commencement) and ritualization, for example, (earning tenure) to differentiate the two ends. Moore & Myerhoff (1971) offered two different titles, heavy ritual (commencement) and secular ceremony (earning tenure) to help capture this distinction.

*The Public and Formal*

Manning's (2000) study of ritual at Mount Holyoke College and Saint Michael's College, both liberal arts colleges similar to Wilkinson College in mission and organization, described distinct rituals that she classified into (1) rituals of reification, (2) rituals of revitalization, (3) rituals of resistance, (4) rituals of incorporation, (5) rituals of investiture, (6) rituals of entering and leaving, and (7) rituals of healing (Manning, 2000, pp. 5-7). These rituals were public rituals with a perimeter of shared cultural significance that circumscribed the college community of students, faculty, staff, alumni, and administrators.

Manning (2000) identified four "significant themes" embedded in her categories of campus rituals that included (1) mirroring the college's values, (2) punctuation and mediation of campus life, (3) power, and (4) criticism and parody (Manning, 2000, pp. 8-9). College values were the referents for these rituals, and so the rituals were invested in meaning because the participants in these rituals shared a meaning making system of significance that revolved around shared campus values. These rituals were described as patterned, ordered, formal, repetitive, and symbolic enactments of the cultural values of the campus. Sometimes these ceremonies also dramatized and reified the power relations of the community, such as the arrangements for seating for the college faculty and administrators.

<u>Academic Ceremonies</u>. Research participants in this study talked about how academic ceremonies were important to them and for the college community. These rituals had the ternate structure that resembles Van Gennep's (1960) three-phase rite of passage. (See Figure 2 below).

Preparation →     Transformation →

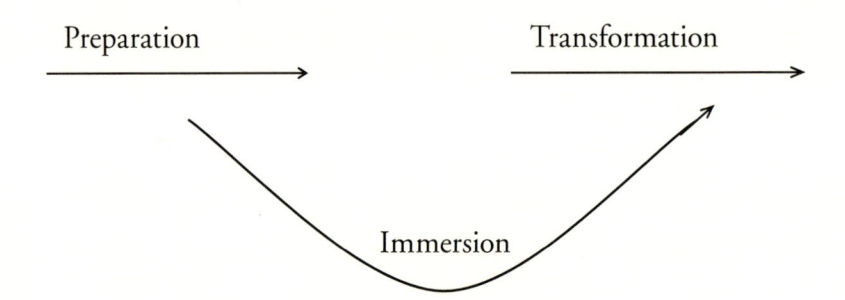

Immersion

Figure 2. – Ritualization/Transition of Significance

They also involved features of ritual performance (Tambiah, 1980). At public academic ceremonies such as Opening Convocation, the Passing (where seniors march through an archway in Kanter Hall after turning in their senior independent theses), Baccalaureate, and commencement, the entire campus community pauses to prepare, participate, and pass through a ritual that transforms participants.

The characterization of ritual as invested with features of performance also offers a potential framework for discerning structures of ritualization in faculty leadership, since, as discussed later in this chapter, much of what is described as leadership is often deemed performative. Charles, the development psychologist, noted that:

> in general, rituals make a difference. That it's important, in terms of transitions, that we have graduation ceremonies and wedding ceremonies, major transitions in life across human cultures going back tens of thousands of years. There have been institutionalized ways of marking those events. And I think it makes people, one, recognize them as important, but also as a shared experience.

For Charles and the other research participants, academic ceremonies served to implant significance across time and space. They remain a valuable cultural resource to ensure the future of the college by embedding memories for former students. Charles noted:

I think humans have this general need for institutionalized, ritualized experiences that, sort of, group celebrations, that later on you remember... When you look back across your life, your fifties, and your sixties, making decisions about where to send your children to school, you'll look back and you'll remember those experiences. And I think if it's been a positive experience, positive life, and it's when alumni start writing checks, when alumni start to send some of their children here, it all perpetuates the health of the institution. Every faculty member here thirty years from now probably won't be here. Many people unfortunately won't even be alive. But, the students that we have taught will be in their fifties and sixties. And they'll be in good jobs, good professions. They'll be... the big donors that come up with million-dollar grants to the college. So what we do ensures the health of the college thirty, fifty years from now. There'll be faculty members here that aren't even born yet.... So it does matter what we do in the long term... the life of the institution is more important than any individual here. That's what we have to keep in mind. The rituals that we have set a structure, that several decades from now will payoff, that ensure the life of the college.

*Seasonal Rituals* As Charles noted, "the rituals that are attendant on a college matter greatly." Academic events and ceremonies punctuated and marked the academic year. Even as they existed as cultural structures with institutional formality and communal significance for the Wilkinson College community, academic ceremonies also had meaning for the research participants in more personally significant ways. For example, the day in the fall when new students arrive on campus marks the beginning of another academic season. The beginning of the year, according to Paula is "a little bitter sweet because you know that the summer is over, and it's time... to get serious again." Paula noted that, "the thing that marks the beginning of the school year is all the first-year students unpacking their belongings." This is a day of significance for nearly everyone on campus. But for

Paula, this day also marks a transition in the year "from scheduling your day however you want, to your day being dictated by the needs of either your classes or your research students and your students... from a fluid kind of day to a very structured bing, bing, bing, bing, bing kind of day."

Opening Convocation is part of a "very long historical tradition of academia," one of the rituals of "entering and leaving" (Manning, 2000) invested with ceremonial and institutional significance. But Convocation also had a particularly local and more personal significance for Paula and her colleagues:

> I like the opportunity to see the seniors there, and just kind of think about: Boy... I really hope that they will take advantage of this, that they really will, that they'll realize that this is their last [year] in... college, and really give themselves the opportunity to do something with it. So it's kind of, I guess maybe nostalgic is the word. You kind of, and you sit there and you think about your own, and you sit there and you look at all of the faculty and you think, oh my gosh, you know, every year I move a little further up in the ranks. So before I was... the last one in the row, and watching all the people in the front row. Now I'm up a row or so... I think it does mark, you know, it's kind of a defined time...

Commencement is another very public ceremony, but also inscribed with personal significance. For Paula, commencement offers another time to make connections, to see students and colleagues, but also to mark the progression of her own career at Wilkinson:

> It's kind of fun to see everybody in their, in their little gowns, you know, the kind of pomp and circumstance of the event. And quite honestly it's the only time I get to see some of my colleagues. They line us up by the year you came in, and so that my little year started out as fourteen, and I think we're down to two. And so I like to get to see those colleagues,

and I'm, I'm also aware of the people that are immediately ahead of me now, and before I wasn't so much. I was more aware of the people who were right there with me, and then the people that came in immediately behind me. But now I am, I guess I'm starting to notice other, other people around me. But I like that, and I like seeing the students... I've gone through my first two full cycles of students now, so I've seen them as first-years, and then seen them as seniors. And so having them walk by, and you just think, boy you've come a long way... you really have come a long way.

commencement also marked the end of an academic season; as Paula noted, "spring is evidenced by the first robin showing up... summer is evidenced by coming and putting your gown... on the hook." In summary, academic ceremonies were important to the research participants, but these ceremonies also had another salient significance that emerged from more personal meaning systems.

*The Personal and Informal*

Manning (1990, 2000) used field observations of academic rituals and ceremonies. I examined ritualization in the leadership work of research participants as interpreted through their own narratives of passage (Grimes, 2000) as members of the Wilkinson College faculty. While Manning (1990, 2000) focused on ritualized campus occasions, I examined the less formally structured ritualization (Driver, 1998) and secular ceremony (Moore & Myerhoff, 1977) surrounding faculty leadership. I found three constellations of informal ritualization: milestones, conversations, and tenure.

*Milestones.* Research participants started long before they arrived at Wilkinson College, beginning with transitions that influenced their academic trajectories. Francesca's first significant intellectual transition occurred when she left home for the first time to live in Germany on a Fulbright Fellowship:

> I had been so serious all the way through college and for me this year was more of a year to be in a different setting and lead a different kind of life, although I did an awful a lot of reading, and a lot of it just my own, just because I was interested. So it was, in lots of ways, a definitive year, it was a year of independence. I was really living very far away from my family, which I had never done before. And that was a good thing to. I did a lot of traveling. And I felt as though I sort of wanted to suck up the world at least as much of it as I could in the European context. So I went to Italy, and I was in Eastern Europe. And I made these long trips on the train, you know, living on sort of rock bottom money, but just experiencing everything that I could pack in that one year.

Charles reported an early and significant transition from a successful career as a Toys-R-Us store manager to an intellectually satisfying role as a faculty member. Reflecting on his old job, Charles noted:

> I hated every single day that I worked there. I worked in Detroit, Washington, and Los Angeles. It was finally after I had been asked to go to the opening in the Las Vegas market. That would have been a big career promotion for me at the time. The next step would have been in the corporate offices. But I decided that I didn't want to do this anymore, that I couldn't. I essentially quit in the management program, although I stayed working for the company and started graduate school and eventually just quit all together. I focused on my graduate work instead.

For Francesca, Paula, Charles, and Rebecca, these personal transitions, what Driver (1998) termed ritualization, occurred in the context of passages (Grimes, 2000) in their careers that were often deeply personal even as they were manifested in public activities. Francesca reported her first few years at Wilkinson as years of fragmentation, and for her a significant transition was successfully emerging out of those early years with more hopeful insights on what she was capable of doing at the college:

> I think the fragmentation and trying to find ways to make the pieces of our lives fit together better was very important at that point as a kind of transition experience. I also learned, and I've learned this again in other contexts, that I could work harder than I ever thought I could, that I could just put in more time, and be more focused, and work harder than I… might have thought possible in the past… those belong to those kinds of transition experiences I guess.

Ritualizing events also include career milestones with a smaller and local significance. One example was Paula's first set of teaching evaluations:

> And that was a challenge to get through, because even though most of them were very good, there were the few that, you know, I wasn't everybody's favorite. So that was one of the first, you know, that hurt a little, recognizing that it's, it's okay to not be perfect, to do the best that you can do.

She anticipated them in preparation, she received and read them and they "hurt a little," and she emerged from the experience with renewed insight. Another milestone, a crisis shared and experienced together as an entire department was when Paula's chemistry faculty had to move out of their dilapidated building so that it could be renovated.

> Moving out of building may have also been kind of a crisis of sort, because we all had… to pack up and move out all of the equipment, all of the chemicals, and got very little help from transportation because they were swamped with doing things for graduation. And we had one week to get out. And get out is what we had to do.… I was concerned because… we do have some people with fairly strong tempers and personalities. And I was concerned, oh my god, that we

can't even behave in normal staff meetings, what's gonna happen now. And we really, everyone really pulled together. And that was, that was nice, because it was challenging enough.

Paula's colleagues had very little time for the preparation, experienced an immersion, and crossed over the experience transformed as "everyone pulled together." Other local milestones reported by research participants included the first professional presentation or publication, the first research grant received, going on the first research leave, and then returning from leave. Each of these milestones greeted an important transition in their careers. It gave each of them the "rewarding feeling that you gather, of seeing something accomplished."

*Conversations* Research participants also narrated a cluster of periodic, transformative activities related to conversations with their colleagues. These conversations, according to Francesca, were "likely to be both professional and… personal at some level," and they were not just for purely social purposes although they occurred inside a web of established relationships. These conversations were about mutually influential and mutually satisfying learning from colleagues. Francesca noted

> there've been times when I think… I've been able to learn something from them, not because I would have done what they did or thought the same way that they did, but I, I learned something by watching them deal with an issue in their context and realizing how I would have dealt with that in mine. So what have I learned from them? …I need to be reminded that it's important to foster, to keep relationships alive, because that's part of being a whole human being.

More often the conversations are scheduled opportunities, such as department and college meetings and forums and times for informal gatherings, where faculty and students reify their connection to each other and to their discipline. Charles described a weekly lunch with faculty colleagues and students in the department:

> Every noon, every Thursday at 12:00… we will go over and many of the psych students and psych majors will come and join us for lunch. It's a lot of fun. We laugh, we sort of talk about the department. Talk about directions. Talk of the new building. Some students talk about their IS's, other projects they're doing. It's a nice relaxed environment for 30 – 45 minutes we're over there. Get a free lunch. We get to meet… there may by six students or so. Sometimes it changes, sometimes more, sometimes less, depending on what they're doing. But I like it very much. It's a good idea. And I wish more students availed themselves of it. The ones that do, I think, enjoy it. I think that as a faculty member I do too. It's really important that they see us outside of the classroom. Because in their junior and senior year we have to work so closely with them on their junior independent study, the senior independent study, I think it's a good idea that they see us outside of class… It just makes everything work better together.

Another opportunity for conversation is the department meeting. This meeting is another time to come together, and in conducting the quotidian business of the department, some larger and more fundamental issues such as curriculum are discussed. Perspectives are shared, and the experience transforms even as it reifies departmental identity. Paula described how she experienced the department meeting as her time to regularly challenge her colleagues, "Are we doing the best we can?" Paula and her colleagues look to the department meeting to help create a "more supportive thriving environment for the faculty."

> We have [department] meetings every week. And I get that opportunity every week. And with my lovely little PDA, all week long as I think of things, I have a little staff meeting note, I keep a running list, and then when we're done the business on the agenda, then I can pull out my PDA and say, "Okay, this week, I want to ask about…" And so I'm pretty regular about it. And… the thing that's nice though is that

> when you bring these questions up, there's always, there's always one or other two people that are like "O, you know… that's a good question! We should look at that." And so that we've got quite a docket of things that we will be discussing over the summer, and into the fall semester. But it's, it's good conversation, and a lot of times, I think, those conversations are lacking because we're so busy taking care of the routine business, and so busy taking care of the, you know, putting out the fires… that we don't really have time to step back from the micro issues to the bigger issues of, you know… are we doing the best that we can do, are there smarter things that we could do? And what are we doing well? …I think that's where my energy goes.

These discussions are not just an exchange of negotiated positions. They are prepared for and passed through, bringing meaningful significance for the participants. These conversations of significance reify connection, they are founded on a shared sense of departmental collegiality, and they enact and re-enact a passage to shared values and commitments. Paula reflected on her chemistry department conversations.

> I think that having those conversations of what we value, what we think should be priorities for the students, for the classes, for the research, for the program, and just kind of get those ideas out on the table. One of the things that I've seen, and I think we will continue to do is… strike a compromise, on the things that are really, really important, quite often we do share those values. And sometimes, and I think where we usually differ is in our ideas about how to get to those, how to accomplish those goals…

Conversations of significance occurred when faculty relationships were strong, and when faculty in the department shared practices and worked in a shared departmental culture. Charles described the necessary setting for conversation in the psychology department:

> We have, as they say, a real good rapport in this department, and so people are back and forth just popping into an office and talking for a few minutes, just checking the hall to see if everything is going okay and stuff. So we have a very sort of casual relationship, which I think is good. Again it builds some solidarity in the department. Makes things go well, I think, just by example as well. [We] are very concerned about students… spend a lot time with them here. We're faculty, when we're here we keep our doors open.

Another conversation opportunity is one that marks the end of the year, and comes during a time of significant public and personal transition for the faculty, the day of commencement. The college hosts a faculty lunch the afternoon after commencement, a time for the faculty to gather after all the graduates have left to celebrate with their families. It's a quiet time for closure. After the lunch, it's time to prepare for the summer. Paula remembered the faculty lunch as

> a nice way to go and [to] fill that void of, of those students being gone… It's a nice closure kind of… experience… And then we leave the lunch and you just kind of stroll back across campus. And you don't have to rush because you don't have anything to grade, and you don't have anything that has to be done that afternoon… I try to… close up this semester as quickly as possible… So that afternoon I like to come back and just, I guess it's a little nesting… I clean up, clean up the papers, get things organized, take care of my emails. Just very relaxed. And usually I make it a point to get out of here at a decent hour. Take an early leave, maybe go home and do a load of yard work. Relax.

*Tenure* At the time the interviews for this research study were conducted, three of the four research participants had earned tenure, and Charles, as the most recently hired junior faculty member, was anticipating tenure in three years. Paula remembered what crossing over to becoming a tenured faculty member felt like, and the new sense of responsibility she felt:

> It's kind of anticlimactic. You're like great, now what. But it also brings some sense of responsibility with it, I mean, you kind of feel like oh well, now. And there's a sense of permanency because you feel like okay now I'm going to get to stay. And so I really should be looking... a year ahead, two years ahead, maybe I should think about five years and ten years, where do I want to see myself in respect to the department and to the campus. Where would I like to see things go?. On one hand it feels good because they've given me a vote of confidence that says, okay, you get to stay. And then on the other hand it feels little intimidating because now I get to stay a next time.

Earning tenure marks the crossing of a significant threshold for faculty. Although not accompanied by much public ceremony at Wilkinson College, tenure candidates studiously prepare themselves and their portfolios, pass through the decision-making process and wait for a letter (the "high moment"), and are then welcomed to a new community of now-tenured and re-invited faculty. Francesca remembered her experience with one of the most significant transitions in her faculty life, earning tenure:

> It was a very... frightening moment for me. I was probably like most other faculty members. I was really nervous about how it was going to go... I knew that I didn't have a big publication and research record... and I was afraid that... that would catch up with me and that I wouldn't be given tenure. Because even then there was this sort of rising focus on publication and research... But, I was worried about that... So getting tenure was, of course, it was a high moment for me. It was a kind of acknowledgement by the institution that I'd been working so very hard for really... that I could stay. And I could be part of it.

In summary, research participants described ritualization as a three phase process of preparation, immersion, and transformation that aided them in constructing meaning and significance for them.

*Secular Ceremony*

Even the more formal academic ceremonies were inscribed for research participants with a personal significance that extended beyond the meaning making of the formal institutional rituals. It is important to distinguish between ritual performance and ritual experience. As Grimes (1995) suggested

> ritual performance is ritual as actually done and witnessed. But even when ritual is performed by a group, it is experienced differently by different individuals… So ritual experience – what one takes away from, or gets out of, a rite – is not the same as ritual performance.

The academic ceremony of commencement gave Paula a personally significant ritualization in her movement along the line. Research participants described their ritualization experiences as rich in significance in personal and informal rites, particularly in their milestones, conversations, and the awarding of tenure. Their reported ritualization experiences aligned with most of the constitutive features of "secular ceremony" (Moore and Myerhoff, 1977) as summarized by Manning (2000).

Milestones, conversations, and tenure transitions, identified by research participants in their narratives, contained (a) repetition in content, form, and occasion, (b) self-conscious or deliberate action, (c) orderly, stylized action achieved through extraordinary actions or ordinary actions dramatized in unusual ways, (d) and a collective dimension expressed in the ritual's message of community and social meaning (Manning, 2000, p. 46).

Moore and Myerhoff (1977) defined secular ceremony as ritualization that communicated everyday beliefs and convictions in a non-religious context. In higher education settings, this definition of secular ceremony would include personal and individual routines and patterned actions charged with personal meaning that mark or greet transitions of personal significance.

# Chapter 10

# People And Meaning

## Pivotal Persons

When Francesca, Charles, Paula, and Rebecca identified significant transitions, they often associated each of their transitions with at least one - - what Paula called - - "pivotal person." Sometimes these early influencers and mentors, associated with critical moments of decisions, and making commitments. And although research participants would not attribute their success and career advancement entirely to such social capital resources (Coleman, 1990), all of them seemed to flourish in a system of mutually beneficial social exchanges (Coleman, 1990) where pivotal persons emerged to connect them to opportunities. Pivotal persons also provided role models that helped research participants envision life in the academy. They were often companions who accompanied the research participants through their significant transitions.

*Early Influencers*

Early influencers included teachers who helped paint pictures of what the life in the academy might be like. Francesca remembered faculty members in graduate school who were

> just wonderful to us and inspired us… you looked at their lives, you looked at the kind of things they were thinking about and doing, and you said to yourself… this is the kind of life I would like to be leading, what these people are dong with students and in their own research, and writing, and so on, and this… is the way I can imagine I would like to spend my life.

Charles, the developmental psychologist was influenced into a passage to intellectual work and subsequently graduate school by an inspiring faculty member in an early class who presented a role model.

> I remember taking a course in the philosophy of law or philosophy of social sciences. And I remember… Dr. K, and politically we were completely opposites. He was… a… socialist, and a theosophist, or at least more conservative than that. But it was such a great course… I can't even remember what the class was about. I remember thinking this is what I want to do. And I… actually didn't go back to graduate school for about eight years after that. But I remember very clearly that was the point that I decided that this is what I want to do. I hadn't decided on psychology at the time. Then I was thinking I'd go back and get a Ph.D. in philosophy and do this.

Paula, the organic chemist, had a teacher in high school who helped ignite her interest in the sciences. In investing in the relationship with Paula, and through his actions, this pivotal person painted an admirable picture of what a teacher's life might be like. Paula remembered that he "took a very personal interest, and cared about what he did. And I think that that definitely reflects on what I do here." Paula then made an early commitment to teaching. Paula also remembered a faculty member in college who not only accompanied her in the passage to a commitment to graduate school, but also helped Paula construct an image of the kind of college faculty member she wanted to be.

> I remember my professor being particularly intent on trying to get me to balance work and socializing, cause he thought all I did was work. By the time... I was a senior, well I guess it was my junior year, I knew that, I knew that I had a pretty good idea that I wanted to teach at college like that. But I wasn't sure if I wanted to do that just because that was what I knew, or because that was really what I wanted to do. And do when I went to graduate school I was really open minded about, maybe I wanted to teach, maybe I don't want to teach, but either way I've got to get a Ph.D.

## *Opportunity Connectors*

Pivotal persons created opportunities for research participants to lead committees, to edit and publish, and to connect the participants to others in the profession. Rebecca remembered her pivotal persons:

> I've had good mentors, and because I've been connected, and because I have white-skin privilege, and because I'm not hideously ugly, and not terrifically overweight, and because I'm fairly articulate, I've had things open up to me. And, and I recognize those advantages. I sometimes say, why me, I'm not smarter than some of these other people. But I realize that that's not all there is, it's just not all there is.

Pivotal persons were sought out, if not always deliberately. Research participants reported finding pivotal persons in their discipline largely through excelling in school and demonstrating incipient passion for the discipline. Rebecca found her pivotal persons by deciding to seek additional social capital, and to expand her social network:

> I need to be in a… bigger pool. It doesn't have to be a bigger teaching pool, but it… does need to be a bigger intellectual pool.… But at the same [time]… here's the intellectual part, one does get social capital, but I'm not really doing it for that.

Pivotal persons can also arrive unexpectedly while experiencing a passage. Whether or not they intended to influence the passage, research participants remembered pivotal persons who were present, sometimes almost accidentally, in their most significant passages. Paula remembered a faculty advisor at Georgetown College who led her to choose the University of North Carolina for graduate school.

> When it was time, when I decided that the Ph.D. was what I needed, I went to my advisor and I told him, "how do I pick a graduate school?" and he told me "where do you want to live?" And I actually told him "you're crazy, that, that cannot be the criteria," you know, "tell me, tell me the real…" And he said, "no I'm telling you," he said, "where do you want to live?"… And I told him, I said, "well, I'm thinking more along the lines of, I would like a big institution, with lots of money, but in a small town, because I don't want to live in a big city somewhere." And he suggested a few institutions. And I went down to visit UNC, and on the drive in I thought, this is the place. And then I met with the various faculty and the students that I met with that day. I accepted the next day.

The same faculty advisor re-appeared in another later transformative decision for Paula. After completing her doctorate at the University of North Carolina, and spending two years in a post-doc position, Paula applied to a number of institutions for teaching positions. She was not interviewed at any institution, she was told, because of the absence of teaching experience, "and I remember talking to one of the chairs and saying to them verbatim, 'and when the hell was I supposed to get this teaching experience?'" Disappointed, Paula started work with a research and development company in Maryland. One day she called her faculty advisor back at Georgetown College.

> So I called my advisor from Georgetown and I said, "I'm going to be in town, you want to get together for lunch?" And his first answer was, "oh you're going to give a seminar?"

I was like, "I knew I shouldn't have called you!" And so I had been at the company about three months, and went and gave a seminar. And then I realized that day, I was in the wrong place, I've got to go back and try again. And that afternoon I went and bought a printer, so that I could print resumes… and sent out about thirty resume packages…

*Admirable Role Models*

Pivotal persons are not just guides and mentors. They are remembered as characters who accompanied them in their momentous passages and significant transitions. Rebecca remembered them as helping her "feel authorized," and to become "serious about political science, and… socialize me to become a professor." Francesca also remembered them as very noteworthy early influences in her own aspirations to be a teacher:

> I had a couple of faculty mentors who were college teachers. And I admired so much of what they did in the classroom, and how they lived their lives in the sense… that it was there, it was working with those people, there were two or three of them in particular, and they were very encouraging to me in turn. So I know that made a difference. But I think it was there that I really began to think seriously about maybe working in a university or college setting, where I can interact with students in the way they interacted with me. And work with ideas and continue to learn, learn, learn because I was enjoying so much the learning that I was doing… I think that probably had a big influence on my wanting to go ahead and earn the doctoral degree and to teach on a post secondary level… I… was encouraged… to consider a career in college teaching… to go on and get a doctorate.

Also for Francesca were the pivotal persons who helped and guided her to prepare for the transition into the dean of the faculty position.

Francesca recounted how she was motivated, not just by her own aspiration to make a difference, but also by another administrator.

> I mean, when DH [former vice president for academic affairs] left here... he said, you know, '[Francesca] I hope you stay at [Wilkinson]' ...He said that you could be a dean someday, maybe not at [Wilkinson], but at some other school. I think that sort of encouragement gave me kind of a... sense [that] I should really try this job because this job is about... it's another level of building skills, and another... It's a risk, but it's another level of stepping out and seeing how the whole college works, and looking for a chance to pull some things together and make them more coherent. So I think that was the road into the Deans Office.

The pivotal persons were remembered in the narratives of research participants because of their roles in a specific significant transition, but they might also be a continuing presence in the lives of the participants, as unforgettable and honored friends, and as intellectual companions. Rebecca noted that

> I do want to honor and recognize them. These are people whose names I remember, with whom I'm still in contact, for the most part... And there is something about knowing people across a long period of time... and I want to keep these... friends not only for the loveliness of the friendship and because I feel so close to them, but because they carry part of my history... [that] can't be retrieved without them.

Research participants remembered pivotal persons who attended and accompanied them through their passages of significance. (See Figure 3 below). They were present in early transitions of significance, they helped connect research participants to the academy as an initial career and to opportunities for professional advancement.

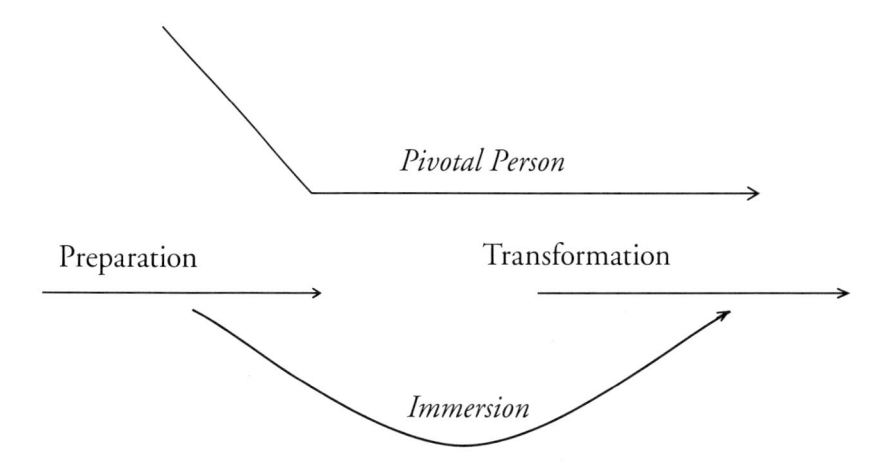

Figure 3. – Pivotal Person in Ritualization

Pivotal persons served as early guides and mentors, opportunity connectors, and admirable role models. Their names and memories were associated with narratives of ritualization and transition.

## Ellipses of Significance

Just as passage narratives are embedded in passage systems (Grimes, 2000), the research participants in this study described their ritualization as firmly implanted in a meaning system that surrounded the rites. I found in their descriptions of this meaning system a constellation of ambient values, convictions, and commitments that orbited their actions and explained their transformations. These values were (1) teaching first, (2) living the academic good life, (3) leaving a legacy, (4) advancing social justice, (5) being women (for three out of the four research participants), and (6) celebrating student success.

### Teaching First

The research participants' narratives reflected the centrality of teaching. They identified themselves as teachers first, and teaching was an element of the academy that they deeply cared about. Charles noted that

> I'm motivated to search for the truth... I guess my most basic motivation is I like this job. I like being part of academia. I like teaching. I like students. I like working with colleagues on interesting ideas... it's perhaps not a, you know, noble goal searching for absolute truth or something like that. I enjoy this life! And that's what motivates me to keep going. I think that's probably true of many of my colleagues. While many are probably motivated for higher ideals than I am, I think we like this life and it's the best life possible.

Francesca's career at Wilkinson was cobbled together with numerous administrative and temporary faculty positions ultimately leading to a deanship, but she still considered herself first and foremost, a faculty member.

> I saw myself primarily as someone teaching German. I think I saw myself as somebody who was trying to bridge fields in my teaching, who was always exploring a new field, a new area, who rarely taught the same course twice, and who was interested in innovative programs at the college.

Teaching was intrinsically valued and valuable to them. Their scholarly work was still a component of their teaching, reflecting an argument made by Boyer (1990), and reflecting a generally accepted view of faculty scholarship at liberal arts colleges (Cech, 2000). As Charles noted, everything revolved around good teaching and its benefits for students.

> I think teaching is the most important thing. And even research, as well, is important because I think engaging students in my research is like teaching. I do lateralization work with birds and things. It's not curing cancer, its not some major life, you know... world-changing thing. But,

it does demonstrate experimental methodology, the logic of hypothetical reasoning, hypothesis testing, and drawing conclusions based on evidence. And I think in that it serves a very good purpose for students to hear, to develop critical thinking and things like that.

Related to Charles' emphasis on teaching was the notion of the centrality of faculty. At the time I was completing the interviews for this study, Wilkinson College had just laid off thirty staff members and middle managers. No faculty positions were compromised and no faculty members were laid off. Charles was very clear about the central role of the faculty in the hierarchy of importance:

> There's administration, there are faculty, there are staff. Our contributions are different. Faculty matter the most. People don't come here because of who cuts the lawn, or who is the president of the college, or who is the food preparer. They come here to be educated. It matters who the faculty are. It doesn't matter who anybody else is… people do not come here because of who the food service is, they come here because of who the faculty are. And that means that there are differences in terms of rewards, there are differences in terms of importance to the college, for the life of the institution. I think it has to be recognized we are held to different standards, in our work we have to publish, we have to do major research. We have to do many things that non-faculty members do not have to do. It makes a difference.

This centrality of teaching and the faculty role at the college is sometimes seen in an oppositional relationship with the administration, particularly with the Board of Trustees. Also at the time I was completing the interviews for this study, Wilkinson College faculty had recently completed a revision of the curriculum, and their recommendations included substituting the previous graduation requirement of at least one course in religious studies with a broader curricular requirement. Rejecting this recommendation, the Board of Trustees reinstated the religious studies course requirement. Reflecting the frustration of many but not all the members of the faculty at Wilkinson, Charles outlined the stance of countervailing opposition to the administration:

> I would like to see the faculty viewed as almost a co-equal branch with the administration, with the Board of Trustees, sort of, supervising the college. I think that's a model that's in place in other schools, where there's a faculty senate that, in fact, has authority, that certain things simply cannot be dealt without their agreement. Well, of course, that's not the case here. The administration, the Board of Trustees, can essentially do what they want without consulting the faculty… they do make decisions that there's nothing that faculty can do about it. I don't particularly care for that. I do recognize their arguments at times, but it would be nice to have a relatively independent faculty. I think that would be a healthier way of running things. That's not the case… The Board will do what the Board wants. They don't have to consult the faculty. Sometimes they become, they can be acrimonious. They get worked up about their positions. But, I think, from my point of view, that's sort of pointless… Voicing opinion is important, but the Board doesn't want to hear… or they only hear what they want to hear.

*Living the Academic Good Life*

Research participants reported that preparing for and participating in academic ceremonies offered opportunities to celebrate the life of the academy, and to reassert values of heritage and tradition (Manning, 2000). Charles wished "we wore our regalia every day." He said that the most important reason for his career move from business executive to faculty member was, "I like tradition, I like the historical sense that we have done this every year in this way… this is the way this has always been done." Charles reflected his preference for rhythm and stability by describing his mostly orderly day:

> I do things very much the same way. I come in. I try to get in by 8:30 every morning. I get my coffee. Hopefully there is a doughnut left over at the faculty lounge. There weren't any today, which is sort of annoying. I got there too late. And I start, I do my email... I either have meetings or appointments before class. So I do my class prep and teach at noon. Come in do prep class prep for 2:00 class. Perhaps see another student. About 4:00 I go home. My day is Tuesdays and Thursdays. I call my parents every afternoon on Tuesday and Thursday. Friday afternoon usually I talk to my brother. At least once a week I talk to my friend over at George Mason, an old colleague. I have a very predictable day. And I like that. Thursday at 11:00 o'clock we have faculty meeting. Tuesdays and Thursdays at noon we go to have lunch with students...

All the research participants enjoyed the stability and rhythm of the academic good life. They remembered that this life, made attractive to them long ago by the example of early pivotal persons, was now the source of their satisfaction and allegiance.

> I am perfectly happy; I have to say this is a good life. I wouldn't trade it. I would... encourage it. Academia is tough to get into because there are not that many jobs. It is highly competitive... But it is a good life. You can make a difference. It is a good life. I wouldn't trade it for anything...

*Leaving a Legacy*

Another strong value that research participants reported were their aspirations for legacy. Research participants in this study were as self-conscious as they were clear about how they wanted to be remembered. They wanted to be remembered primarily for their work with students, and secondarily for their work in their departments. Paula hoped people would remember her for

> my integrity and for my equitable treatment of the students... I want to be remembered for my work on behalf of the students... whether it be teaching in my class, whether it be challenging them to think outside of the box, in terms of what are you going to do, what do you like to do, where are you gonna be. I think I want to be remembered for how I worked with the students... I guess I feel that's where I can make the most difference. The research is important, but I'm not gonna solve the world's problems. The departmental activities are important because, you know, we've gotta have a good department for the future students. The college activities are important cause you've gotta have a college that's sound for the future students. But the students themselves, they're what's most important to me. What, what kind of foundation I give them both as a person and as a scholar, intellectually and socially, so they can go and do what ever they go and do. I feel like that's my, my best contribution.

Students were "the most important group" to Francesca. She wanted them to remember her for the things

> that they got, they were challenged but they got a certain level of encouragement. Or that they, you know, thought about something in a different way or, or that they had the feeling I can do this, I can learn beginning German or whatever it is. It's those kinds of things, I mean, just learning a foreign language, that's a huge hurdle for a lot of people... those kinds of things.

Rebecca would like for her students to think well, and think clearly, and be "just humans and just citizens."

> For my students, I hope they go on to do really good research. I hope they... will think back and think, right here's where I got some good advice, or here's where [Rebecca] did something that really showed me the way. This has really, you know, this has really helped me; now I'm gonna do a

good job, too. I'm going to make sure that, you know, I need a high mark for my own scholarship, that I'm going to be a really, really good teacher, that when I'm feeling exhausted and crabby I'm going to take that one last minute to help that student... not who just... needs to have their hand held but a student who's made an effort, recognize it and, and help that student down the line. So, you know, I hope people will think back in that regard, and whatever kind of legacy I can leave in terms of democratic citizenship, that has encouraged students to take themselves seriously. And to take themselves seriously as morally political people working in the world, who aren't fascist, who aren't racist.

Rebecca wanted most of all to be remembered by her students for her work. She wanted to leave a legacy of people who were scholars and active intellectuals who could critically interrogate their political world. In turn, she would like students to recall her as

> Someone... who did a good job, who [was a] professional, who was a good scholar, who... set a high mark. I guess, I'd like that. And beyond that, I mean I really can't, you know, do I want administrators to somehow honor me or remember me? No. No, I guess not.

Charles wanted his legacy not in terms of durable buildings or rooms, but in having made "those kids' lives different." He wanted to be a part of changing his students' expectations of their abilities:

> Those are the kids that I like working with the best. The ones that you don't expect to turn out well... you take a C student and they graduate with honors. That would be the legacy that I would want. Not a room or a building, or you don't need to remember me. I made those kids' lives different. Hopefully I had a hand in that. That made a difference. That is going to get me out of purgatory.

In addition to improving the lives and work of students, research participants also reported aspirations for making revisions and improvements in the curriculum, and changes in the department, discipline, and the college. At the time I was conducting the interviews for this study, the psychology department was preparing to move in the next few months to a new building, with much awaited classroom, office, and laboratory spaces, including an animal lab. Charles stated:

> Fortunately we all had sort of a shared dream of were we would like for the psych department to go in the next couple of decades. I hope people remember [the] role that I played, as well. We got into the new building. We established greater ties with the bio department.... People have a new respect for the psych department.

Paula would like to have her legacy associated with a revised curriculum sequence and a revitalized chemistry program:

> And so that when my time comes, and it's time for another organic chemist to take over, I want to be able to hand them a good organic chemistry program, that's founded in modern techniques, both pedagogically and scientifically. And so, so the way it exists right now is not the way that it'll be in twenty-four years or thirty years. So I want to, I want to be able to hand in a good program. And make it stronger.

As the research participant closest to retirement, Francesca wanted people at the college to remember her as someone who

> had helped initiate a lot of programs, that in one way or another, are still part of what we do… and someone who cared, in some sense, about the, the overall development and welfare of students, beyond simply their absorbing a certain amount of material.
>
> I have no illusions about this, as I watch people retire, the college moves on very, very quickly. And you find yourself,

I think, as a retired person, how ever much of a leader you were at the time that you were on campus. You find yourself as a retired person, someone that people really have to rush by… And I think it's sad for people to kind of hang around and want to be on the inside when they've retired. And so I have to illusions about that. I think the college has to move on, and can't spend a lot of time remembering the people who even made major, sort of, contributions to things. But, I think, I, I just simply don't expect that there be some sort of institutional memory about people, because that fades as personnel change, unless you got your name on a building, you know, something like that… I think… it's very great when your colleagues remember well, you know, we have this going on, and these are the people who were involved in initiating it, or in fostering it, whatever 'it' is…

*Penetrating Privilege*

Research participants also reported that the purpose of education was to serve a large social justice agenda. They recognized that a liberal arts college education was itself a privilege, and that the vast majority of students at Wilkinson College had relatively privileged middle and upper-middle family origins. However, not all students at Wilkinson were intellectually prepared. Charles talked about especially reaching out to teach the less well-prepared students, so that they also can make a difference in the world.

> Often faculty… want to work with the best students, the A students. You don't notice the C students. Or the students that don't do that well and sit in the back and don't talk. You have to notice them…. You can make the biggest difference with them. The A students they are going to do well no matter what you do with them. They may develop personal bonds with you. You may work with them. I have worked with many A students as well. But they are going to do well regardless of whom their teachers are. They also do. They are

smart. They are motivated. The lives have sort of worked out well. They are going to go on and do well. You can't forget the C students… I hope that is one thing that people will look back at, those students that I worked with and I was most concerned about. I enjoyed being around them.

For Rebecca, pursuing her own rights as a citizen included enacting a critical pedagogy to help prepare future citizens as engaged intellectuals who could connect their work to broader social concerns that deeply affect how people live, work, and survive (Gramsci, 1971). She wanted her students to learn about injustice and systemic oppression in the world so that they may then penetrate through their privilege:

> There's a lot of injustice in the world. And we're a very privileged nation, and students at this institution are so privileged in ways they don't even realize. And it seems to me that, that level of privilege in a political system like this and a society like this absolutely binds them to act in just ways and binds all of us to acting as well as we can, in terms of justice. And also because I really do believe that democracy is, for all of it's flaws and all it's permutations… is… really the best theoretical set of political arrangements for making a better world, making better people, making people happier, and more, although that's really idealistic, but those are some of my values. And so that makes it important to me. And because, you know, they do come into my classroom and they do go out in the world and I do teach politics, you know, seems like that's one difference I can in the world, you know even if that's my own role as a citizen, and other things I might do outside the classroom.

*Being Women*

All three of the female research participants - - Francesca, Paula, and Rebecca - - brought up considerations of gender, and how being women had influenced their thinking, their decisions, their lives, and their careers. Francesca was at first a trailing spouse, accompanying her husband to Wilkinson College. She remembered the early years as an experience of "tremendous fragmentation," when she occupied a series of leave, replacement, and fractional faculty and administrative positions before she finally secured a full-time position.

> It was my job with to deal with the childcare issues, to deal with the housekeeping and so on issues. I could work, but I still had to deal with those things. And it wasn't that my spouse didn't help with all of those things, but I was the one who sort of had to do the organizational thinking. And I felt the responsibility in a very direct sort of way. So I think that… yes there was an impact there. It contributed to what I guess… a sense of fragmentation, because there was always that feeling wherever you are whatever you're doing, you should be in the other place and you should be doing the other thing. And I think it played out in other ways. I was very, I was much more aware of the fact that students seemed to perceive male and female faculty differently and have different expectations.

Rebecca's academic interest in the study of women and politics grew out of her personal experiences and strong critical convictions about women's experiences in the academy and in the larger society. She remembered:

> When I was in high school, playing high school basketball, in girl's basketball you could dribble three times and then you had to stop and pass the ball. That was it. You know, we couldn't play full-court basketball… And you couldn't go to Harvard, you couldn't go to Yale, you couldn't go to Princeton, those were for men schools only. You couldn't serve as a page on the floor of the US Congress, which infuriated me because that's something I wanted to do. So we weren't encouraged to think… about… some career some big future.

In the early years at Wilkinson College, Francesca remembered that male faculty were addressed as "Dr." while female faculty were called "Miss" or "Mrs." Students appeared to have different expectations of the faculty based on gender.

> Students really did expect a kind of different approach or a different, more nurturing, more supportive… interaction with female faculty members. And so if you… were supportive and encouraging, and willing to go the extra mile and so on, then when you turned around and gave that student a grade that they might not have been very happy with, then it felt to the student like 'my gosh I was betrayed here, you know, there were… she was so nice to me and then she gave me a C.' Whereas, I think, with a male faculty member that kind of very supportive interaction that, with women gets read as nurturing, with men it gets read as mentoring.

The challenges and issues related to their gender deeply influenced the thinking of Francesca, Paula, and Rebecca. They reported being acutely aware of how their lives were affected, and each of them lived commitments to make changes at the college. Francesca remembered spending her early years at Wilkinson participating in questions about gender and change at the college:

> Those kinds of questions were being raised, everything from the structure of the faculty, who has tenure, what the salary structure in relation to gender? All the gender questions were coming to the fore. So I was very aware of those things, and because I was aware of them, I did see the impacts. I was aware that, that it made a difference whether you were a male or female faculty member.

Francesca, Paula, and Rebecca maintained that much remained to be done at Wilkinson. Gender was an active dimension of their work at the college, and they vowed to sustain a conversation with their colleagues. Rebecca maintained that Wilkinson was still a chilly climate for women:

> I think it's really important to talk about the difficulties of being a woman in this job at this institution, because that is a real important issue. And although, the college in many ways… is receptive and positive in regards to gender. In other ways… it creates what has been called a chilly climate. And it has made things, I think, very difficult for female faculty, especially female faculty who increase in power across time, and most particularly for those who are head administrators.

*Celebrating Student Success*

The research participants reported they placed a premium on students transforming themselves as a result of their education. Serving as pivotal persons for these students was a distinct source of satisfaction. Paula reported how she served as a pivotal person for a student.

> I am proud that my first senior independent study student just got her Ph.D. She is a rock star… the amount of work that she published as a graduate student, the people that are clamoring to get her to come work for them. She's a nice genuine person, and… I had only a small role in that but I am proud, I am proud of that. And I'm also proud of my other student from that year who is the director of a reading program down in Athens.

Charles remembered the satisfaction he felt about one particular student:

> I remember one student, Charley who as being a good C student and didn't do very well. At graduation his dad pulled me aside and said that you made the difference that he was not headed for anything but down. Charley is working in psychology now. He is married. He is very happy with his

job. That made me feel real good when the dad came by and said you know we really thank you for what you did.

Another time, noting that she was "really good about tooting other people's horns," Paula talked about one student, whose accomplishments she was proud to have been a part of.

> A student contacted me the other day, and he's been accepted to a Masters of Health Administration program, a joint Ph.D./MD program. And he's gotten a... fellowship that will cover most of his costs. And he says thank you... So you feel like... you really have the opportunity to make a difference for those people who go make a difference for somebody else... It's the adrenaline, seeing things happen that make some small positive difference somewhere.

For the other research participants, the most important constituency for their work, the most important reason for their transitions of significance was their work with students. Reflecting this general sentiment, Paula articulated this conviction:

> The students themselves, they're what's most important to me. What... kind of foundation I give them both as a person and as a scholar, intellectually and socially, so they can go and do what ever they go and do. I feel like that's my, my best contribution.

I found in the narratives of research participants recurrent motifs of values and commitments that surrounded their work and their ritualization. These ambient values and commitments surround their transitions of significance. Transitions of significance for research participants were embedded in this system of meaning that circumscribed the ritualization in a perimeter of values and commitments that I call the surrounding *ellipse of significance* (see Figure 4 below). The ellipse of significance serves as a "container" with elements of meaning that include at least the elements I found in the research participants' narratives: (1) teaching first, (2) living the academic good life, (3) leaving a legacy, (4) penetrating privilege, (5) being women, and (6) celebrating student success.

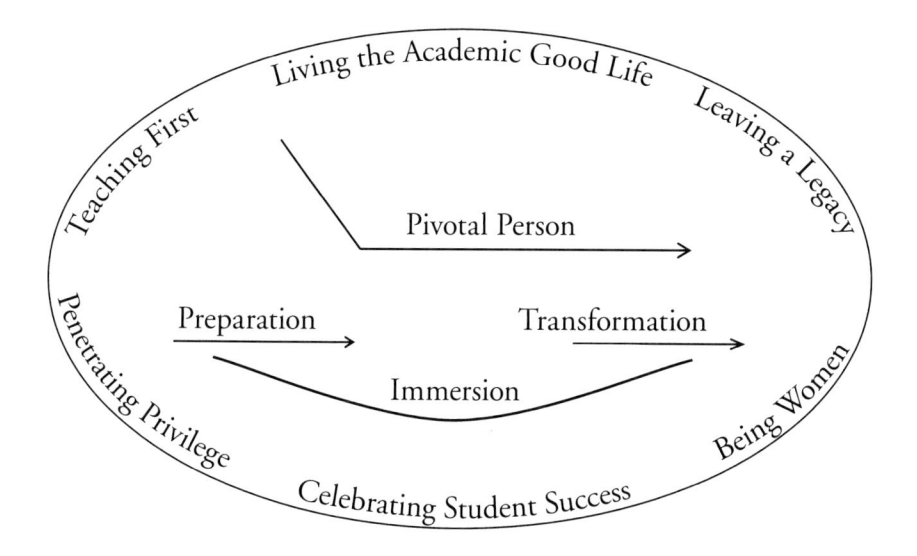

Figure 4. – Ellipse of Significance

# Chapter 11

# Leadership

In the narrative reflections of their leadership work, Francesca, Charles, Paula, and Rebecca, generally experienced their work absent of conventional hierarchical roles. With the exception of Francesca's administrative experience as dean of the faculty and Rebecca's tangential mention of her previously having served as department chair, these research participants principally described their work of leadership in terms of post-heroic explanations of leadership (Rost, 1991), that is leadership as an activity or process, rather than leadership as an appointed role. In examining the narratives of research participants I located self-described leadership work along a continuum between one end of formal academic administrative positions and roles and the other end of informal faculty leadership work. Given the nature of their formal campus roles as members of the faculty almost all the descriptions in the narratives of research participants emphasized informal leadership work.

*Post-Heroic Explanations*

In post-heroic explanations of leadership, all members of the community are presumed to be able to serve as potentially both leaders and followers, sometimes simultaneously depending on the domain and context, and all of them working towards a shared purpose. Post-Heroic explanations stand in stark contrast to classical understandings of leadership, where leaders are positioned in heroic roles, often entitled with discretionary authority, power and appointed position.

In her studies of leadership in higher education, Adriana Kezar (2000) extended a more comprehensive understanding of positionality. For Kezar (2000), positionality considerations included not just formal appointments, but the sum of historically, culturally, and socially constructed considerations that influenced how the work of leadership was interpreted in higher education settings. Kezar (2000) asserted that

> *Positioned individuals* (assuming that individuals co-construct their location culturally, organizationally, and historically while interacting with others) *possessing multifaceted identities* (assuming that individuals are shaped by formative conditions such as family, culture, community, religion, etc.) *within a particular context* (assuming most contexts are fairly unique and particular) *influenced by conditions of power* (assuming power relationships and dynamics pervade culture, social structures, and history) *construct* (develop understandings based on their situatedness or positionality and particular context and negotiate this understanding with other individuals' understandings) *leadership in unique (individual level) and collective (group level) ways simultaneously* (assuming independent webs of situated individuals connected by their changing positions on various issues) (Kezar, 2000, p. 727).

Exploring leadership outside the structures of hierarchies and positions requires constructing broader notions of leadership that include the experiences and perspectives of leadership without formal role authority.

## Formal Administrative Roles

Two of the faculty participants in this study, Francesca and Rebecca had previously occupied formal roles in academic administration, Francesca as former dean of the faculty, and Rebecca as a former chair of her department. Both of them saw their time at these positions as temporary episodes in their more essential roles as teachers and scholars. The formal positions of chair and dean of the faculty were perceived primarily as opportunities for position holders to support and nourish the work of their faculty colleagues. Francesca remembered the deanship as an extension of her faculty role.

> The kinds of things I tried to do in the Deans office, I had been trying to do as a faculty member in a lot of ways. I just had more freedom… and more opportunity to try to make connections between people and programs… One of the things that I was really interested in, was simply to take piece-meal, things that we had in place in a sort of piece-meal way, and make policies more consistent, so that they were clear to people and, and it was easier… to move forward… I was very concerned… with making… policies in relation to some of those things much more coherent, and consistent, and clearer. And… that was, in a way, a carry over from some things that I'd done as a faculty member.

Rebecca remembered her tasks and responsibilities as department chair as opportunities to advance the work of her department faculty colleagues, particularly women faculty at Wilkinson.

> When I was chair I didn't give them dreadful teaching loads. I put helpful things their way, publication opportunities or information about money. I'd write letters of recommendations for them. I'd review their review files before they're submitted to make sure nothing's missing… I think I've been decent, not just to junior faculty in my department, but also junior women, which I think is really

important. [I was] really supportive in regard to things like resolving maternity leave policy and stuff like that. And then, I think my other role is, is to be a fierce defender of our role as scholars…

In her formal role of administrative leadership, Rebecca was able to enact her critical stance toward the experiences of women at Wilkinson. Describing the perspective of a faculty "follower," Charles described the various task and roles that his department chair played:

> I think… he presents the department in a strong light… I think he really represents us very well. He gets across our needs and what significance we have to the college. But within the department I think it is a very democratic… process… we all have regular faculty meetings every Tuesday we get together. We discuss everything. We usually arrive at a consensus. Fortunately we all think the same way about the direction of the department… I think he has more of a low-key kind of approach to leadership. I think it works very well. It's not, who will do this or what do you all think. And then fortunately we all get along… It's more of a, it's not a purely hierarchical position, he is sort of our representative. And he consults us on everything. And we get feedback… So I like it. I think there are seven of us. He keeps us all on track… It is very egalitarian. I appreciate that.

Among the four research participants, Charles is the youngest and most junior member of the faculty. He had described previous experiences with formal leadership roles as a store manager and junior executive at Toys-R-Us. Now that he was at Wilkinson, he reflected the ambivalence of faculty perspective on the formal role and "burden" of the department chair position:

> I have also talked to people and they do find the administration part rewarding as well because you can make a different kind of difference. Perhaps in the decade to come

if I am alive that long and I am still here... It is a lot work not with a lot of praise or reward to it. I guess it is also a burden that we also share equally, which is a good idea.

Francesca was first introduced to more formal leadership roles on campus when a newly-arrived vice president for academic affairs hired her on as a special assistant, based on her previous experience in a number of administrative coordination roles. This was a gateway opportunity for her to work in the midst of major academic affairs policy matters, and prepared her for the opportunity to be elected to the dean of the faculty position. At Wilkinson the candidate for dean of the faculty is nominated and elected to the office by the faculty at large. Francesca remembered her journey to her decanal position, beginning with her role of special assistant to the vice president for academic affairs:

> I organized the forum events then for him and I ran the summer session. And I did a lot, I did other things for him. And so I had my first real taste of doing more college wide administration. And I think... that being able to branch out, to get to know more aspects of the college and how they worked, how the pieces fitted together, and the sense that I had some influence over what was happening here. That was really very exciting for me.

The vice president of academic affairs was a connector for Francesca, and served as a pivotal person for Francesca's transition to the formal role of dean of the faculty. At the time the interviews for this were conducted, Francesca had left the dean of the faculty position for a year. She considered herself to be recovering from the experience.

> I felt very good about everything for the first year or so. And I thought that I got lots of positive feedback from my colleagues on the faculty. That feeling however did wear away, and things shifted as they inevitably would. I mean, there were more and more problems that arise that need to be solved. Someone is always unhappy about the solution

regardless of what it is. And, I was also in the Deans office during a period of enormous transition in the administration. I served under two different presidents and three different vice presidents for academic affairs. And each one of those VPAAs... they had very, very different approaches, work styles, expectations, kind of styles of interaction with their colleagues and the administration. So every two years I was relearning how to interact with my immediate, my most immediate colleague, and always starting out on new projects that that person wanted done. Each every two years it was a whole kind of new agenda or set of priorities. So it was very challenging and often exhausting. And that coupled with the sort of rising number of faculty unhappiness about various things, many for which I wasn't responsible for, but just sort of generally aimed at the administration, was very, very discouraging... So I think by the time I came out of the Deans Office I had certainly a different sense about the institution as a whole and how it functioned, and lots of ideas about things that could happen here. But I also had a, a very strong sense about my own limitations. And, in fact during the course of those, of those six years, I just, I made up my mind not to continue in academic administration...

While Francesca appreciated the initial opportunity to serve as dean of the faculty, she tired of the experience after several years. Her descriptions of the experience of the role of dean of the faculty represented dynamic fluidity in personnel and disequilibrium, descriptions that contrast with the elements of stability and tradition impressed in the academic good life of the faculty. Could this help partly explain her decision not to continue with academic administration?

Still, as Francesca compared her experiences in an administration role with her work as a faculty member, she noted a significant difference: Despite the constant change "it felt more like a community to me in administration" than when she worked as a faculty member. She thought faculty were

> very independent operators in lots of ways. And they will come together around a particular issue or a problem, and they'll form an alliance in relation to that, but those alliances break part again and get reformed in relation to others, where they may be in quite adversarial relationships with each other.

But in administration, it seemed, the focus was much more concerned about the entire institution and it's future over the long term. The focus was

> not just my department, or my program, or my area, or my issue; you have to look at all of it. And you have to look at it as a piece. And you may be working on one piece at a time, but you have to be remembering the other pieces and what's going to be the impact here, and what's going to be the effect there, and... for me that was just hugely satisfying. So I do think it's a different experience of collaborative work and community, a very different experience.

Formal roles of academic administration served as episodes of opportunity for advancing the work of the faculty. While it felt more "collaborative," than the world of faculty "independent operators," significant transitions into formal leadership roles – (s)election to the dean of the faculty, or department chair – may not have sufficiently resonated with the elements of the ellipse of significance identified earlier in the previous chapter.

*Informal Work*

Much of the faculty leadership work that research participants described in their narratives were experienced outside formal roles in the form of assignments and commitments that Paula described as part of the "faculty administrative roles." Assignments included work in which research participants reported serving the department and the college as chairs or members of search committees and other ad-hoc decision-making and consultative groups. Their commitments comprised a posture or stance that research participants adopted for shaping their work of faculty leadership. Research participants also reported in their narratives that informal leadership included opportunities for them to serve their students and colleagues as their pivotal persons.

<u>Assignments</u>. Senior faculty members with some institutional history were typically considered ideal candidates for these appointments because, according to Francesca, "it was not a bad thing to have a person with some long-term perspective and experience involved… maybe I have a longer-perspective on things and… a kind of accumulated experience." Research participants reported in their narratives carrying a repertoire of assignments, tasks, and roles that they fulfilled for their students and their colleagues.

Informal leadership work also included the individual initiatives that served students, the department or the college. For example, Paula developed, sought grant-funding, and facilitated a campus summer outreach program that brought 120 sixth grade girls to campus, which is followed by a summer workshop for high school chemistry teachers "with the idea… if you can teach the teachers then you can impact a lot more students for a longer period of time." As I explore later in this chapter, Paula's work is an instance of informal faculty leadership that resonates with, and is inscribed by many of the elements of the ellipse of significance.

One of the self-appointed informal roles of performing faculty leadership work was to enact and maintain an oppositional stance towards the administration. This was a role for remaining vigilant about administrative decisions, and articulating critical responses when appropriate. Rebecca reflected that she thought she was expected to

> stand up to the administration. This is the virtue of being tenured. And I'm maybe not as responsible in as I should be but there are some things that I will just say publicly that junior faculty members won't say.

This role is reserved only for those who have successfully attained tenure. Charles, the only yet-to-be-tenured faculty member participating in this study, commented that "as a faculty without tenure I will reserve my comments until after I am under the protections of tenure."

Another space for informal faculty leadership is the larger community of the discipline or area of research interest. Although all the research participants mentioned connections with their discipline, one participant, Rebecca, described how she developed and maintained a large and international network of scholars in the field, which she readily made available to students.

> I'm known as a scholar. And my role in that larger community is, is one that I have made myself because you're not hired or recruited or formally installed some place, you have to [be] more entrepreneurial... you have to initiate things, to have a role in that wider community. And it's, it's not that one does that all by oneself, I'm sure I talked... about the various people who've been so helpful to me.

Francesca reported her activities as an informal leader in the faculty, which included serving on various committees, helping to making connections between colleagues, acknowledging and recognizing their accomplishments. Francesca speculated that it was this informal faculty leadership that may have been recognized by her colleagues, and which may have led to her election as dean of the faculty. Francesca's active informal leadership may have also helped her decide to take a chance at academic administration.

> One of the roles I did play as a faculty member... was to try to share information and make contacts between and among people who wouldn't otherwise have been touch with each other. And I think because I worked on so many different committees, and in different programs, and even in different parts of the institution that weren't necessarily strictly academic, I knew more about what was going on around the college. And I... tended to try to make contacts between

people in departments or just… share information around, build connection. And I think that that was maybe one of the things that I liked to do best. And I think that that was one of the things that sent me into administration… You kind of translate from one group to another, but also just in making connections… that was one of the things that I did as a faculty member…I was always trying to prompt people… to congratulate them on something they'd done, or be, push them, help think about themselves as moving into another, into a next stage. So it was a sort of a mentoring… I wasn't trying to become a mentor to someone, I was just saying, 'you know you did so well on this'. It didn't matter what it was, something I'd read that they'd written, something they said in a faculty meeting, or some performance on a committee… that I would, that I would encourage them, now go on and do this or have you thought about that. And, in, in fact I do think that I've played that role with students, a lot, in informal or more formal course-related ways.

<u>Commitments</u>. The "faculty administrative role" emanated out of a strong sense of responsibility and identification with the department and other faculty colleagues. Research participants reported that these commitments were active self-conscious stances. These commitments included adopted positions of fidelity to students, the department, and the college, and influenced their work of faculty leadership. Paula reflected on her stance:

I feel a stronger allegiance to my responsibilities in the chemistry department… But then I also feel a strong responsibility to the colleagues… I've only missed one faculty meeting in six years. I feel responsible, I feel the need to be a responsible member of the community… One of my roles is try to give the administration feedback when I think things need improvement. And I also try to make it a point to give them feedback when I think things have gone well. So, I think, I guess, that's kind of my faculty administrative role.

Paula added that this strong sense of responsibility was shared by many of her faculty colleagues. During her early years as a faculty member before stepping up to the dean's position, Francesca remembered feeling that her colleagues could count on her.

> I think people would have thought that… they could probably count on me to pick up the responsibility for something and carry it forward. They could probably count on me to spend much too much on any project that I was working on. They could probably figure that if they could get me involved in something, you know, it would eventually get done, that I was willing to take on responsibility for lots of different kinds of things.

These commitments include a stance toward challenging and influencing students so that they "get the most out of their college experience." Paula detailed this stance of influencing students:

> When I say I push them I don't think I push them in terms of learning the material from my class, I think I push them in terms of encouraging them to think about options, encouraging them to think about what do they want to do. And I think I try to encourage the students to do what they want, and to do what they'll be good at. And I think some of the most important advising I do in organic chemistry, is essentially giving students permission to drop the class. And to go on and do something different with clear conscience, and not feeling like they should take organic chemistry, and they should be a chemistry major, or whatever. So I think that some of the best influence I've had is encouraging people to do what they really want to do rather than what they feel will make the most money or will be the most prestigious, or whatever. And then also the students that do stay in chemistry, or in another science, trying to help them think about… what are different things… I want them to do what's good for them, but sometimes I think it's comfortable for them just to follow the example that we set, rather than, you know, look into being some bioengineer, or look into

being a congressional representative. So I, so I really try to challenge the students to get outside of the box.

The commitment to challenge and influence also extended to faculty colleagues in the form of an interrogative stance that sought to continually clarify and improve their teaching. Paula described her stance toward her chemistry faculty colleagues:

> My colleagues, I think I challenge them on a regular basis... I'm the one that's always asking the questions, "Why do we do it that way?" "Do we do it that way because that's the way we've always done it, or do we do it that way because it's the best way?" "How do these things fit together?" "I know about my little part of the curriculum, but I don't know much about the rest of the curriculum, can we, can we talk about this." So really, I think that I'm the one that constantly pushing and poking, are, are we doing the best we can do.

The sense of security that tenure accords, and the status of having become a member of the senior faculty results in opportunities for challenge and conversation to extend to mentoring colleagues. Research participants described an emerging assertive commitment to get involved in the matters of the department and the college, and becoming more vocal and active about mentoring junior colleagues because it ultimately improves the educational experience for students. A year after receiving tenure, Paula reflected on how her commitment to the department has grown stronger as she became one of the four senior members of the department faculty when four of her colleagues retired:

> I think we could do better. And now I'm saying it a little more strongly because I believe it a little more strongly... I've been here long enough now, that for some of the bigger issues, I'm starting to have opinions. I feel like I have enough data, and enough personal experience to start having opinions about whether I think this policy is good, or whether I think this administrator is doing a good job, or this faculty member is a

> good colleague. And maybe this faculty member is not such a good colleague... so I've been here long enough that... I'm starting to have some opinions. And for me that's a big deal. I mean, cause I don't... form opinions quickly. And once I have an opinion, once I have a commitment about... I think this program needs to be changed. Or I think... this aspect needs to be improved... then I'm willing to do that... when it comes time for me to take a leadership role in the department, [and] being deliberate about my decisions and my opinions.

Maintaining this continuing stance of informal leadership involves developing a strong visibility and presence on campus, continually seeking opportunities to engage in conversations about matters around campus. Rebecca reported how she maintained and nourished her stance by employing a set of strategies she called "being scary."

> And by being scary, I mean I publish a lot, and I let people know it. You know... when something comes out, I send it over to the VPAA. I list it in the *[Wilkinson Reports]*. I let people know, and so... that's the resource that, you know, I can't be this, I can't be this myth. I'm out-spoken, and in many ways, right. And other faculty see that, and that's a resource... and that's... actually a strategy that is... very helpful to them.

<u>Pivotal Persons</u>. Research participants also noted their leadership as pivotal persons for others in significant transition. Rebecca found it satisfying to serve as the "fairy godmother" for students, using her professional network to "[snaps her fingers] and make something happen for the student, and that is so wonderful." Rebecca added that:

> because I am so networked out in the wider world, the role of advisor is a really important one, and I can do some of that for first-year students and non-majors, but I can really do good helpful things for a student when they begin to major

in political science. There's... just tons of stuff I can do and I love doing that.

Research participants also described opportunities for serving as pivotal persons for their faculty colleagues, supporting them in their work with encouragement, the benefit of their experiences, and referrals to resources. Francesca noted

> one of the major things that... other people have done for me, and that sometimes I've been able to do for them is encourage them to go forward with something, to take a risk, to, to move to the next stage. I think that's an important part of these friendships and relationships. I think it's, it's becomes then a kind of mentoring relationship even if you are peers. You're, you're supporting each other in stepping out, and moving into a new role, or taking on a new responsibility, and taking a certain amount of risk in doing that. And I think that that would be true for all of the relationships that I would count as important ones... Certainly I know that that's true with some other people. And certainly that would be... one of my main experiences out of all these relationships, that I was encouraged to think that I could do something beyond what I might have thought I could do.

As one of the emerging senior faculty members in the chemistry department, Paula looked forward to sharing her experiences with the junior faculty. Francesca, with her long experience at Wilkinson as faculty and then dean of the faculty, looked forward to providing leadership on campus by making connections between faculty colleagues and resources. Charles reported talking to students about his experiences in the world of business.

Rebecca reported cultivating her international network over the years of her career, carefully weaving together a group of colleagues and personal friends around the country. Some of the members of her network were mentors and peers in graduate school, others were academic colleagues she met along the way, as she co-published and co-edited publications with them, and as she held offices in the American Political Science Association. Rebecca shared her strategy for building academic networks:

> You do what you're supposed to do, professionally, you meet people, you talk with them, you make a good impression or you don't, you do good things for other people and they do good things for you. And so then you can get established in that way. And, and so this is [the] combination, you have to have your own initiative, you have to work, you also have to rely on the help of other people.

Taking on self-designated or appointed assignments, making commitments to challenge and support their students, their department, and the college, and actively seeking opportunities to serve as pivotal persons for students and faculty colleagues were three general areas in which the research participants engaged in informal faculty leadership.

## Ritualization and Leadership

When the examination of the work of faculty leadership with post-heroic explanations (Rost, 1991) is combined with an examination of ritual with explanations of ritualization (Driver, 1998) and transitions in personally meaningful passages such as secular ceremony (Moore and Myerhoff, 1971), the intersection presents a connection between ritualization and faculty leadership work.

The work of faculty leadership can be located along an axis that extends from an endpoint of the formal to an endpoint of the informal. When the various leadership work efforts noted by the research participants are plotted along this continuum, an axis of leadership – from formal to informal is generated (See Figure 5 below):

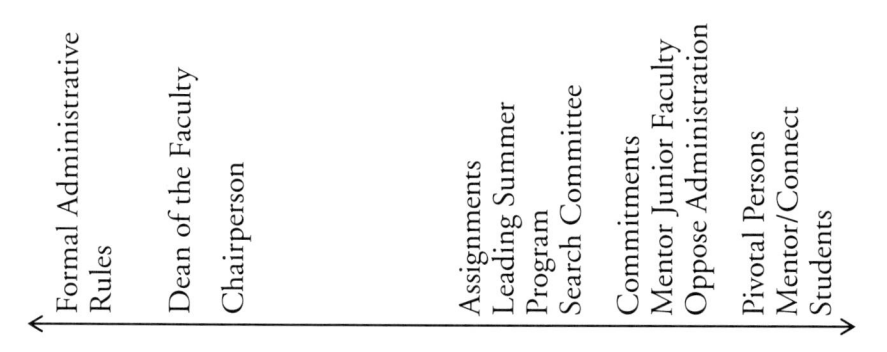

← Formal Administrative Rules | Dean of the Faculty | Chairperson | Assignments | Leading Summer Program | Search Committee | Commitments | Mentor Junior Faculty | Oppose Administration | Pivotal Persons | Mentor/Connect | Students →

Figure 5. – Leadership

Ritual (ceremony) and ritualization reported by the research participants of this study can also be located on an axis that extends from an endpoint of the formal ceremony to an endpoint of the everyday ritualization that attends transitions of significance. (See Figure 6 below).

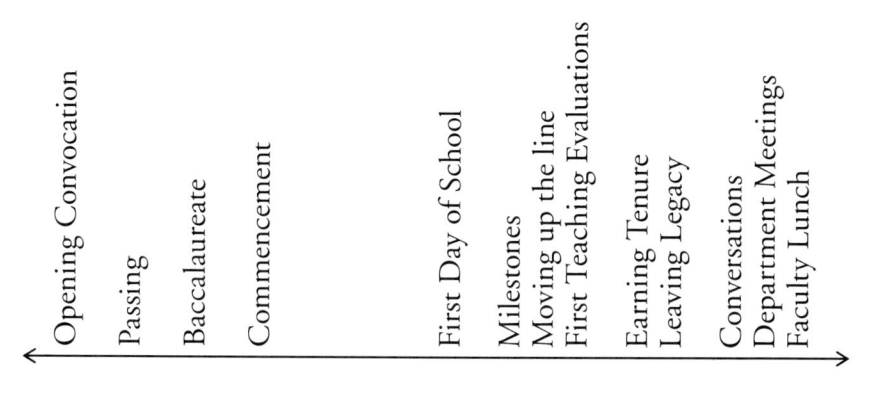

← Opening Convocation | Passing | Baccalaureate | Commencement | First Day of School | Milestones | Moving up the line | First Teaching Evaluations | Earning Tenure | Leaving Legacy | Conversations | Department Meetings | Faculty Lunch →

Figure 6. – Ritualization

When the axis of ritualization is intersected with the axis of leadership (see Figure 7 below), a matrix of meaning making is generated with four spaces of engagement, four spaces of how the research participants constructed meaning for their work at teacher-scholars at Wilkinson College.

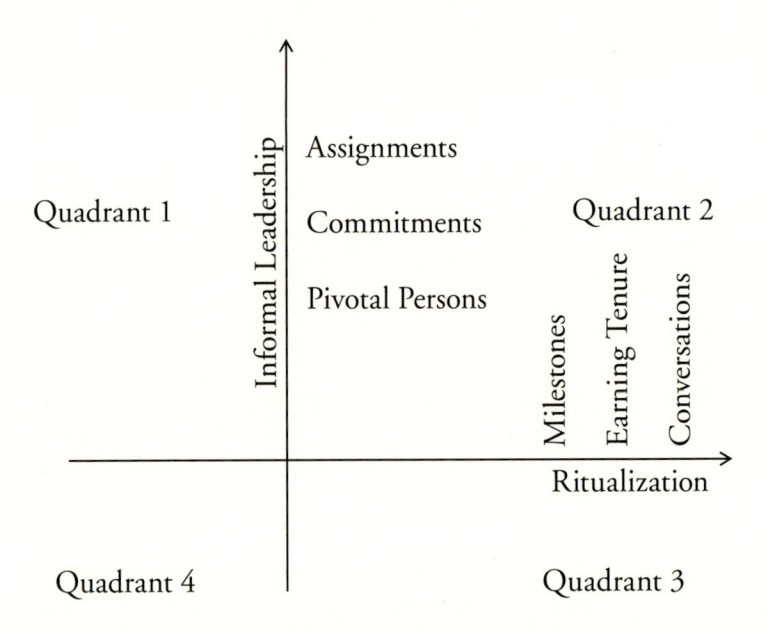

```
                    ↑
                    │  Assignments
                    │
   Quadrant 1       │  Commitments           Quadrant 2
                    │
           Informal Leadership
                    │  Pivotal Persons
                    │                  Milestones  Earning Tenure  Conversations
                    │
────────────────────┼──────────────────────────────────────→
                    │                                Ritualization
                    │
   Quadrant 4       │                         Quadrant 3
```

Figure 7. – Ritualization and Leadership

The majority of faculty work reported by research participants occurred in the space of Quadrant 2, where ritualization and informal leadership meet. This is the space where the work of faculty leadership work at Wilkinson is experienced is ritualized. This is also the space where Francesca, Charles, Paula, and Rebecca made meaning of their faculty leadership work, particularly in terms of the values and convictions of a shared ellipse of significance (Figure 3 in the previous chapter).

The work of faculty leadership reported by research participants occurred in the space between informal leadership and ritualization (see Figure 7 on page 278). While two of the research participants discussed their experiences as dean of the faculty and department chair, they described them as not insignificant sojourns away from their faculty work. Additionally, in their retrospective reflections about their time in administration, they also framed the experiences as opportunities for them to assist their faculty colleagues. It is worth noting, of course, that their reflections were influenced by the fact that the specific formal roles they occupied were academic administration positions. Their work of informal leadership surrounded the self-appointed assignments they acquired, the commitments they adopted, and the pivotal roles they played in the lives of their students and their colleagues.

Francesca, Charles, Paula, and Rebecca described and explained their work of faculty leadership, among other ways, in terms of Kezar's (2000) *positionality considerations* of higher education leadership: background, campus role, and power conditions. Their backgrounds as teachers and scholars, their campus roles as faculty, and the relative power they perceived they had, influenced their leadership work in both formal positions (as dean and chair) and informal assignments, commitments, and pivotal roles. This understanding of leadership work aligns with a post-heroic explanation of leadership (Rost, 1991), which locates leadership in activity and process instead of in formal positions. In the post-heroic explanation of leadership all faculty are presumed to be constantly doing leadership work in an organic and dynamic system.

Wilkinson College is a *cybernetic system* (Birnbaum, 1988) with a predominantly *collegial* culture (Bergquist, 1992), in which faculty work independently and adaptively as individual contractors, who coalesce only occasionally to make shared decisions. In this context, faculty leadership work was to serve students, colleagues, and the institution (Greenleaf, 1977), and to legate to them contributions through self-assigned efforts, enacted commitments, and service as pivotal persons for students and colleagues.

Francesca, Charles, Paula, and Rebecca made meaning of their work of faculty leadership with ritualization that helped them through the passages of their career, transitions of significance that they prepared for, immersed in, and emerged out of transformed (Van Genepp, 1960). Three thematic motifs in this ritualization emerged from their narratives: milestones, earning tenure, and conversations. They reported making meaning of their passages in the academy through individual and local milestones such as early decisions to become an academic and to come to Wilkinson, earning tenure, and coming together for conversations. These conversations were also settings to share their assignments and commitments. Formal academic ceremonies served as occasions for them to publicly celebrate and to personally confirm their own individual passages, such as moving up the faculty line, gathering for conversation with colleagues, and attending to students marking their success. Academic ceremonies were also opportunities for faculty to re-actualize a transformational *sacred time* (Eliade, 1957), returning to the beginning to remember again why they chose a life in the academy.

The research participants also recalled the presence of pivotal persons who attended their transitions by guiding them through early decisions and commitments, inspiring them as personal examples of the academic life, and connecting them to opportunities. They remembered that their pivotal persons were teachers, mentors, and professional colleagues.

Ritualization is informed and sanctioned by myths that provide the ideological content that surrounds the ritualization (Honko, 1984). Francesca, Charles, Paula, and Rebecca identified a set of ambient values that included teaching first, the academic good life, leaving a legacy, penetrating privilege, being women, and celebrating student successes. These values circumscribed their ritualization in an ellipse of significance. (See Figure 4). The values in the ellipse of significance both informed and confirmed the research participants' ritualization. Their ritualization helped them make sense of their leadership work and their academic lives.

An examination of the narrative profiles resulted in finding major themes of personal and informal ritualization. Francesca, Charles, Paula, and Rebecca remembered that ritualization marked transitions of significance that were accompanied by pivotal persons who ignited incipient interest in teaching and scholarship, who helped make professionally useful connections, and who served as admirable role models. I also found a set of ambient values, commitments and convictions that I call an ellipse of significance that surrounded and inscribed the ritualization experiences of research participants. Their narrative profiles also yielded major themes of informal faculty leadership. They remembered their faculty leadership work as comprising self-appointed initiatives that served students, the department, and the college, commitments or stances toward their work and their colleagues, and opportunities to serve as pivotal persons for students and colleagues in their transitions of significance.

# Chapter 12

# Implications

In the preface to his book, *Liberating Rites: Understanding the Transformative Power of Ritual* (1998), Tom Driver proposed that "rites can be liberating, provided their character is rightly understood and their practice creatively linked to the actual needs of living persons and groups" (p. xii). I believe the narratives of Francesca, Charles, Paula, and Rebecca have more than adequately testified to the transformative power of their ritualization to greet and make meaning of their significant transitions. The potential of liberating rituals in the lives of teachers and scholars still remains out of the reach of any significant conversation regarding faculty work, particularly faculty leadership work. This study was just one attempt to inch a little closer toward the prospect of Driver's (1998) notion of liberation.

A decade after completing this study, Francesca retired and lives nearby, a continuing loyal member of the Wilkinson community, although now distant from the daily operation of the college she once helped guide as dean of the faculty. Rebecca left Wilkinson for a much larger instituion that could offer her more expansive opportunities in her discipline of political science. Charles and Paula are still teaching at Wilkinson, continuing to perform their work with students and colleagues. In this final chapter, I summarize and explore the implications of the findings on ritualization and leadership. I review the passage of the study itself, particularly in terms of my interpretive influence as the researcher, narrative analysis and narrative inquiry. I explore the implications of the findings in this study for further research, for professional practice, and for me personally.

## Reflections of the Study

Charles, the developmental psychologist, noted that, "it is not necessary to acquire knowledge, to have pure objective standards." Charles's own research work was in experimental psychology, and yet he noted that "it's hard to eliminate subjective biases… but if we recognize them and state them up front" then it's possible to advance knowledge.

*The Researcher as Instrument*

I want to confirm that my own subjectivity actively influenced what I have learned in this study. This is appropriately in accordance with Lincoln and Guba's (1985) second axiom that the inquirer and the object of the inquiry interact to influence one another. I constructed and asked the questions and I selected the follow-up questions. I focused on faculty leadership work in a liberal arts college because of its familiarity to my personal experience. I was sufficiently acquainted with the research site – Wilkinson College – and my own experiences as a faculty member and administrator focused my interest on faculty leadership work. I have no doubt that these experiences influenced what I elected to *attend to* (first level) in the interviews, what I selected to *tell* (second level) in constructing the narrative profiles, and what I selected to *transcribe* and code as the themes in the narratives (Riessman, 1993).

Lincoln and Guba's (1985) fifth axiom, that "inquiry is value bound" also applies here. This axiom has the following corollaries:

> Corollary 1: Inquiries are influenced by *inquirer* values…;
> Corollary 2: Inquiry is influenced by the choice of the *paradigm*…;

> Corollary 3: Inquiry is influenced by the choice of *substantive theory*...;
> Corollary 4: Inquiry is influenced by the values that inhere in the *context*;
> Corollary 5: Inquiry is either *value-resonant* (reinforcing or congruent) or *value-dissonant* (conflicting)... (Lincoln & Guba, 1985, p. 38).

As I described above, my experiences with Wilkinson College, higher education, and my conceptions of leadership influenced what I elected to *value* in this inquiry. I selected the *paradigm* for this research, I selected the models and *theories* of leadership and ritualization to help examine the data, and I selected the *context*, in terms of the research site and methodologies for this study.

All the research participants of this study commented on how the process of the research interviews functioned for them as self-exploration. Paula, who I interviewed the year she received tenure, said

> It's been good... I've enjoyed it. It's inspired me to get out my copy of *Good Start* (Gibson, 1992) and start thinking about some things again... I'm in a different stage now, and so it's time, it's time to think about things maybe from a different perspective.

Charles, in his second year at Wilkinson had received a tempting offer from an institution back in his home state of Virginia. He noted that the experience of the three interviews helped him clarify his ultimate decision to stay at Wilkinson. He experienced the interviews as

> [a] way [for] reflecting... crystallizing it in my own mind. I think it has helped me say, 'you are right, I am content enough to be here and the transition is over.' My commitment here is pretty solid now. I am not going to look for another job. This is where I am going to stay... Actually this has helped me, in many ways, think back about all those things and convince myself again that I did the right thing.

*Joint Construction of Findings*

This study was conducted with a research methodology that mutually shaped and influenced the experience of the researcher and the research participants. The research methodology of this study is firmly rooted in the interpretivist paradigm (Sipe and Constable, 1996), and in this paradigm, ontological assumptions about reality are subjective and constructed; there is little to distinguish between the knower and the known. Interpretivist research is dialogic and therefore what is learned is jointly constructed by the researcher and the research. In this study what was learned is a product of my interpretive filters combined with the narrative filters of Francesca, Charles, Paula, and Rebecca remembering their experiences. This was a study of what meaning they made of their experiences, and I pursued what Cohen and Manion (1994), citing Husserl (1948/1973), termed meaning *reflexivity*, which can only be obtained retroactively through a process of extemporaneous self-description, such as the research interviews I conducted with the research participants.

I began this project intuiting a potential connection between leadership and ritualization. As a result of this study, Francesca, Charles, Paula, Rebecca and I have jointly constructed an attempted explanation that connects ritualization and faculty leadership work in one liberal arts college in the Midwest.

## Implications for Practice

The meaning making of faculty leadership work with ritualization offers some implications for refining our understanding of leadership in the academy in general, and of the profession of faculty work in particular. Leadership and ritualization are worth extending into the realms of the professoriate where alignment between values and practice are often threatened.

In a study of the professions of genetics and journalism, Gardner, Csikszentmihalyi, and Damon (2001) outlined a model of the professional realm in which a professional interacts with her/his profession, which in turn interacts with the larger society that the profession serves. This model for the *professional realm* (Gardner, Csikszentmihalyi, and Damon, 2001) offers an opportunity to explore how a mindful examination of ritualization might be relevant to the practice of the professoriate.

Gardner, Csikszentmihalyi, and Damon (2001) identified four components of a professional realm. The first component comprises the *individual practitioners* who characterize the "specific knowledge, skills, practices, rules, and values that differentiate them from the rest of the culture" (Gardner, Csikszentmihalyi, and Damon, 2001, p. 21), and who then essentially facilitate the advance of the profession. As faculty members in specific disciplines, the research participants were individual practitioners. They chose to pursue a life of advancing specialized knowledge and skills, and worked with rules, practices, and values that were unique to their chosen discipline.

The community of practitioners develops the thresholds for the profession, including related skills and competencies so that "when enough specialized knowledge has been codified for smooth transition to new practitioners" a *domain* is established as the second component of the professional realm (p. 22). Francesca, Charles, Paula, and Rebecca each talked about their faculty experiences in terms of their academic disciplines and their lives as teachers and scholars. Their narratives for the most part described domains "encompassing both the procedural and ethical standards of their profession" (p. 24), and how they spent their lives constructing a career in their domains.

The third component of a professional realm was what Gardner, Csikszentmihalyi, and Damon (2002) called the *field*, the collection of individual practitioners who "actually practice a domain's procedures" (p. 24). Each of the research participants located their professional experiences in relation to other members of the field, their academic discipline, and in the case of Charles and Rebecca, their sub-disciplines. They reported being inspired and mentored by, and having trained with "expert practitioners" (p. 25) or pivotal persons, while serving as their "apprentices or students" (p. 25) in graduate school, and as research collaborators and junior faculty. Some of them, like Rebecca and Francesca, reported assuming formal positions, becoming members of their field's elite "gatekeepers who preside over the destiny of the professional realm and judge which changes in the domain should be sanctioned" (p. 24).

In addition to individual practitioners, the domain, and the field, Gardner, Csikszentmihalyi, and Damon (2002) listed the fourth component of the professional realm, the *other stakeholders* (p. 26) in the society at large, consisting of external stakeholders. For Francesca, Charles, Paula, and Rebecca, other stakeholders included the people outside their domains with significant influence over their work. This list included the college administration, students and their families and parents. Sometimes they saw students, particularly in their research work, as insiders in their domain as apprentices for the field, and college administrators as partners inside their domain.

According to Gardner, Csikszentmihalyi, and Damon (2002), professional realms are most robust when "the expectations of stakeholders match those of the field, and when domain and field are themselves in sync" resulting in an ideal situation they called *authentic alignment* (p. 27). Although Gardner, Csikszentmihalyi, & Damon (2002) discussed only the professional realms of genetics and journalism, extending their model to the professional realm of the professoriate exposes a number of fissures, and threats to alignment between the values prized by the domain of higher education and college teaching (Young, 1998) and the expectations of external stakeholders.

Critics of higher education have indicted the domain of higher education for everything from being unresponsive to societal expectations (Sykes, 1988) to being ineffectively and inefficiently organized and run (Keller, 1983). Francesca, Charles, Paula, and Rebecca worried about external stakeholders seeing their domains and fields as out of touch with societal expectations. Charles worried that the college may need to be run more like the Toys-R-Us business he used to work for, in order to stay relevant. Ultimately, one of the sources of threats to alignment may be the decline in societal trust in higher education in general and liberal arts college education.

Another source of threat to alignment is the shifting dynamic of practice within the field itself. Practitioner members of the field need to be able to count on a mutually agreed upon set of domain values. Wilkinson College trustees, managing the boundary between the domain and external stakeholders, recently overruled one of the faculty's recommendations for a revised curriculum. The College administration, mindful of the public questioning of the relevance of the pure liberal arts, recently asked the faculty to consider teaching more interdisciplinary courses. The research participants of this study saw these as uncomfortable portents for their field. What if we re-imagined these emerging questions about higher education?

Observations connecting ritualization and leadership invite consideration of some implications for helping to attenuate the threats to alignment identified by Gardner, Csikszentmihalyi, & Damon (2002). What if threats to alignment, such as terminating the employment of 30 members of the staff and reinserting the religious studies requirement, were framed less in terms of discrepant positions that need to be negotiated, mediated or resolved? What if they were framed instead in terms of a complexity that requires an expanded view of managing uncertainty by ritualizing through change, such as passing through how the institution must change structurally, and reasserting a value in the founding mission of the college?

William Bridges (1980) used Van Gennep's (1960) three-phase structure of ritual – preparation, immersion, and transformation – to develop an analogous model for managing transitions in complexity and change. Bridges (1980) essentially proposed a change-management model, in which the ending and loss of transition can best be managed by preparing for and engaging the disruption, and then entering a "neutral zone" to reorient, renew, and creatively re-pattern, and then finally re-emerging to transformatively act on new commitments.

The notion of ellipses of significance might offer a pathway to manage the threats to alignment in higher education. Engaging in ritualized conversation about the shared values and practices of the domain would engender a returning to the beginning as a way of letting go of loss (layoffs, countermanded decision) and emerging with a transformative commitment. People don't resist change as much as they mourn the loss of what was true. This would not just constitute managing conflict through effective group process. Instead, it would be the re-imagined pursuit of change management through co-constructing meaning through a process of shared ritualization, similar to what Francesca, Charles, Paula, and Rebecca reported essentially in their experiences with department meetings and other gatherings.

We can also potentially expand our currently limited working definitions of leadership in higher education beyond formal appointments and positions. Not only would this help to embrace the less than formal work of faculty leadership, but it would also legitimate the work of the many others in our campus communities who labor to serve the institution and make a difference outside the boundaries of their assigned positions. We can identify and valorize the preparation, performance, and positive outcomes obtained on campus from the freely offered gifts of assignments, commitments, and pivotal persons. When faculty and others extend themselves to students and others to benefit their professional communities, they are being informal leaders on ampus. When campus community members step outside their position responsibilities to respond to an incident or crisis, they are performing the work of leadership on campus. Including informal work in our understanding of leadership re-imagines leadership with a more inclusive, generative, and pluralistic understanding of post-heroic leadership. For the faculty in particular, and a campus community that values the faculty for what they contribute to the college, attending to informal, less-than-public, often personal secular ceremony – in milestones, conversations, and what tenure represents – honors how these professionals make meaning of their career commitments. There is an increasing awareness that faculty attuned to meaning-making are more effective in assisting their students to clarify their future career and life trajectories (Clydesdale, 2015). They are also more clearly remembered by their students for their contributions to students as they develop purpose for their lives (Nash & Murray, 2010). Francesca, Charles, Paula, and Rebecca appreciated the meaning-making value of their ritualization as much as they enjoyed the occasions of formal campus rituals.

## Implications for Research

This study is one of the first to examine and connect constructions of ritualization and leadership. The literature on ritualization reviewed earlier in the second chapter, for the most part, focused on heavy ritual. Although some studies have explored everyday ritualization (Driver, 1998; Grimes, 1996, 2000; Wall & Ferguson, 1998), literature on ritualization in the domains of higher education and the professoriate has largely being absent. Astin & Astin (1999) and Palmer (1998) have made some useful contributions that address the notions of faculty making meaning of their work. Human beings ritualize and utilize ceremony to make sense of their transitions of significance. My hope remains that this introductory response to the gap in the literature opens conversation about how individual faculty members construct meaning through ritualization and secular ceremony.

Numerous studies have been produced on leadership, and as I noted in my review of literature, much of this literature surrounds constructions of leadership in terms of organizational positionality or individual behaviors and traits. In the realm of higher education, with rare exceptions (such as Astin & Leland, 1991; Astin & Astin, 2000), studies of leadership have helped to generally explain, and hopefully improve, the leadership of department chairs, deans, vice presidents, provosts and presidents. While useful in their contexts, these heroic constructions of leadership cannot help entirely explain the leadership work of faculty. Faculty in liberal arts colleges serve their students, their departments, and their institutions by engaging in leadership work often without positional authority. The absence of explanatory models for how faculty provide leadership at their institutions without the vestment of organizational authority is a gap that potentially ignores their contribution, and remains a promising area for future research.

This particular study was conducted at a very specific site: a selective liberal arts college in the Midwest. The rich diversity of higher education in institutional organization and type opens a world of questions about ritualization and faculty leadership at institutions unlike the site of this study. Studies similar to this research conducted with the faculty of community colleges, comprehensive, and research institutions, as well as comparative studies of faculty at different types of institutions could potentiallly yield rich information and insights that would help honor the contributions of the faculty at all institutions.

The scope of this study focused on members of the faculty. In most institutions of higher education, approximately two members of a group, commonly identified as non-managerial staff workers, support the work of each faculty member. Much of their work is as diverse in specialization and complexity as the work of faculty, and yet their valuable work is rarely present in conversations about serving the campus without authority. An examination of the leadership work of staff in terms of post-heroic constructions of leadership, and their everyday ritualization would honor and make more visible their leadership engagement with the campus.

Finally, it would theoretically be possible to replicate this study in each *domain* (Gardner, Csikszentmihalyi, & Damon, 2002) or profession that shares a generally common set of values and practices. Does each domain generally share the same elements of an ellipse of significance? If so, what are the elements of the ellipses of significance? What types of ritualization might the elements of the ellipses of surround? If not, what surrounds and helps contextualize the everyday ritualization in that domain?

## Implications for Me

While our conventional understanding of higher education ritual focuses on public and stylized ceremonies such as commencements, inaugurations, (see Manning, 1995, 2000), "most of life is not lived in the high drama of major transitions but in following routines...with peaks and valleys,... other sorts of ritual are necessary for weathering the plains of ordinariness" (Grimes, 1995, p. 216). I began this project several years ago in search of how faculty members generally made sense of their professional work and personal lives. More particularly, I wanted to make sense of how my greatest teachers had made sense of their work, their transitions of significance in their career journey. In examining the ritualization reported by the research participants, I (re)learned the power of ritual to transform, and I began to explore ritualization in my professional and personal life.

During the early writing of this chapter I re-read Ronald Grimes' *Marrying and Burying: Rites of Passage in a Man's Life* (1995). Dedicated to Tom Driver, *Marrying and Burying* (1995) is a largely autobiographical narrative, full of elliptical ruminations, poems and descriptions of dreams. Grimes (1995) utilized this deeply personal account of loss and passage in his personal and professional life as the narrative text to examine for ritualization. A scholar, teacher, and prolific author on ritual, Grimes had also collaborated with Victor Turner, and drew much of his work on Moore and Myerhoff's (1977) and Myerhoff's (1978) notions of secular ritual.

I know ritualization is ubiquitous and entailed in my everyday actions and decisions. I seek them now in my teaching, in my administrative work, and in my life. I search my patterned actions and utterances for everyday transitions of significance with a renewed vigilance for clues to ritualization and transformation. I want and need to be able to recall and retell stories about the pivotal persons in my life. I want to be able to remember again the ambient values around the ellipses of significance that have informed my transitions. As it was for Francesca, Charles, Paula, and Rebecca, my wish is for transformative remembering.

# References

Adams, H. (1988). *The academic tribes* (2nd ed.). Urbana, Illinois: University of Illinois Press.

Aldrich, H.E. (1999). *Organizations evolving*. Thousand Oaks, California: Sage Publications.

Alexander, B.C. (1991). *Victor Turner revisited: Ritual as social change*. Atlanta, Georgia: Scholars Press.

Astin, A.W., & Astin, H.S. (1999). *Meaning and spirituality in the lives of college faculty*. Los Angeles, California: Higher Education Research Institute, University of California Los Angeles.

Astin, A.W., & Astin, H.S. (2000). *Leadership reconsidered: Engaging higher education in social change*. Battle Creek, Michigan: W.K. Kellogg Foundation.

Astin, H.S., & Leland, C. (1991). *Women of influence, women of vision: A cross-generational study of leaders and social change*. San Francisco, California: Jossey-Bass Publishers.

Autry, J.A. (1994). *Life and work: A manager's search for meaning*. New York, New York: William Morrow & Company.

Bain, K. (2004). *What the best college teachers do*. Cambridge, Massachusetts: Harvard University Press.

Balderston, F.E. (1995). *Managing today's university: Strategies for viability, change, and excellence*. San Francisco, California: Jossey-Bass Publishers.

Barber, R. (1991). *Pilgrimages*. Woodbridge, Suffolk, UK: Boydell Press.

Barnard, C. (1938). *The functions of the executive.* Cambridge, Massachusetts: Harvard University Press.

Bass, B.M. (1981). *Stogdill's handbook of leadership: Theory and research* (2nd ed.). New York, New York: The Free Press.

Bass, B.M. (1990). *Bass & Stogdill's handbook of leadership: Theory, research, and managerial applications* (3rd ed.). New York, New York: The Free Press.

Bell, C. (1997). *Ritual: Perspectives and dimensions.* New York, New York: Oxford University Press.

Bensimon, E. (1991). The meaning of "good presidential leadership": A frame analysis. In M. Peterson (Ed.), *ASHE reader on organization and governance in higher education* (pp. 421-430). Needham Heights, Massachusetts: Ginn.

Bensimon, E., & Neumann, A. (1993). *Redesigning collegiate leadership: Teams and teamwork in higher education.* Baltimore, Maryland: The Johns Hopkins University Press.

Berger, P., & Luckmann, T. (1967). *The social construction of reality.* Garden City, New York: Doubleday.

Bergquist, W.H. (1992). *The four cultures of the academy: Insights and strategies for improving leadership in collegiate organizations.* San Francisco, California: Jossey-Bass Publishers.

Bergquist, W.H. (1993). *The postmodern organization: Mastering the art of irreversible change.* San Francisco, California: Jossey-Bass Publishers.

Birnbaum, R.L. (1988). *How colleges work: The cybernetics of academic organization and leadership.* San Francisco, California: Jossey-Bass Publishers.

Birnbaum, R.L. (1992). *How academic leadership works: Understanding success and failure in the college presidency.* San Francisco, California: Jossey-Bass Publishers.

Birnbaum, R.L. (2000). *Management fads in higher education: Where they come from, what they do, why they fail.* San Francisco, California: Jossey-Bass Publishers.

Blackburn, R.T., & Lawrence, J.H. (1995). *Faculty at work: Motivation, expectation, satisfaction.* Baltimore, Maryland: Johns Hopkins University Press.

Blake, R.R., & Mouton, J.S. (1964). The managerial grid. Houston, Texas: Gulf.

Block, P. (1993). *Stewardship: Choosing service over self-interest.* San Francisco, California: Berrett- Koehler Publishers.

Bogdan, R.C. & Biklen, S.K. (1998). *Qualitative research for education: An introduction to theory and methods.* Needham Heights, Massachusetts: Allyn and Bacon.

Bok, D. (1986). *Higher learning.* Cambridge, Massachusetts: Harvard University Press.

Bolles, E.B. (1991). *A second way of knowing: The riddle of human perception.* New York, New York: Prentice Hall Press.

Bolman, L.G., & Deal, T.E. (1991). *Reframing organizations: Artistry, choice, and leadership.* San Francisco, California: Jossey-Bass Publishers.

Bolman, L.G., & Deal, T.E. (1995). *Leading with soul: An uncommon journey of spirit.* San Francisco, California: Jossey-Bass Publishers.

Bormann, E.G. (1981). *The application of symbolic convergence communication theory to organizations.* Paper presented at the SCA/IA Conference on Interpretive Approaches to the Study of Organizational Communication. Alta, Utah.

Boyer, E.L. (1990). *Scholarship reconsidered: Priorities of the professoriate.* Princeton, New Jersey: Princeton University Press.

Bridges, W.P. (1980). *Transitions: Making sense of life's changes.* Boulder, Colorado: Perseus Publishing.

Bridges, W. (2001). *The way of transition: Embracing life's most difficult moments.* Cambridge, Massachusetts: Perseus Publishing.

Bridges, W.P. (2003). *Managing transitions: Making the most of change.* Boulder, Colorado: Perseus Publishing.

Briskin, A. (1998). *The stirring of soul in the workplace.* San Francisco, California: Berrett-Koehler Publishers.

Bruner, J. (1990). *Acts of meaning*. Cambridge, Massachusetts: Harvard University Press.

Buber, M. (1958). *I and thou*. New York, New York: Author.

Burns, J.M. (1978). *Leadership*. New York, New York: Harper and Row.

Cashman, K. (1998). *Leadership from the inside out: Becoming a leader for life*. Provo, Utah: Executive Excellence Publishing.

Cech, T.R. (2000). "Science at liberal arts colleges: A better education?" In Koblik, S. & Graubard, S.R. (Eds.). *Distinctively American: The Residential Liberal Arts Colleges*. New Brunswick, New Jersey: Transaction Publishers, pp. 195-216.

Cialdini, R.B. (1993). *Influence: The psychology of persuasion*. New York, New York: William Morrow.

Cialdini, R.B. (1995). *Influence: Science and practice*. 3rd ed. New York, New York: HarperCollins College Publishers.

Clandinin, D.J., & Connelly, F. M. (2000). *Narrative inquiry: Experience and story in qualitative research*. San Francisco, California: Jossey-Bass Publishers.

Clark, B. (1992). *The distinctive college*. New Brunswick, New Jersey: Transaction Publishers.

Clydesdale, T. (2015). *The purposeful graduate: Why colleges must talk to students about vocation*. Chicago, Illinois: University of Chicago Press.

Cohen, L., & Manion, L. (1994). *Research methods in education*. (4th ed.). New York, New York: Routledge.

Cohen, M., & March, J. (1986). *Leadership and ambiguity: The American college president*, (2nd ed.). Cambridge, Massachusetts: Harvard University Press.

Coleman, J.S. (1990). *Foundations of social theory*. Cambridge, Massachusetts: Harvard University Press.

Crainer, S. (2000). *The management century: A critical review of 20th century thought and practice*. San Francisco, California: Jossey-Bass Publishers.

Creswell, J.W. (1998). *Qualitative inquiry and research design: Choosing among five traditions*. Thousand Oaks, California: Sage Publications.

Csikszentmihalyi, M. (2003). *Good business: Leadership, flow, and the making of meaning.* New York, New York: Viking Books.

Cushman, E. (1998). *The struggle and the tools: Oral and literate strategies in an inner city community.* Albany, New York: State University of New York Press.

Curtis, B. (1978). Introduction. In B. Curtis & W. Mays, (Eds.). *Phenomenology and education.* London, Methuen.

Daloz, L.A.P., Keen, C.H., Keen, J.P., & Parks, S.D. (1996). *Common fire: Leading lives of commitment in a complex world.* Boston, Massachusetts: Beacon Press.

DePree, M. (1989). *Leadership is an art.* New York, New York: Dell Publishing.

DePree, M. (1992). *Leadership jazz.* New York, New York: Dell Publishing.

DePree. M. (1997). *Leading without power: Finding hope in serving community.* San Francisco, California: Jossey-Bass Publishers.

Donmoyer, R. (1997). Paradigm talk reconsidered. In V. Richardson et al (Eds.), *Handbook of research on teaching*, 4th ed. Washington, D.C.: AERA.

Driver, T.F. (1998). *Liberating rites: Understanding the transformative power of ritual.* Boulder, Colorado: Westview Press.

Eisner, E.W. (1991). *The enlightened eye: Qualitative inquiry and the enhancement of educational practice.* Old Tappan, New Jersey: Macmillan.

Eliade, M. (1957). *The sacred and the profane: The nature of religion.* San Diego, California: Harcourt Brace & Company.

Eliade, M. (1958). *Rites and symbols of initiation: The mysteries of birth and rebirth.* Woodstock, Connecticut: Spring Publications.

Emery, F.E., & Trist, E.L. (1960). Socio-technical systems. In C.W. Churchman and Others (Eds.), *Management sciences, models and techniques.* London: Pergamon.

Evans, M.G. (1970). The effects of supervisory behavior on the path-goal relationship. *Organizational behavior and human performance,* 5. (pp. 277-298).

Evans, R. (2000). The authentic leader. In *The Jossey-Bass reader on educational leadership*. (pp. 287-308). San Francisco, California: Jossey-Bass Publishers.

Fayol, H. (1949). *General and industrial management*. (Constance Storrs, Trans.). London: Sir Isaac Putnam.

Fiedler, F.E. (1967). *A theory of leadership effectiveness*. New York, New York: McGraw-Hill.

Fisher, J.L. (1984). *Power of the presidency*. New York, New York: Macmillan.

Fisher, J.L., Tack, M.W., & Wheeler, K.J. (1988). *The effective college president*. New York, New York: American Council on Education.

Fisher, W.R. (1987). *Human communication as narration: Toward a philosophy of reason, value, and action*. Columbia, South Carolina: University of South Carolina Press.

Fitzpatrick, J., Secrist, J., & Wright, D.J. (1998). *Secrets for a successful dissertation*. Thousand Oaks, California: Sage Publications.

Fleishman, E.A. (1973). Twenty years of consideration and structure. In E.A. Fleishman & J.G. Hunt, (Eds.). *Current developments in the study of leadership*. Carbondale, Illinois: Southern Illinois University Press.

Follett, M.P. (1924). *Creative experience*. New York, New York: Longmans, Green.

Fox, E.M., & Urwick. L. F., (Eds.). (1982). *Dynamic administration: The collected papers of Mary Parker Follett*. New York, New York: Hippocrene Books.

French, J., & Raven, B.H. (1959). The bases of social power. In D. Cartwright, (Ed.). *Studies of social power*. Ann Arbor, Michigan: Institute for Social Research.

Frost, P.J., & Taylor, M.S. (Eds.). (1996). *Rhythms of academic life: Personal accounts of careers in academia*. Thousand Oaks, California: Sage Publications.

Fulton, O. (1998). Unity or fragmentation, convergence or diversity: The academic profession in comparative perspective in the era of mass higher education. In W.G. Bowen & H.T. Shapiro, (Eds.).

*Universities and their leadership*. Princeton, New Jersey: Princeton University Press.

Gallagher, W. (1993). *The power of place: How our surroundings shape our thoughts, emotions, and actions*. New York, New York: HarperCollins Publishers.

Gardner, H. (1995). *Leading minds: An anatomy of leadership*. New York, New York: BasicBooks.

Gardner, H. (1999). *Intelligence reframed: Multiple intelligences for the 21$^{st}$ century*. New York, New York: Basic Books.

Gardner, H., Csikszentmihalyi, M., & Damon, W. (2001). *Good work: When excellence and ethics meet*. Basic Books.

Garfinkel, H. (1967). *Studies in ethnomethodology*. Englewood Cliffs, New Jersey: Prentice Hall Press.

Gee, J.P. (1985). The narrativization of experiences in the oral style. *Journal of education*, 169(1), pp. 9-35.

Giamatti, A.B. (1988). *A free and ordered space: The real world of the university*. New York, New York: W.W. Norton & Company.

Gibson, G.W. (1992). *Good start: A guidebook for new faculty in liberal arts colleges*. Bolton, Massachusetts: Anker Publishing

Glaser, B.G., & Strauss, A.L. (1967). *The discovery of grounded theory*. Chicago, Illinois: Aldine Press.

Gramsci, A. (1971). *Selections from the prison notebooks*. (trans. & ed. Hoare, Q. & Smith, G.). New York, New York: International Publishers.

Grant, G., & Murray, C.E. (1999). *Teaching in America: The slow revolution*. Cambridge, Massachusetts: Harvard University Press.

Greenleaf, R. (1977). *Servant leadership: A journey into the nature of legitimate power and greatness*. New York, New York: Paulist Press.

Grimes, R.L. (1976/1992). *Symbol and conquest: Public ritual and drama in Santa Fe*. Albuquerque, New Mexico: University of New Mexico Press.

Grimes, R.L. (1995). *Marrying and burying: Rites of passage in a man's life*. Boulder, Colorado: Westview Press.

Grimes, R.L. (1996). (Ed.). *Readings in ritual studies.* Upper Saddle River, New Jersey: Prentice-Hall.

Grimes, R.L. (2000). *Deeply into the bone: Reinventing rites of passage.* Berkeley, California: University of California Press.

Guba, E.G., & Lincoln, Y.S. (1989). *Fourth generation evaluation.* Newbury Park, California: Sage Publications.

Guillory, W.A. (2000). *The living organization: Spirituality in the workplace.* Salt Lake City, Utah: Innovations International.

Halpin, A.W., & Winer, B.J. (1957). A factorial study of the leader behavior descriptions. In R.M. Stogdill & A.E. Coons (Eds.), *Leader behavior: It's description and measurement.* Columbus, Ohio: Ohio State University, Bureau of Business Research.

Hastie, R., & Dawes, R.M. (2001). *Rational choice in an uncertain world: The psychology of judgment and decision making.* Thousand Oaks, California: Sage Publications.

Haviland, W.A. (1993). *Cultural anthropology,* (7th ed.). Fort Worth, Texas: Harcourt Brace Jovanovich.

Hecht, I.W.D., Higgerson, M.L., Gmelch, W.H., & Tucker, A. (1999). *The department chair as academic leader.* Phoenix, Arizona: American Council on Education/Oryx Press.

Heifetz, R.A. (1994). *Leadership without easy answers.* Cambridge, Massachusetts: Harvard University Press.

Heil, G., Bennis, W., & Stephens, D.C. (2000). *Douglas McGregor revisited: Managing the human side of the enterprise.* New York, New York: John Wiley & Sons.

Hersey, P., & Blanchard, K.H. (1969). Life cycle theory of leadership. *Training and development journal, 23.* (pp. 26-34).

Hersey, P., & Blanchard, K.H. (1982). *Management of organizational behavior: Utilizing human resources, 4th ed.* Englewood Cliffs, New Jersey: Prentice-Hall.

Higher Education Research Institute. (1996). *Guidebook for a social change model of leadership development.* Los Angeles, California: Graduate School of Education and Information Studies, University of California.

Holliday, V.L. (2000). Rhetoric, iconography, and leadership in classical antiquity: Pericles and Augustus. In V.L. Holliday (Ed.), *Classical and modern narratives of leadership* (pp. 11-44). Wauconda, Illinois: Bolchazy-Carducci Publishers.

Holstein, J.A., & Gubrium, J.F. (1995). *The active interview.* Thousand Oaks, California: Sage Publications.

Honko, L. (1984). The problem of defining myth. In A. Dundes, (Ed.) *Sacred narratives: Readings in the theory of myth.* Berkeley, California: University of California Press. (pp. 41-52).

Horowitz, H.L. (1984). *Alma mater: Design and experience in the women's colleges from their nineteenth-century beginnings to the 1930s.* Amherst, Massachusetts: University of Massachusetts Press.

Horowitz, H.L. (1987). *Campus life: Undergraduate cultures from the end of the eighteenth century to the present.* Chicago, Illinois: University of Chicago Press.

House, R.J., & Dressler, G. (1974). The path-goal theory of leadership: Some post-hoc and a priori tests. In J.G. Hunt & L.L. Larson (Eds.), *Contingency approaches to leadership.* Carbondale, Illinois: Southern Illinois University Press.

Hughes, R., Ginnett, R., & Curphy, G. (1996) *Leadership: Enhancing the lessons of experience, 2nd ed.* Chicago, Illinois: Irwin.

Hurst, C.E. (2000). *Living theory: The application of classical social theory to contemporary life.* Needham Heights, Massachusetts: Allyn & Bacon.

Husserl, E. (1948/1973). *Experience and judgment: Investigation in a genealogy of logic* (J.S. Churchill & K. Amerikas, Trans.). Evanston, Illinois: Northwestern University Press. (Original work published 1939)

Jaworski, J. (1996). *Synchronicity: The inner path of leadership.* San Francisco, California: Berrett-Koehler Publishers.

Josselson, R., & Lieblich, A. (1999). *Making meaning of narratives.* Thousand Oaks, California: Sage Publications.

Katz, D., & Kahn, R.L. (1978). *The social psychology of organizations. (2nd ed.).* New York, New York: Wiley.

Kegan, R. (1983). *The evolving self.* Cambridge, Massachusetts: Harvard University Press.

Keller, G. (1983). *Academic strategy: The management revolution in American higher education.* Baltimore, Maryland: Johns Hopkins University Press.

Kelley, G. (1963). *A theory of personality: The psychology of personal constructs.* New York, New York: W.W. Norton.

Kennedy, D. (1997). *Academic duty.* Cambridge, Massachusetts: Harvard University Press.

Kernan, A. (1999). *In Plato's cave.* New Haven, Connecticut: Yale University Press.

Kerr, C., & Gade, M.L. (1986). *The many lives of academic presidents: Time, place and character.* Washington, D.C.: Association of Governing Boards of Universities and Colleges.

Kezar, A.J. (1996). *Reconstructing exclusive images: An examination of higher education leadership models.* Unpublished doctoral dissertation. Ann Arbor, Michigan: University of Michigan.

Kezar, A.J. (2000). Pluralistic leadership. *Journal of Higher Education, 71*(6), pp. 722-743.

Kirk, J. & Miller, M.L. (1986). *Reliability and validity in qualitative research.* Newbury Park, California: Sage Publications.

Kluge, P.F. (1993). *Alma mater: A college homecoming.* Reading, Massachusetts: Addison-Wesley.

Koblik, S. & Graubard, S.R. (Eds.). (2000). *Distinctively American: The residential liberal arts colleges.* New Brunswick, New Jersey: Transaction Publishers.

Koestenbaum, P. (1991). *Leadership: The inner side of greatness.* San Francisco, California: Jossey-Bass Publishers.

Komives, S.R., Lucas, N., & McMahon, T.R. (1998). *Exploring leadership: For college students who want to make a difference.* San Francisco, California: Jossey-Bass Publishers.

Kotter, J.P. (1985). *Power and influence.* New York, New York: Free Press.

Kouzes, J.M. & Posner, B.Z. (1987). *The leadership challenge: How to get extraordinary things done in organizations.* San Francisco, California: Jossey-Bass Publishers.

Kvale, S. (1996). *Interviews: An introduction to qualitative research interviewing.* Thousand Oaks, California: Sage Publications.

Landsberger, H. (1958). *Hawthorne revisited.* Ithaca, New York: Cornell University Press.

Lather, P. (1991). *Getting smart: Feminist research and pedagogy with/in the postmodern.* New York, New York: Routledge.

Lather, P. (1997). Validity as an incitement to discourse. In V. Richardson et al (Eds.), *Handbook of research on teaching, 4$^{th}$ ed.* Washington, D.C.: AERA

LeCompte, M.D. (1987). Bias in biography: Bias and subjectivity in ethnographic research. *Anthropology & Education Quarterly, 18.* (pp. 43-52).

Lee, R.J., & King, S.N. (2001). *Discovering the leader in you: A guide to realizing your personal leadership potential.* San Francisco, California: Jossey-Bass Publishers.

Leider, R.J. (1997). *The power of purpose: Creating meaning in your life and work.* San Francisco, California: Berrett-Koehler Publishers.

Lightfoot, S.L. (1983). *The good high school: Portraits of character and culture.* New York, New York: Basic Books.

Lightfoot, S.L., & Davis, J.H. (1997). *The art and science of portraiture.* San Francisco, California: Jossey-Bass Publishers.

Likert, R. (1961). *New patterns of management.* New York, New York: McGraw- Hill.

Lincoln, Y.S. & Guba, E.G. (1985). *Naturalistic inquiry.* Thousand Oaks, California: Sage Publications.

Little, J.W. (2000). Assessing the prospects for teacher leadership. In *The jossey-bass reader on educational leadership.* San Francisco, California: Jossey-Bass Publishers. (pp. 390-418).

Mackoff, B. & Wenet, G. (2001). *The inner work of leaders: Leadership as a habit of mind.* New York, New York: AMACOM/American Management Association.

Madsen, D. (1992). *Successful dissertations and theses. (2nd ed.)*. San Francisco, California: Jossey-Bass Publishers.

Manning, K. (1990). *Campus rituals and cultural meaning*. Unpublished doctoral dissertation. Bloomington, Indiana: Indiana University.

Manning, K. (2000). *Rituals, ceremonies, and cultural meaning in higher education*. Westport, Connecticut: Bergin & Garvey.

Manning, P. (1987). Semiotics and fieldwork. Newbury, California: Sage Publications.

Manning, P., & Cullum-Swan, B. (1994). Narrative, content, and semiotic analysis. In N.K. Denzin, & Y.S. Lincoln (Eds.), *Handbook of qualitative research*. Thousand Oaks, California: Sage Publications. (pp. 463-477).

Maslow, A.H. (1954). *Motivation and personality*. New York, New York: Harper and Row.

Maslow, A.H. (1965). *Eupsychian management*. Homewood, Illinois: Richard D. Irwin.

Mayo, E. (1947). *The human problems of an industrial civilization*. Boston, Massachusetts: Harvard University Press.

McAdams, D.P. (1993). *The stories we live by: Personal myths and the making of the self*. New York, New York: The Guilford Press.

McGregor, D. (1960). *The human side of enterprise*. New York, New York: McGraw-Hill.

Meloy, J.M. (1994). *Writing the qualitative dissertation: Understanding by doing*. Hillsdale, New Jersey: Lawrence Earlbaum Associates, Publishers.

Meyerhoff, B. (1978). *Number our days*. New York, New York: Simon & Schuster.

Merriam, S.B. (1998). *Qualitative research and case study applications in education*. San Francisco, California: Jossey-Bass Publishers.

Middaugh, M.F. (2001). *Understanding faculty productivity: Standards and benchmarks for colleges and universities*. San Francisco, California: Jossey-Bass Publishers.

Milgram, S. (1974). *Obedience to authority: An experimental view*. New York, New York: Harper and Row.

Miller, L.M. (1989). *Barbarians to bureaucrats: Corporate life cycle strategies.* New York, New York: Fawcett Columbine.

Miller, R.W. (1987). *Fact and method: Explanation, confirmation and reality in the natural and the social sciences.* Princeton, New Jersey: Princeton University Press.

Mintzberg, H. (1983). *Structure in fives: Designing effective organizations.* Englewood Cliffs, New Jersey: Prentice-Hall.

Mishler, E.G. (1986). *Research interviewing: Context and narrative.* Cambridge, Massachusetts: Harvard University Press.

Moore, S.F., & Myerhoff, B.G. (1977). Secular ritual: Forms and meaning. In S. Moore & B.G. Myerhoff (Eds.). *Secular ritual.* (pp. 3-24). Assen, Netherlands: van Gorcum.

Moore, S.F., & Myerhoff, B.G. (1975). *Symbol and politics in communal ideology: Cases and questions.* Ithaca, New York: Cornell University Press.

Morgan, D.L. (1997). *Focus groups as qualitative research. 2nd ed.* Thousand Oaks, California: Sage Publications.

Morgan, G. (1989). *Creative Organization Theory.* Thousand Oaks, California: Sage Publications.

Moxley, R.S. (2000). *Leadership and spirit: Breathing new vitality and energy into individuals and organizations.* San Francisco, California: Jossey-Bass Publishers.

Mumby, D.K. (Ed.) (1993). *Narrative and social control: Critical perspectives.* Newbury Park, California: Sage Publishers.

Mumby, D.K., & Stohl, C. (1991). Power and discourse in organizational studies: Absence and the dialectic of control. *Discourse and Society,* 2, (pp. 313-332).

Nadler, D.A., & Gerstein, M.S. (1992). Designing high-performance work systems: Organizing people, work, technology, and information. In D.A. Nadler, M.S. Gerstein, & Associates, *Organizational architecture: Designs for changing organizations.* (pp. 110-132). San Francisco, California: Jossey-Bass Publishers.

Nair, K. (1997). *A higher standard of leadership: Lessons from the life of Gandhi.* San Francisco, California: Berrett-Koehler Publishers.

Nash, R.J., & Murray, M.C. (2010). *Helping college students find purpose: A campus guide to meaning-making.* San Francisco, California: Jossey-Bass Publishers.

Northouse, P.G. (2001). *Leadership: Theory and practice.* 2$^{nd}$ ed. Thousand Oaks, California: Sage Publications.

O'Brien, G.D. (1998). *All the essential half-truths about higher education.* Chicago, Illinois: University of Chicago Press.

Oshry, B. (1996). *Seeing systems: Unlocking the mysteries of organizational life.* San Francisco, California: Berrett-Koehler Publishers.

Oshry, B. (1999). *Leading systems: Lessons from the power lab.* San Francisco, California: Berrett-Koehler Publishers.

Owen, H. (1987). *Spirit: Transformation and development in organizations.* Potomac, Maryland: Abbott Publishing.

Owen, H. (1999). *The spirit of leadership: Liberating the leader in each of us.* San Francisco, California: Berrett-Koehler Publishers.

Palmer, P.J. (1998). *The courage to teach: Exploring the inner landscape of a teacher's life.* San Francisco, California: Jossey-Bass Publishers.

Palmer, P.J. (1998). Leading from within. In L.C. Spears (Ed.), *Insights on leadership: Service, stewardship, spirit, and servant-leadership.* New York, New York: John Wiley & Sons, Inc.

Palus, C.J., & Horth, D.M. (2002). *The leader's edge: Six creative competencies for navigating complex challenges.* San Francisco, California: Jossey-Bass Publishers.

Patton, M.Q. (1989). *Qualitative evaluation methods.* (10$^{th}$ printing). Beverly Hills, California: Sage Publications.

Peshkin, A. (1985). Virtuous subjectivity: In the participant-observer's I's. In D. Berg & K. Smith (Eds.), *Exploring clinical methods for social research.* Beverly Hills, California: Sage Publications. (pp. 267-282).

Peshkin, A. (1988). In search of subjectivity – one's own. *Educational Researcher 17* (7), pp. 17-22.

Pfeffer, J. (1992). *Managing with power: Politics and influence in organizations.* Boston, Massachusetts: Harvard Business School Press.

Polanyi, M. (1958/1962). *Personal knowledge: Towards a post-critical philosophy.* Chicago, Illinois: University of Chicago Press.

Polkinghorne, D.E. (1988). *Narrative knowing and the human sciences.* Albany, New York: State University of New York Press.

Pottenbaum, G.A. (1992). *The rites of people: Exploring the ritual character of human experience.* Washington, D.C.: The Pastoral Press.

Punch, M. (1994). Politics and ethics in qualitative research. In N.K. Denzin, & Y.S. Lincoln (Eds.), *Handbook of qualitative research.* Thousand Oaks, California: Sage Publications. (pp. 83-95).

Quinn, R.E. (1996). *Deep change: Discovering the leader within.* San Francisco, California: Jossey-Bass Publishers.

Quinn, R.E. (2000). *Change the world: How ordinary people can accomplish extraordinary results.* San Francisco, California: Jossey-Bass Publishers.

Readings, B. (1996). *The university in ruins.* Cambridge, Massachusetts: Harvard University Press.

Riessman, C.K. (1993). *Narrative analysis.* Newbury Park, California: Sage Publications.

Rost, J.C. (1991). *Leadership for the twenty-first century.* New York, New York: Praeger.

Roethlisberger, F.L., & Dickson, W. (1939). *Management and the worker.* New York, New York: John Wiley & Sons.

Rubin, H.J., & Rubin, I.S. (1995). *Qualitative interviewing: The art of hearing data.* Thousand Oaks, California: Sage Publications.

Rudestam, K.E., & Newton, R.R. (1992). *Surviving your dissertation: A comprehensive guide to content and process.* Newbury Park, California: Sage Publications.

Schein, E.H. (1985). *Organizational culture and leadership.* San Francisco, California: Jossey-Bass Publishers.

Scholes, R., & Kellogg, R. (1966). *The nature of narrative.* London: Oxford University Press.

Schuman, D. (1982). *Policy analysis, education, and everyday life.* Lexington, Massachusetts: Heath.

Schutz, A. (1967). *The phenomenology of the social world* (G. Walsh & F. Lehnert, Trans.). Evanston, Illinois: Northwestern University Press. (Original work published in 1932).

Seidman, E. (1985). *In the words of the faculty: Perspectives on improving teaching and educational quality in community colleges.* San Francisco, California: Jossey-Bass Publishers.

Seidman, I. (1998). *Interviewing as qualitative research: A guide for researchers in education and the social sciences, 2nd edition.* New York, New York: Teachers College, Columbia University.

Seligman, M.A. (1990). *Learned optimism.* New York, New York: Pocket Books.

Sipe, L., & Constable, S. (1996). A chart of four contemporary research paradigms. *Taboo: The Journal of Culture and Education, 1,* pp. 153-163.

Spears, L.C. (1995). *Reflections on leadership. How Robert K. Greenleaf's theory of servant-leadership influenced today's top management thinkers.* New York, New York: John Wiley & Sons, Inc.

Spears, L.C. (Ed.). (1998). *Insights on leadership: Service, stewardship, spirit, and servant-leadership.* New York, New York: John Wiley & Sons, Inc.

Spreitzer, G.M., & Quinn, R.E. (2001). *A company of leaders: Five disciplines for unleashing the power in your workplace.* San Francisco, California: Jossey-Bass Publishers.

Stewart, K. (1996). *A space on the side of the road: Cultural poetics in an "other America."* (Princeton, New Jersey: Princeton University Press.

Strauss, A.L. & Corbin, J. (1998). *Basics of qualitative research: Grounded theory procedures and techniques, 2nd edition.* Thousand Oaks, California: Sage Publications.

Sykes, C.J. (1988). *Profscam: Professors and the demise of higher education.* New York, New York: St. Martin's Griffin.

Tambiah, S. J. (1996). A performative approach to ritual. In *Readings in ritual studies.* (R.L. Grimes, ed.). Upper Saddle River, New Jersey: Prentice-Hall. (pp. 495-511).

Taylor, F.W. (1947). *Principles of scientific management.* New York, New York: Harper Brothers.

Terkel, S. (1972). *Working.* New York, New York: Pantheon Books.

Tieger, P.D. & Barron, B. (1992). *Do What You Are.* New York, New Your: Little Brown and Company.

Tompkins, J. (1996). *A life in school: What the teacher learned.* Reading, Massachusetts: Perseus Books.

Trice, H.M. (1985). Rites and ceremonials in organizational cultures. *Research in the Sociology of Organizations, 4.* (pp. 221-270).

Trice, H.M., & Beyer, J.M. (1984). Studying organizational cultures through rites and ceremonials. *Academy of Management Review, 9.* (pp. 653-669).

Turner, V. (1969). *The ritual process: Structure and anti-structure.* New York, New York: Aldine de Gruyter.

Useem, M. (1998). *The leadership moment.* New York, New York: Three Rivers Press.

Van Gennep, A. (1960). *The rites of passage.* Chicago, Illinois: The University of Chicago Press.

Vaughan, G.B. (1986). *The community college presidency.* New York, New York: American Council on Education/Macmillan.

Vaughan, G.B. (1989). *Leadership in transition: The community college presidency.* New York, New York: American Council on Education/Macmillan.

von Bertalanffy, L. (1950). The theory of open systems in physics and biology. *Science,* (3), pp. 23-29.

von Bertalanffy, L. (1968). *General system theory.* New York, New York: George Braziller.

Walkerdine, V. (1997). *Daddy's girl: Young girls and popular culture.* Cambridge, Massachusetts: Harvard University Press.

Wall, K., & Ferguson, G. (1998). *Rites of passage: Celebrating life's changes.* Hilsboro, Oregon: Beyond Words Publishing.

Weber, M. (1947). *The theory of social and economic organizations.* New York, New York: Free Press.

Weick, K.E. (1979). *The social psychology of organizing.* (2nd ed.). Reading, Massachusetts: Addison-Wesley

Weick, K.E. (1995). *Sensemaking in organizations.* Thousand Oaks, California: Sage Publications.

Weingartner, R.H. (1996). *Fitting form to function: A primer on the organization of academic institutions.* Phoenix, Arizona: American Council on Education/Oryx Press.

Weiss, R.S. (1994). *Learning from strangers: The art and method of qualitative interview studies.* New York, New York: Free Press.

Wheatley, M.J. (1994). *Leadership and the new science: Learning about organization from an orderly universe.* San Francisco, California: Berrett-Koehler Publishers.

Whyte, D. (1994). *The heart aroused: Poetry and the preservation of the soul in corporate America.* New York, New York: Currency Doubleday Books

Whyte, D. (2001). *Crossing the unknown sea: Work as a pilgrimage of identity.* New York, New York: Riverhead Books.

Willis, P. (1977). *Learning to labor: How working class kids get working class jobs.* New York, New York: Columbia University Press.

Wolcott, H.F. (1994). *Transforming data: Description, analysis, and interpretation.* Thousand Oaks, California: Sage Publications.

Yin, R.K. (1994). *Case study research: Design and methods.* Thousand Oaks, California: Sage Publications.

Young, R.B. (1997). *No neutral ground: Standing by the values we prize in higher education.* San Francisco, California: Jossey-Bass Publishers.

Yukl, G.A. (1994). *Leadership in organizations (3rd ed.).* Englewood Cliffs, New Jersey: Prentice-Hall.

Made in United States
North Haven, CT
08 April 2022